CW00674563

INTERPRETING
THE
Orient

TRAVELLERS IN EGYPT AND THE NEAR EAST

INTERPRETING
THE
Orient

TRAVELLERS IN EGYPT AND THE NEAR EAST

EDITED BY
PAUL AND JANET STARKEY

ITHACA

INTERPRETING THE ORIENT
Travellers in Egypt and the Near East

Ithaca Press is an imprint of Garnet Publishing Limited

Published by
Garnet Publishing Limited
8 Southern Court
South Street
Reading
RG1 4QS
UK

Copyright © Paul and Janet Starkey 2001

All rights reserved.
No part of this book may be reproduced in any form or by
any electronic or mechanical means, including information
storage and retrieval systems, without permission in writing
from the publisher, except by a reviewer who may quote
brief passages in a review.

First Edition

ISBN 0 86372 258 X

British Library Cataloguing-in-Publication Data
A catalogue record for this book is available from the British Library

Jacket design by Garnet Publishing
Typeset by Samantha Barden

Printed in Lebanon

Contents

Introduction

Paul and Janet Starkey

Egypt and the Near East have enchanted many people, both from within the region and from outside it. Travellers from the West, in particular, have journeyed to the region over the centuries for a variety of motives, both good and bad: they have travelled on pilgrimages; they have set out in pursuit of knowledge, of power, diplomacy and trade; they have travelled for pleasure and adventure, to plunder and to discover the exotic – or sometimes simply to discover themselves. Some have been influenced more than others by what they saw; others have brought back tangible evidence of their visits in the form of antiquities or other collectors' items; many have used their experiences and observations for their own literary or artistic ends.

The collection of papers in this book has its origin in the conference: 'Travellers to Egypt and the Near East' held at St Catherine's College, Oxford, in July 1997. The conference was a successor to that held in Durham in 1995, papers from which were published as *Travellers in Egypt* (London, 1998). Like its predecessor, the Oxford conference was a multidisciplinary affair, notable as much for the enthusiasm of the contributors as for the academic excellence of their contributions. Like its predecessor, much of the conference, for understandable reasons, also centred on the nineteenth century; however, a significant group of contributions took a wider perspective, extending the chronological and intellectual horizons of the participants and stimulating much lively discussion. This is the second of two volumes of fascinating material presented at the conference. The first volume is titled *Unfolding the Orient: Travellers in Egypt and the Near East* and includes papers on Mary Wartley Montagu, James Silk Buckingham, Lord Belmore and James Burton. For convenience, the papers in the collections are arranged approximately in chronological order though with so many common themes running through them it has proved impossible to order them in a strict sequence according to a single criterion. In addition to the chronological sequence, the reader will detect a number of common themes – religion, gender, economics, colonialism, perceptions of literature and art and so forth – that haunt the essays and form webs of interconnection between them.

The theme of the Western image of the Near East is continued in this volume of essays, which discuss a number of nineteenth-century painters of 'Oriental' subjects. In 'About-Face: Sir David Wilkie's portrait of "Mehemet Ali"', Emily Weeks argues that in Wilkie's last portrait of Muhammad Ali (1841), the Pasha was as involved in the compositional decision-making process (and dominates the portrait in contrast to Wilkie's portrait of Sultan Abdülmecid) as the artist himself. Weeks outlines the political background of the Pasha's rise to power and his relations with Britain to argue that an about-face occurred, both in the artistic encounter between artist and subject and also in the politics of Muhammad Ali himself. In 'Carl Haag 1820–1915: Fact or Fantasy?', Cornelia Oelwein discusses the Middle Eastern experiences of the watercolour artist who travelled to Cairo in 1858 with the painter Frederick Goodall, before journeying to Palestine where he sketched the Holy Places, including Islamic monuments in Jerusalem; the impressions of his journeys inspired him for years, for many of his paintings are clearly based on his romantic memories. In 'John Frederick Lewis: "In Knowledge of the Orientals Quite One of Themselves"', Briony Llewellyn and Charles Newton discuss the work of an artist who adopted local dress and lived in Ottoman style for ten years in Cairo, from 1841. Lewis was concerned to paint specific everyday scenes of people and places that he knew well as accurately as possible, and his pictures of harem life have a narrative firmly grounded in reality. Sometimes classed as an Orientalist, Lewis's attitude to Egyptian society was marked by an obvious empathy – in marked contrast, for example, to that of William Holman Hunt's Visits to Eygpt, discussed by Judith Bronkhurst in 'William Holman Hunt: Passion, Prejudice and Truth to Nature'. Hunt's images of Egypt, which he visited in 1854 and 1857, were strongly influenced by feelings of Protestant English superiority, while fantasy was an essential element of his response to the Near East. A pre-Raphaelite, initially enchanted by Egypt and the Nile, he observed the landscape in the light of its religious associations, but his reactions to Cairo, like those of Kinglake, were almost entirely negative.

A somewhat different aspect of cross-cultural influence is discussed in 'David Urquhart and the Role of Travel Literature in the Introduction of Turkish Baths to Victorian England', in which Nebahat Avcıoğlu argues the importance of travel literature in transporting the architecture of one culture to another. After working in Istanbul, David Urquhart, diplomat, linguist and traveller, returned to Britain to take up the causes of political reform and the improvement of working-class conditions. The introduction of Turkish baths formed part of his philanthropic programme, and his achievements demonstrated the possibility of cultural mobility from East to West, the Other reinterpreted as a means of changing Self.

The next two essays investigate attitudes to religious minorities in the area. Since the early nineteenth century the Church Missionary Society had sent missionaries to minority groups in the Near East. In 'J. Wolff and H. Stern: Missionaries in Yemen', Aviva Klein-Franke considers the effectiveness of two German Jews who converted to Christianity and travelled to Yemen as missionaries: J. Wolff, who travelled there in 1836; and the charismatic H. Stern, who visited twenty years later. Klein-Franke outlines the contemporary Yemeni political and economic environment and considers the impact (or lack of it) of the missionaries' visits; the information they published on their travels is particularly important in view of the general lack of data from Yemen of that period. 'The Copts of Egypt: Neither Christian nor Egyptian?', by Hoda Gindi, discusses Europe's view of the Copts, who in most nineteenth-century travel writings were ignored, or at best seen as 'degenerate descendants' of the Ancient Egyptians. Gindi argues that European writers saw the Copts as legitimate targets for Protestant missionaries, and that travellers' attitudes towards them support Edward Said's view of the 'doctrine of European superiority'. As Eastern Christians of non-European extraction, the Copts found themselves without a role in the Oriental discourse created by Europe, and nineteenth-century accounts that mentioned them were ususaly critical and, at worst, accused them of heresy.

In 'Gender Politics in a Colonial Context: Victorian Women's Accounts of Egypt', Sahar Sobhi Abdel-Hakim discusses theories on 'gendered Orientalism' and questions some of the polarities that have developed in the debate. Abdel-Hakim investigates the relevance of these theories by exploring the work of Sophia Poole, Harriet Martineau and Lucie Duff Gordon in the 1840s–1860s, concluding that Victorian women writers did not challenge male discursive strategies but rather played a crucial role in the promotion of colonialism.

Cairo has long been established as the centre of the Muslim world. Loubna A. Youssef's essay on 'The Image of Nineteenth-Century Cairo as a Medieval City in Kinglake's *Eōthen*' focuses on the author's view of Cairo as a plague-ridden city, an image of hell: he found the desert en route to Cairo more inspiring than Cairo itself. With a distorted image of Islam and no knowledge of Arabic, he was unable to observe Cairene life intelligently, and the resulting account, based on a three-week stay in 1835, is characterised by misrepresentation and even by ill will towards the city.

'While I was in Egypt, I finished *Dr. Thorne*' by Nadia Gindy describes Trollope's visit to Egypt in 1858 to arrange a postal treaty for the GPO. Although Trollope described some of the officials whom he met, the visit did not lead to a travel book; instead, he used Egypt as the backdrop for two short stories in which he deflated the stereotyped notion of the exotic Orient and ridiculed the ordinary British tourist. His breadth of vision stands in marked contrast to that exhibited, for example, by Kinglake and Holman Hunt.

'On Translating *The Englishwoman in Egypt* into Arabic', by Azza Kararah, discusses the problems of translating the book named in the title, which was written by Sophia Poole and first published in 1844. As sister to the Arabist E.W. Lane, Sophia enjoyed a deep insight into the local culture, and this enabled her to describe accurately the minutiae of daily life, including details about life in the harem, which few men were able to enter. The translator, however, has to accommodate not only her sympathy for the Arab world, but also her Victorian snobbishness. The task requires not only care and understanding, but also a sense of humour.

Two essays in the collection deal with the career of Amelia Edwards. In 'Amelia Edwards: From Novelist to Egyptologist', Patricia O'Neill describes how Amelia Edwards' visit to Egypt in 1873–4 represented a turning point in her career, transforming her from a romanticist and popular novelist to a champion of Egyptology. Although she arrived in Egypt without Arabic and with little knowledge of

Egyptian history, her second travelogue, *A Thousand Miles up the Nile* (1877), became a classic both of travel literature and of women's travel writing. Her observations reflected her keen artistic perceptions, transforming her readers from passive tourists into discoverers of knowledge, while in turn she contributed to the admission of women into masculine realms of scholarship as a result of her absorption with the development of Egyptology in the West. A fascinating sidelight on her career is provided by Brenda Moon's essay 'Amelia Edwards, Jennie Lane and Egypt', in which Brenda Moon describes how Amelia Edwards' maid, Jennie Lane, also kept a diary of the journey. At times there are striking differences in tone between the two accounts, as Jennie Lane tempers with chronological details the licence that Amelia occasionally exercises in the cause of art.

Russian writers' interest in the Orient differed from that of many other European authors, as Russia did not perceive the East as exotic. Marianna Taymanova's essay, 'Oriental Motifs in the Poetry of Nikolay Gumilev', considers the effect on Gumilev's philosophy of his journeys to Abyssinia at the turn of the twentieth century. Gumilev saw life as a permanent metamorphosis, in which East and West were reconciled in a dual unity; the multifaceted world he experienced was transformed into the essence of his poetry with its concrete, colourful impressions.

Like that on Gumilev, the final two essays take us geographically somewhat outside the main focus of the collection, to Persia and Morocco. Katharine Chubbuck's essay, '"Ah! That the Desert were my Dwelling Place": The Romance of Persia in the Early Writings of Gertrude Bell', recounts the experience of the pragmatic Oxford graduate who failed to find a husband on the London circuit and was sent to Persia in the 1890s, where she fell in love with Henry Cadogan, wrote of her experiences and translated Persian poetry. Having eventually found her spiritual home in Baghdad, she died there after many years in the service of the British government.

Finally Amy Johnson discusses the position of Moroccan women in her essay 'Orientalism and Gender: The Condition and Status of Women in Morocco'. Johnson analyses the views of a number of British and American women writers on Morocco to determine whether the theories of Billie Melman in *Women's Orients* (1992) also apply to the western Middle East. Johnson concludes that these writers saw the Orient in terms of their own gender experience and in the light of their own idea of gender relations, and is able to conclude that Melman's theories also apply to Morocco.

Like those of the earlier volume, the various essays in this collection provide a fascinating array of perspectives on a set of historical, literary and cultural relationships about which lively debate is certain to continue well into the twenty-first century. It is to be hoped that they will prove as enjoyable and stimulating to the reader as they were for those who heard the original papers, and participated in the discussions that accompanied them, at the Oxford conference.

1

About-Face:[1]
Sir David Wilkie's Portrait
of 'Mehemet Ali'[2]

Emily M. Weeks

When discussing Orientalist paintings, such as Sir David Wilkie's portrait of 'Mehemet Ali', art historians and others, having read their Edward Said, almost invariably concern themselves primarily with the Western artist involved. It is the artist who is revealed to us, rather than the comparatively boring and lifeless sitter.

In the detail of Sir David Wilkie's picture, however, lies a wealth of information about the past actions, present situation and future political intentions of the Pasha. Specifically, it brings to light his clever courtship of England and his desire for Egyptian independence. Moreover, in the circumstances surrounding its creation, aspects of Muhammad Ali's personality are revealed. It is he who becomes our focus, and Sir David Wilkie who is relegated to the margins of the story.

Accordingly, my purpose in discussing Wilkie's painting is two-fold. First, I hope to construct something of a political and personal biography of the Pasha by means of this portrait. Second, and more broadly, I wish to argue that an Orientalist painting need not always rely upon Edward Said's notion of Orientalism for an explanation of its meaning.[3] In fact, what this painting reveals is no less than a clever inversion of Said's discourse, in which Western power is noticeable only for its absence.

In 1841, the Scottish artist, Sir David Wilkie, painted his last picture, a portrait in oils of 'Mehemet Ali' (fig. 1). It was not Wilkie's only depiction of the Pasha: a small, unfinished watercolour sketch in the Searight Collection preceded it by a few days, and was meant as a study

FIGURE 1
His Highness 'Mehemet Ali' **by Sir David Wilkie**
(by courtesy of the Tate Picture Library)

for this larger work.[4] In the watercolour version, the Pasha grips his sword. He is shown to the knees, his body enclosed in an oval frame, and he wears the red Turkish fez. The oil, now in the Tate Gallery, London, retains some of these features, but is more striking for its departure from them. The oval frame is gone; the hand no longer grips the sword. 'Mehemet Ali' is shown full-length. His dress is more carefully recorded. Why were these changes made? And, more significantly, who demanded them?

Wilkie's large portrait of 'Mehemet Ali' arrived in London shortly after the artist's death in 1841.[5] When it was hung in the 1842 Royal Academy exhibition, it attracted a great deal of attention, primarily for its subject matter. Prince Puckler Muskau noted that 'Mehemet Ali' had been a subject of 'daily conversation' in England at this time.[6] Progressive Victorians admired this self-made man, as well as the ambitious social and economic reforms he had enacted in Egypt over the last few decades. As early as 1827, Josiah Condor had stated:

> That Mohammed Ali is an extraordinary man cannot be disputed . . . his restless activity and spirit of enterprise . . . justly entitle him to be considered as one of the most accomplished . . . and one of the greatest of Mohammedan princes, that have ever vaulted into a throne.[7]

It was natural that the countenance, and not merely the politics, of the Pasha should be of great interest to the Victorian public as well. Visitors to Egypt lucky enough to have an audience with Muhammad Ali described his features in painstaking detail, down to the shapes of the bumps on his head.[8] Body type, or physiognomy, was thought to be a reliable indicator of personality, intelligence and social status in Victorian England, and was therefore given much attention. Portrait 'reading' was a popular pastime for men and women and, for those who could not go to Egypt, to now have the opportunity to read the Pasha's features for themselves must have been exciting indeed.

A critic writing on the 1842 exhibition in the *Athenaeum* had this to say:

> There is force and despotism, not merely in his shrewd eyes and firm lips, but in the attitude and in the hands which grasp nervously, with scimitar-like fingers, the elbows of the chair . . . It was a fine bit of coquetry . . . to introduce the glass full of innocent flowers so near the sword-point of the peremptory Lion of Alexandria.[9]

This was a curious reading. It was by no means the political message Muhammad Ali had intended to send, nor the impression he had wished to make in England. In fact, he had worked diligently to construct something quite different, as we will now see.

The Pasha's commission for this portrait was the result of one of the many inconveniences of nineteenth-century travel. Wilkie had been touring the Holy Land with the art dealer, William Woodburn, and had intended to leave Jerusalem in April, visit Beirut briefly and then return home to England. However, reports of plague at the port in Jaffa forced a diversion to Alexandria, where they chose to remain until the next ship for London was due to depart.[10] Mr Green, the local agent for the P. & O. steamer company, informed Wilkie that the Pasha had heard of his arrival and desired a meeting. On 5 May 1841, Woodburn and Wilkie went to the Pasha's summer palace and were presented to him in the garden. Wilkie recorded later: 'On being told I had painted the Sultan [of Turkey], the previous year . . . His Highness . . . desired I would make a picture for him of himself . . .'[11] Wilkie, with nothing else to do, and art materials at the ready, agreed.

On 14 May 1841, Wilkie wrote of Muhammad Ali to his brother Thomas: 'His Highness is an interesting character, has a fine head and beard, and I think makes the best portrait I have met with in my travels. He took much interest in it, and appeared with his attendants pleased with it.'[12] The Pasha's pleasure did not come without hesitation, however. During the sittings, four in all on 7, 8, 10 and 11 May, Muhammad Ali repeatedly voiced concerns and complaints. As Sarah Searight has noted, the Pasha was even liable to leap up, seize the brush from Wilkie's hand and try to alter any feature he disliked.[13] Translators explained to Wilkie that the Pasha thought he looked 'too young' in the picture, and that the 'marks in the brow and round the eyes ought to be made stronger'.[14] Wilkie had de-emphasised the lines in these areas, a practice he had undoubtedly grown accustomed to in his position as a society portraitist and as Painter-in-Ordinary to England's royal family.[15] Wilkie's answer to the Pasha's dissatisfaction was that he wanted to paint his expression and features rather than little details, in order to give [his] flat picture 'life and movement'.[16] The Pasha seemed satisfied with this reply, though he still insisted on checking Wilkie's progress regularly.

The Pasha had also been troubled by the initial position of his left hand. At first, Wilkie painted the Pasha's hand upon the hilt of his sword, as can be seen in the watercolour sketch. But Muhammad Ali declared that this 'menacing gesture' was inappropriate, for the British had 'deprived [him] of [his] sword' at the recent Battle of St Jean d'Acre.[17] Wilkie altered the composition as the Pasha wished, moving the hand to the more acceptable, 'peaceful' position seen in the oil version.

This last compositional change, though small, is important for two reasons. First, it reveals, as does the account of this portrait's creation as a whole, something of the forceful and energetic character of Muhammad Ali. It demonstrates that the artist did not 'capture' the Pasha's likeness, or 'stuff and mount' him, as Edward Said's 'Orientalist' encounter would have us expect. The Pasha would not allow this. He was as much a part of the decision-making process about the composition as the artist himself. Said's discourse has here, in effect, been reversed – compromise, collaboration and the Pasha's active intervention, rather than a lop-sided, Western-empowered 'Orientalism', were at work in the creation of this Orientalist painting.

Second, this alteration of the position of the hand provides a clue to Muhammad Ali's political ambitions and intentions in commissioning this portrait. Why was he so anxious in May 1841 to appear less 'menacing' to the British public? Why have his portrait painted at all, when he had been defeated so recently in the Battle of Acre? Less profound, but equally important and politically-motivated, are the questions why is he wearing those particular clothes and why is he sitting in that particular elbow chair?

When Wilkie painted this portrait in 1841, Muhammad Ali had been the virtual dictator of Egypt for over thirty years. Before his rule, Egypt had been occupied by a string of foreign powers – Roman, Byzantine, Arab and Ottoman – and was consequently overshadowed by them. At the end of the eighteenth century, however, Egypt became the focus of international attention, due to the actions of two great soldiers, Muhammad Ali and Napoleon Bonaparte.[18]

Jean Léon Gérôme's 1863 portrait of Napoleon Bonaparte makes a striking contrast to Wilkie's portrait of the Pasha (fig. 2). Both pictures depict foreign conquerors of Egypt, but one epitomises domination and conquest, the other, placid deliberation. One figure is set boldly into an Egyptian landscape; the other sits upon a chair, placed in no obvious geographical location. Napoleon looks to other, unspecified, lands that may soon be his. His eyes are averted, his profile worthy of a Roman coin. 'Mehemet Ali', on the other hand, looks at us, though indirectly. His lips are curled in a bemused half-smile. He does not challenge us, nor

FIGURE 2
Napeleon in Egypt by Jean-Léon Gérôme
(by courtesy of the Art Museum, Princeton University)

aggressively confront us. Rather, he coyly courts us. We, the audience, are ignored by the one figure and are made the objects of flirtatious interest – even desire – by the other. It is our land he looks upon. These formal differences are worth bearing in mind, for they are not only the result of aesthetic decisions made on the part of the respective Western artists, but also, I would argue, political ones made on the parts of their ambitious patrons.

Napoleon's invasion of Egypt in 1798 quickly attracted the attention of England, which now recognised the strategic importance of the country and the access it offered to India. It also attracted the attention of Egypt's nominal overlord, the Ottoman Sultan. British and Ottoman Turkish forces united in 1802 to drive the French out.[19] They were aided by an Albanian contingent led by Muhammad Ali. Napoleon fled, the British and Turks returned home with their anxieties temporarily relieved, and Muhammad Ali remained in Egypt.[20]

Though still subject to the Ottoman Emperor, Muhammad Ali declared himself the independent sovereign of Egypt in 1806. Five years later, he massacred the entire Mamluk guard in the courtyard of his Citadel in Cairo.[21] In 1831, exploiting his great and growing power, and with thoughts of an Egyptian empire stirring in his mind, Muhammad Ali invaded Palestine and Syria.[22] This aggressive push again worried Ottoman and English powers. Thus, on 4 November 1840, England and Ottoman Turkey, with some aid from Austria, again joined forces, this time in Syria, at the Battle of St Jean d'Acre. Muhammad Ali was defeated. After lengthy negotiations, he was granted hereditary rule of Egypt, but was deprived of all territories outside it.[23]

Ever the cunning diplomat, the Pasha saw in his defeat a window of opportunity. Since he was in a less threatening position now, 'deprived of his sword' as it were, British favour might gradually be gained. The Pasha had long realised that temporary aid from Britain, both financial and administrative, could help Egypt modernise and become a world power. Egypt could then embark more effectively on the campaign for the Egyptian empire Muhammad Ali so desired. Anxious to show his admiration for Western ways, and with these political ends in mind, Muhammad Ali courted Europe (France and England in particular), extending invitations to foreign diplomats, promoting tourism and strengthening political ties. Western educational systems were implemented, a printing press established, Western trade encouraged and Western industries introduced into Egypt.[24]

What we see again here, this time in the politics of Muhammad Ali, is the inversion of the East/West power relationship as defined in Said's *Orientalism*. As with the execution of Wilkie's portrait, the question of who holds power and who does not is not always clear. Egypt in 1841 was not a helpless nation awaiting its inevitable colonisation, but rather one working hard to subvert and resist it. The Pasha was down for now, perhaps, after his defeat in Syria, but was by no means out of the political picture. In the Middle East, and, as the Pasha hoped, soon in the world at large, Egypt was going to become a powerful force and a coloniser itself.

In the climate of increasing closeness between England and Egypt encouraged by Muhammad Ali in these years, news between the countries travelled fast. Word of Wilkie's portrait reached the London press by 19 May – that is, only 12 days after the first of the sittings.[25] Before his departure from Alexandria, Wilkie had recorded the stipulations of the commission: he was to put the finishing touches on the oil painting in London, have it framed there and then send the original back to the Pasha. The Pasha also granted the artist permission to make a copy of it that would remain in England.[26] Though Wilkie died on the return voyage home, and this plan was never realised, it is important to keep it in mind.[27] We now see that this portrait had a dual function, and was meant to express two political agendas: it had messages for both an audience in England and an audience in Egypt.

In both countries, Wilkie's portrait of 'Mehemet Ali' would have served important ideological functions. To better determine what these were, it will be helpful to look also at Wilkie's portrait of the new Ottoman Sultan Abdülmecid 'Abd al-Majid, the painting that had inspired the Pasha's commission, in the Royal Collection (fig. 3). The two pictures actually hung side by side at the Royal Academy exhibition of 1842, making a comparison between them inevitable.

Abdülmecid is represented with sword in hand, perhaps in a reference to his recent victory over Muhammad Ali at the Battle of Acre. He is in French military uniform and his beard is closely cropped, both features being representative of the new Western dress codes enforced by the Ottoman sultans from 1829. These decrees forbade traditional Eastern dress, requiring boots instead of slippers, trousers instead of baggy pants and frock coats instead of caftans. Long beards were forbidden and the fez was required headwear.[28]

The clothes of 'Mehemet Ali' now take on greater significance. He wears the fez, in obedience with the Ottoman decrees, but is otherwise in traditional – and forbidden – dress. His beard is full, not cropped. He wears slippers, not boots, and baggy pants, not trousers. A separate

FIGURE 3
Abu-ul-Mejid, Sultan of Turkey **by Sir David Wilkie**
(by courtesy of Her Majesty Queen Elizabeth II)

identity is claimed and established. Wary Egyptians, perhaps still unsure of this foreign usurper and uncomfortable with the vigour of his reforms, might have found comfort in this peacefully posed figure, dressed in familiar clothing. His dress, moreover, could have offered them a timely symbol of Egyptian nationalism around which to rally. This was no

'Frenchified' Abdülmecid, but a man who took pride in the indigenous traditions of his adopted country. By choosing to be painted in this way, Muhammad Ali could forcefully, deliberately but unaggressively (so as not to alienate potential allies), claim Egypt's independence from empires, Ottoman, French and British, in a pictorial language that would have been understood in any country in 1841.

The difference in poses between the two figures would have been noted as well. Abdülmecid looks to the side, perched tensely on the edge of an embroidered couch. 'Mehemet Ali' also sits on a piece of furniture, but here is where the similarity ends. His frontal pose, a position that has connoted authority since antiquity, demands the audience's attention. He sits placidly, but not idly. He is attentive and watchful. Though he looks askance at the viewer, he never releases him or her from his line of vision. The viewer is forced to remain aware of the Pasha, and is centralised in front of this impressive presence, for, unlike Abdülmecid, 'Mehemet Ali' is not a diminutive figure lost upon a large field of patterned fabric. He dominates the picture, solid and massive. He is, in effect, enthroned.

The actual 'throne' depicted here was a gift from Moses Montefiore, a favourite of the Pasha's.[29] Its inclusion in this portrait is important for two reasons. It not only elevates Muhammad Ali to a dignified status in Western eyes, as Wilkie assured him it would, but also serves as a powerful reminder of the Pasha's Western reforms.[30] 'Mehemet Ali' could, then, through this piece of furniture and his clothing, satisfy two needs at once – he could be viewed as both Egyptian and Western, as he needed to be in order to send the appropriate messages of political propaganda to his two separate audiences.

The repositioning of the hand away from the sword, the Egyptian dress and the chair are, I have argued, important clues to this portrait's political meaning. But there is one element left to consider. The lack of background is significant in this picture as well: it thwarts any attempt to safely lock 'Mehemet Ali' into the East. Though painted in a large Turkish room of his summer palace, replete with Islamic patterns and designs, no Eastern details are included at all. The flowers on the right, the only intruders in the otherwise bare background, are not particularly exotic. They are not even placed in an 'Oriental' vase. No cultural barrier has been erected. West and East are allowed to merge into one, just as the Pasha would have wished it.

This absence of any cultural separation, in a period obsessed with social, racial and cultural barriers is, I would argue, what doomed the success of 'Mehemet Ali's' message in Victorian England. The critic in the previously mentioned article in the *Athenaeum* felt acute discomfort when viewing this portrait, not because the Pasha's political message failed to be understood but because it succeeded all too well. He recognised in the Pasha's pointed and penetrating gaze, his forceful attitude, his Western throne and his ambiguous setting, his desire to become a part of Europe – and, more specifically, England. The critic realised that the Pasha intended to enter it as a ruler of an independent country, rather than as a bruised and battered 'good colonial' subject. He was troubled not merely because the Pasha seemed to him a threatening figure, but because 'Mehemet Ali', in this portrait, presented a threat to the entire British Empire.

We have interpreted this image of 'Mehemet Ali' not as followers of Edward Said might wish us to, as another damning example of Western imperialist strategies, but as the Pasha would have wanted us to in May of 1841, as a statement of Egyptian independence and diplomatic goodwill. The East/West power relationship that Said introduced to us has been turned inside out and upside down. An 'about-face' has occurred – first in the artistic encounter between the artist and his subject, and then in the politics of Muhammad Ali. The Pasha's strength of character, his clever political activity and his astute use of Western means – from Western industries to portrait-painting – to achieve his own ends, have at last been acknowledged. Finally, Wilkie's painting has shown that Orientalist paintings do not necessarily smack of Said's Orientalism, and that Eastern hands are not always as idle as they might appear to be – even when they are placed, as here, on the arms of a large elbow chair.

NOTES

1 The essay is a version of an article published in Julie F. Codell and Dianne Sachko Macleod (eds.), *Orientalism Transposed: The Impact of the Colonies on British Culture* (Aldershot, Ashgate, 1998).

2 Wilkie's portrait is entitled 'Mehemet Ali', an Anglicised form of the Turkish standard spelling 'Mehmet Ali', and where reference to Wilkie's portrait is made, the term 'Mehemet Ali' is used in this essay. Elsewhere, the Arabic form 'Muhammad Ali', is employed, as throughout this book. [Editors' note.]

3 I use the term 'Orientalist painting' in its broadest and most politically neutral sense. It can be loosely defined as a painting of non-Western countries/subject matter by a European artist. Since the publication of Edward Said's seminal book *Orientalism* in 1978 (New York, Vintage), such pictures have been the source of renewed interest among scholars, particularly art historians, for the messages of imperialism they are thought to contain. See, for example, Linda Nochlin, 'The Imaginary Orient', *The Politics of Vision* (New York, Harper and Row, 1989), pp. 33–59.

4 This sketch was used as the frontispiece of Wilkie's posthumous publication, *Sir David Wilkie's Sketches in Turkey, Syria and Egypt, 1840–41, Drawn on Stone by Joseph Nash* (London, Graves and Warmsley, 1843).

5 William J. Chiego (ed.), *Sir David Wilkie of Scotland (1785–1841)* (Raleigh, NC, North Carolina Museum of Art, 1987), p. 270. Wilkie died in June aboard the ship *Oriental*, after travelling in the Middle East and the Holy Land. His body was buried at sea; the event was memorialised by J.M.W. Turner in 'Peace: Burial at Sea'.

6 Prince Puckler Muskau, *Egypt Under Mohammed Ali* (London, 1845), p. 102.

7 Josiah Condor, *The Modern Traveller* (London, 1827), p. 162.

8 See Chiego, *op. cit.*, p. 270 for a few brief mentions of this (i.e. from 1841: 'His stature is undersized [5' 2"], and his figure . . . is now rather stooped, and corpulent . . . He has . . . [a] lofty forehead and aquiline nose, with the flexible brow so strongly indicative of quick changes of thought and passion.' Again, in 1840 his surgeon drew attention to: his prominent and open forehead, markedly curved eyebrows, deeply-seated, light chestnut eyes, the nose a little flat at the end, small mouth, upward-curling mustaches, the beard white and not thick, small hands and feet – adding that his headgear was generally inclined toward the right.)

9 *Athenaeum* (7 May 1842), 411.

10 The alternative route via Malta and Marseilles was far more tiresome and strenuous.

11 Chiego, *op. cit.*, p. 268. Muhammad Ali might not have been quite so keen to have this particular artist memorialise him on canvas, had he known of Wilkie's reputation as a face-painter in England. A state portrait he had painted of Queen Victoria was called 'so atrocious' that the Queen '[could] not send it as a present abroad' *(ibid.*, p. 57). Equally unflattering were the words of the First Earl of Ellesmere, who referred to Wilkie's venture into the field of portrait-painting as a 'national misfortune' *(ibid.*, p. 49). Of course, choice was not an issue for the Pasha – Wilkie was likely to be the only portrait painter in Alexandria at the time, and, more importantly, the only Painter-in-Ordinary to the Queen of England.

12 Allan Cunningham, *The Life of Sir David Wilkie with His Journals, Tours and Critical Remarks on Works of Art and a Selection from His Correspondence* (London, 1843), vol. 3, p. 493. Cunningham was Wilkie's friend and biographer, and his work is of inestimable value to the modern scholar. In these volumes are recorded numerous letters sent by Wilkie to various friends, relatives and patrons, as well as the majority of Wilkie's own journal entries.

13 Sarah Searight, *The British in the Middle East* (London, Weidenfeld and Nicolson, 1969), p. 172.

14 Chiego, *op. cit.*, p. 268.

15 In 1823, Wilkie succeeded Sir Henry Raeburn as the King's Limner for Scotland, a position that entailed much portrait painting. Similarly, when he succeeded Sir Thomas Lawrence to become Painter-in-Ordinary to King George IV (a position he retained under William IV and Queen Victoria), it was portraiture that occupied most of his time. In total, Wilkie created 150 portraits of royal and aristocratic figures. For a good discussion of Wilkie as a portraitist, and his own genuine dislike of the practice, see H.A.D. Miles' essay 'Wilkie as a Portraitist: Observations on "A National Misfortune"', Chiego, *op. cit.*, pp. 49–58.

16 Cunningham, *op. cit.*, pp. 468–9. Wilkie's intention to suggest the 'general effect' of the Pasha's countenance rather than its details is also typical of contemporary theories on portraiture. In his comments on painting (written in 1830 but never published), Wilkie wrote: 'In truth, a strictly accurate likeness is by no means necessary for recognition.' He seems to have taken Joshua Reynolds' Fourteenth Discourse (*A Discourse delivered to the students of the Royal Academy, on the distribution of the prizes, Dec 10th 1788*) (London, 1789) to heart, like so many other painters working in England at the time, repeating almost verbatim Reynolds' recommendation that the 'idea' of the sitter should be painted, rather than the exact physical likeness. For a good discussion of Reynolds' theories of portraiture and their influence on the English portrait tradition, see David Piper, *The English Face* (London, National Portrait Gallery, 1978).

17 Wilkie, *op. cit.*, pl. 1.

18 J.C.B. Richmond, *Egypt 1798–1952: Her Advance towards a Modern Identity* (London, Methuen, 1977), p. 17. The French had no vested interest in Egypt itself at this time, but saw its value as a piece on the diplomatic chessboard. Egypt was correctly recognised as a vital shipping link between East and West. Holland, Denmark, Sweden and other countries with trading interests in this area of the world would be grateful for any action that would challenge England's maritime despotism. Such allies could later benefit France, when Napoleon carried out his plan to oust England from the East by force, and eventually control world shipping between Europe and the Far East himself. French civilisation would then be spread towards India and up the Nile into Africa. It is worth mentioning that Napoleon was a hero to Muhammad Ali, and it is even said that the Pasha chose the same birth-date as Napoleon, out of sheer adulation.

19 The British desired to prevent Turkey's disintegration at the hands of Russia and other foreign powers, and thus were willing to help prop up its tottering Empire for a time. The possibility of a 'power vacuum' might disrupt the political balance that had been carefully constructed in the East and that met with their approval. The favour with which recent Ottoman sultans regarded the British promised policies conducive to British goals. If Egypt could be kept within the Ottoman Empire, then access to India would be ensured, even if only nominally. Moreover, the trials, tribulations and expenses of administering (another) overseas colony would be avoided.

20 Valentine Chirol, *The Occident and the Orient* (Chicago, University of Chicago Press, 1924), pp. 71–72.

21 Richmond, *op. cit.*, p. 40. Though ruling 'in the name of the Ottomans', in reality the Mamluks (descendants of Circassian slaves) answered to no one and enjoyed an unchallenged reign of terror in Egypt.

22 Today, the province of Syria comprises Syria, Lebanon and parts of Israel, Palestine and Jordan.

23 For a good, detailed account of the events of this complicated affair, see Frederick Stanley Rodkey, 'The Turco-Egyptian Question in the Relations of England, France and Russia, 1832–1841', *University of Illinois Studies in the Social Sciences*, 11:3–4 (September–December 1923), *passim*. For a more recent, and briefer, overview, see M.S. Anderson, *The Eastern Question 1774-1923: A Study in International Relations* (London, Macmillan, 1974), pp. 77–109.

24 Richmond, *op. cit.*, p. 65. Amazingly, given Egypt's later situation and its present state, Muhammad Ali initiated these reforms without the incurrence of any substantial foreign debt.

25 Chiego, *op. cit.*, p. 270.

26 *Ibid.*, p. 268.

27 A London newspaper reported in September that the portrait was sent back to the Pasha, with a price of 200 guineas, but was soon returned by him. Chiego writes, and I agree, that this 'seems unlikely' (Chiego, *op. cit.*, p. 270).

28 Enid M. Slatter, 'The Princess, the Sultan and the Pasha', *Art and Artists* (November 1987), 16.

29 See Frederick William Robert Stewart, Lord Castlereagh, Marquess of Londonderry, *A Journal to Damascus, through Egypt, Nubia, Arabia Petraea, Palestine and Syria* (London, Henry Colburn, 1947), vol. 1, pp. 223–4. Sir Moses Montefiore (1784–1885), a British citizen of Italian origin, was a philanthropist and champion of the Jewish cause at home and abroad. His first visit to Egypt, and audience with the Pasha, was in 1827. His goal of establishing Jewish colonies in Syria led him to return to the Middle East in 1839, and to request another meeting with the Pasha. A third audience was held in September 1840, when Montefiore pleaded on behalf of Jewish prisoners held in Damascus. For a brief biography of Montefiore, see the *Dictionary of National Biography* (London, Smith, Elder, 1909), pp. 725–7. For accounts of Montefiore's travels in and around Egypt, see Lady Montefiore's *Private Journal of a Visit to Egypt and Palestine by way of Italy and the Mediterranean* (8 vols., London, 1836), and the *Diaries of Moses and Lady Montefiore*, ed. Dr L. Loewe (London, 1890).

30 Chiego notes that Muhammad Ali first wished to be seated upon a divan, but Wilkie objected to this, explaining that though this was 'most picturesque', he thought to European eyes this 'wanted dignity' (Chiego, *op. cit.*, p. 268). Also, Wilkie wrote that he was first asked to paint the Pasha in the *chiouch* [kiosk] of the palace's summer garden, but that he had objected to the light there (*ibid.*). Both of these features (the kiosk and the divan) would have given the portrait a decidedly more 'Eastern' look. They would also seem to indicate that the execution and composition of the portrait were not entirely dictated by Muhammad Ali. However, I think there is sufficient evidence to support my claim that Muhammad Ali was indeed an active participant in the painting's overall creation. What is more confusing is that it was Wilkie who argued in favour of the chair, pointing out that it would lend the Pasha an air of dignity in Western eyes. Wilkie was, if anything, pro-Turkish in his sentiments and would therefore not have felt any obligation to present Muhammad Ali to the British public in a positive light. Why honour the Pasha in this way? Why deliberately aid him in his attempt to 'put his best face forward' in England? This curious

state of affairs serves the purposes of this chapter well, I believe. Just as Muhammad Ali's status as a 'colonised' object is problematic, so too is Wilkie's status as a Western coloniser. Said's paradigm is again proven to be inadequate for an explanation of this portrait.

2

Carl Haag 1820–1915:
Fact or Fantasy?

Cornelia Oelwein

In his time, Carl Haag was a well-known and successful painter of watercolours. His pictures are still sought after today and sell for high prices, especially in England. However, there is no modern book describing the artist's life and his work besides Delia Millar's excellent *Queen Victoria's Life in the Scottish Highlands Depicted by her Watercolour Artists*,[1] which concentrates only on his works for the Queen in Scotland.

A short article was published in 1996 by Briony Llewellyn in the *Dictionary of Art*[2] and individual pictures are described elsewhere, for example in Yehoshua Ben Arieh's recent *Painting the Holy Land in the Nineteenth Century*.[3] There are also some old articles from the last century or the beginning of the twentieth century.[4] To work out an œuvre catalogue is nearly impossible, however, for most of his paintings are in private collections spread all over the world and only a few are shown in public museums, such as the Victoria and Albert Museum's Searight Collection.[5] Occasionally one of Haag's pictures is offered for sale.[6]

Although some of Carl Haag's descendants still live in England, it seems that they know little about their famous great-grandfather. The 55 diaries written by Carl Haag in German between 1864 and his death in 1915 were given by his family to a dealer in antiques who requested what he called 'a considerable sum of money' to refrain from selling them and just allow interested persons to look at them. I am currently researching for a publication on the artist Carl Haag,[7] and in this essay shall endeavour to present some preliminary findings in two parts: first, I discuss Carl Haag's life and work, with special emphasis on his time in the Near East and related works; second, I try to answer the question: do his pictures depict fact or fantasy?

Carl Haag's life and work

Carl Haag was born the son of a baker in Erlangen, near Nuremberg in Bavaria, on 20 April 1820. A small sign on his father's house, in the middle of the town at Theaterstraße Nr. 2, commemorates his residence there. In 1836 he joined the Nuremberg art school to work with Albert Christoph Reindel (1784–1853), who was a famous engraver. Haag, however, loved working in colours. A few pictures are known from his early days, showing the neighbourhood of his home town: for example a small sepia drawing from Frauenaurach in 1839.[8]

In 1844 he studied at the Munich Academy of Arts. He did not take courses on a regular basis – he was not even formally registered – but learned the use of brushes and colours from the then famous Romantic painters, Peter von Cornelius, Wilhelm von Kaulbach and, especially, Carl Rottmann. While a student in Nuremberg, he had kept an album in which he tried to collect keepsakes of his friends, including their autographs and their likenesses. He elaborated on most of these and the eventual results were excellent coloured miniatures. The fame of this portrait album had preceded Haag to Munich, and his reputation resulted in him being employed to paint small effigies in the same style. Haag proved very successful at painting likenesses, most of them being worked from memory, but this work did not satisfy his desires and aims as an artist. He also designed illustrations and practised in oils, but his preference was always for watercolours.

After about two years, Carl Haag left Munich to travel to Paris. On the way, however, he took a detour into Belgium to visit some artist friends. Haag stayed for several months in Brussels, during which time he painted a portrait of a noble lady at her special request. Then he abandoned the idea of visiting Paris and travelled to England, because British *aquarelles* were being talked about on the Continent. Artists such as William Turner (1775–1851) had developed new techniques and were famous for their watercolours, and Haag was eager to study them.

On his arrival in London, in April 1847, he went to a watercolour exhibition. The event obviously impressed him deeply, for he set up house in London and applied to join the Royal Academy. After the winter – which he spent in Rome – he was accepted as a student there in 1848. Two years later, he exhibited at the Society of Painters in Watercolours, and he was elected a full member in 1853. For the following fifty years no exhibition was without some Haag paintings or sketches. Altogether

Carl Haag exhibited 274 watercolours[9] and became an extraordinarily successful watercolour painter of portraits, narrative subjects and scenes from everyday life.

Ernest, Duke of Sachsen Coburg Gotha, whom Haag met in 1852 on a journey through the Alps, introduced him to Queen Victoria. He was invited to Balmoral by her in the autumn of 1853 and started a series of different pictures showing the royal family and the Queen's guests at Balmoral Castle, hunting, salmon spearing and other holiday joys. Delia Millar described them as working holidays. The pictures still belong to the royal family today, though some are sent on touring exhibitions abroad. The most famous of them, *Morning in the Highlands*, was recently hung in the exhibition 'Victoria & Albert, Vicky & the Kaiser' in Berlin.[10] The story of Queen Victoria's patronage of Haag closes on rather an ugly note, as Delia Millar tells us. The reason was – as it is so often – money, but this incident happened 15 years after the first invitation. A happier postscript completes the story. When Haag made his final appearance at Windsor in 1899, the Queen wrote in her Journal: 'I knew him very well formerly, having had lessons with him and possess many fine pictures by him . . .'[11]

In the 1850s Haag stayed abroad for most of the time, preferring to base himself in Rome, though he also travelled to Dalmatia and to Montenegro. During the winter of 1857–8 he visited Munich again and, finally, after some months in England, he went to Cairo, together with the painter Frederick Goodall (1822–1904), in autumn 1858. This period marked the start of Haag's career in Orientalist art. The two artists spent the winter in Egypt, sketching together in the streets of Cairo and in the surrounding desert, finding many 'grand and picturesque subjects', as Haag wrote home in a letter to the secretary of the Old Water-Colour Society Mr Jenkins. 'Tell those', he continued, 'that are in search of new ground of subjects for their pencil that there is but one Cairo! and artists ought to see it.'[12]

Haag stayed in the Near East for about 18 months. In the spring of 1859 he travelled to Palestine, arriving in Jerusalem in time for the Easter festivals. There he was mainly occupied in sketching the Holy Places, but he also made some fine pencil drawings of more general views of the city,[13] as well as painting the exceptionally interesting watercolour *General View of Jerusalem from the Mount of Olives*.[14] Haag commented:

I greatly enjoyed my sojourn in the desert, where I lived in an ordinary canvas tent and painted for hours every day. Desert life is most agreeable. I rode nearly all the way from Cairo to Jerusalem on the back of a camel, and I never experienced anything more exhilarating.[15]

Sketching in Islamic areas was not without danger, however. In an interview years later, Haag said:

I had to be protected against outbursts of fanaticism, and as I was under the wing of the Sultan, so to speak, the Pasha, who was responsible for my well-being, had to make all sorts of arrangements before he could satisfy himself that there was no danger of my being molested.[16]

It was a rare event for a Christian to penetrate into the temple area of Jerusalem. Sometimes Haag even had to be accompanied by officers and a shaykh of the mosque, who once advised some dangerous-looking individuals to keep away from him if they did not want their images to appear in the pictures. 'From that moment I was free to paint as much as I pleased', Haag said,

and during the whole time I was at Jerusalem I never saw those awful blacks again. They feared me like the plague, because they have a superstition that as long as a picture containing their portraits exists they will never have rest in their graves.

Continuing his travels in summertime, Haag went north to Samaria and Galilee, living among the local Bedouin tribes and studying their daily life and their costumes. One of these was the Hawara tribe, near Mount Tabor, whose shaykh, Agile Agha, was visited by several European travellers at this time, including the Prince of Wales in 1862. A water-colour, *Camp of Agile Agha*, was recently offered by Spink & Son (London), signed and dated 1859. Several sketches exist of the Bedouin shaykh and his camp. Some years later, Haag painted a large watercolour for the Royal Collection, having been commissioned by the Prince of Wales on 8 July 1862, to commemorate the Prince's meeting with Agile Agha. Haag was not present on that occasion but had visited the shaykh two years before, and was, therefore, able to reconstruct the scene using his sketches, in conjunction with sittings from the Prince and several of his retinue. A portrait of the shaykh himself by Haag is also in the Royal Collection.[17]

In the autumn 1860, Haag travelled to Syria. Staying in Damascus, he met Lady Jane Digby el Mezrab, an English lady who had married the popular shaykh Medjuel el Mezrab, of the Anazeh Bedouins.[18] Lady Digby, the former Lady Ellenborough, was something of a tourist attraction and Haag was introduced to her by the British consul in Damascus and shown the lady's collection of drawings. 'If I am a ruined man all my life, or if I walk there in Bedouin sandals, I *must* go to Palmyra!', Haag said[19] after he had seen her pictures of the ruins, the colonnade and the triumphal arch. He asked shaykh Medjuel and his Bedouins to accompany him to Palmyra and documented that trip in some wonderful watercolours, two of them showing the shaykh and his wife in the ruins of Palmyra. Another is the excellent watercolour the *Triumphal Arch*, which is now in the Searight Collection.[20]

Accompanying the travelling party to Palmyra were two young English ladies, the Beaufort sisters. Back in England, Emily Beaufort-Strangford published her travelling journal in two volumes, with the title *Egyptian Sepulchres and Syrian Shrines*. 'M. Haag', she noted, 'made sketches of the faces round us – some superhumanly ugly, but some remarkably pretty'.[21] Emily Beaufort also gave us an insight into the artist's character: 'Haag, who dressed like a Bedoueen, and was always full of jokes, was a favourite with them, and the chief songs were about him, with good-natured fun about his continually dropping asleep.'[22]

Throughout his trips Haag looked for new and exciting subjects. He not only visited famous ruins and historical sites, but made numerous drawings of everyday life in the desert. After leaving Palmyra, Haag travelled to Baalbek in order to sketch the great classical temples there. However, in 1860 Haag left the Levant. The year before, he had written to Mr Jenkins: 'The coming summer and autumn will find me travelling about in Syria and among the Greek Islands; the winter in Cairo again.'[23] There is no documentary evidence that Haag really went to Greece, but I am convinced that he visited the Islands before returning to London. I have a good reason for this belief: several Hellenistic pictures, dated 1861, can still be seen today in the Benaki Museum in Athens.[24]

In 1866 Haag returned for a short time to Germany to marry Ida, the only daughter of the German General Büttner, in Lüneburg.[25] Eventually, they were to have three sons and one daughter. After his marriage he bought a house in Hampstead near London, named it 'Villa Ida' after his wife, and built it as an 'Oriental' studio, furnished with artefacts that he had brought back from Egypt and the Near East.[26] The rooms are reminiscent of Haag's studio in Cairo, which he depicted in several of his works.[27]

In 1873, Haag felt the need to renew his experience of the East, when he was entertained by the Khedive of Egypt after an introduction by the Prince of Wales. He travelled to Egypt again and spent several months sketching in and around Cairo. His impressions of these journeys inspired him for years. Many of his Oriental pictures – highly finished watercolours, full of ethnic details – were exhibited. One of the best known was *Danger in the Desert*, which was also engraved in 1878 by Leo Flameng. It was first exhibited at the Royal Water-Colour Society, in 1871, and later in Paris, in 1878, and gained an Art Medal at Vienna.[28] It seems that Haag had come to specialise in Oriental themes, perhaps because there was a big demand for such works. He had obviously caught the current taste of the people and was well rewarded with medals and awards. Haag was not a poor artist; on the contrary, his paintings made him a wealthy man, and allowed him, for example, to buy – besides 'Villa Ida' – a medieval tower on the river Rhine in Oberwesel, Germany, in the 1860s.

At the age of 83, and having long become naturalised in England, Haag retired to Germany and spent the last 12 years of his life in his medieval tower. He died there on 24 January 1915, at nearly 95 years of age. He had never returned to his home town of Erlangen, but towards the end of his life he had had some communication with its local authority. On the occasion of his eightieth birthday Haag was honoured by an inscription on his father's house; ten years later a street was named after him. In return, he presented a self-portrait to the town, and it hung in the town hall until 1962. Today it is stored in the local museum.[29]

Fact or fantasy?

The portraits of Lady Jane Digby el Mezrab and her husband were both watercolours, made in Palmyra during the summer 1859, and they were sold at Sotheby's, London, in 1982. Today they are in a collection in Kuwait. It seems that Lady Jane did not see the finished portraits at the time they were painted. Years later she wrote to her brother: 'Carl Haag sent me the *Illustrated* with Medjuel's portrait, but not a bit like. . . . He is, I think, much better looking.'[30] Maybe she was seeing it through the eyes of a woman in love, because a portrait by Emily Beaufort, showing exactly the same man, as well as a small drawing by Jane herself, show the accuracy of Haag's likeness. More important for us is Haag's description of their costumes, for he did not paint fantasy costumes. Emily Beaufort showed exactly the same costumes, and photographs of Bedouins from the end of the nineteenth century also reveal exactly the same styles. There is no picture to compare Lady Jane's portrait with (the last one was made years before), but her costume was described in some travel journals and it seems to be quite similar to those descriptions.

One can compare these portraits with those of another couple: two years later, Haag painted a Greek man and a woman in their costumes. Today the pictures are in the Benaki Museum of Athens. While the shaykh and his wife are very static, the Greek couple are much more alive. The picture of the shaykh has no background; while behind Lady Jane one can recognise the colonnades of Palmyra. The Greek pictures show many more details. The costume of the Greek man is easy to identify as the costume of a *palikare*, an irregular soldier, one of whom was described by Lord Byron in *Childe Harold's Pilgrimage*. The landscape is easy to identify: it shows the ruins of the Apollon Epicurius Temple in Bassä, in Arcadia, which was famous for its architecture as well as for its spectacular location. It seems that Haag did not include this background by accident, but wanted to make the soldier more dignified.[31] A woman in her typical costume is shown spinning in the landscape of Arcadia. There are no ruins, but typical plants of the Greek highlands. Women engaged in spinning were a scene of everyday life in the countryside.[32]

In all Haag's pictures we find very exact likenesses of costumes as well as of the supporting items – the saddles of the camels, for example – all of which are painted with great attention to detail. The treatment of architecture and landscape is the same, to the extent that everything – the different gates for example – appears real.

Haag used some motifs several times. On occasions, it seems that he composed a new picture in his studio, taking the details from different sketches that he had made on his tours. The pictures of Agile Agha's camp are one example; another example is the picture group, *Mecca Pilgrims returning to Cairo*, dated 1894,[33] which shows exactly the same street as the watercolour *A Gateway in Cairo*.[34] The scenery of *A Bridal*

Procession in Damascus, dated 1892 (fig. 1),[35] and the study for the picture are also very similar.[36]

Haag painted only an ideal situation, as did most of his contemporaries. An example is the watercolour *War*, dated 1871, which belongs to the Searight Collection. The wounded drummer boy is borne back to camp on his camel, and the battle nearby is further indicated by assorted weapons carried by the soldiers.[37] *War* is a typical example of Haag's perception of reality. Every detail is correct, but it seems to be a bright and sunny day without any pain – even in the face of the wounded soldier. Haag is reflecting details of persons and subjects precisely, but also making a concession to the taste of his potential customers. In fact *War* is a typical mixture of fact and fantasy.

From about 1860, no signs of artistic development are apparent in Haag's work. He had his motifs as well as his methods, and they had made him a rich man. He was an artist of the nineteenth century: more a talented and excellent artisan than an ingenious artist. He did not adopt the 'modern style' methods of artists such as Carl Rottmann or William Turner, let alone the artistic developments of the turn of the century. He neither made experiments, nor did he show any wild fantasy. Most of Haag's paintings are detailed genre pictures, based on many sketches drawn in the Near East, and loved by the public. People liked travelling in these exciting and exotic areas and wanted to recognise them again in a romantic way, as in the words of Lord Byron or the pictures by the painters of the nineteenth century. To satisfy this demand Carl Haag reproduced a romantic, ideal reality of consistently excellent quality.

FIGURE 1
A Bridal procession in Damascus by Carl Haag
(by courtesy of Mathaf Gallery Ltd)

NOTES

1 Delia Millar, *Queen Victoria's Life in the Scottish Highlands Depicted by her Watercolour Artists* (London, Philip Wilson, 1985). Delia Millar also edited *The Victorian Watercolours and Drawings in the Collection of Her Majesty the Queen* (London, Philip Wilson, 1995), which contains some examples of Haag's Orientalist art.

2 Briony Llewellyn, 'Carl Haag', *The Dictionary of Art* (London, Macmillan, 1996), p. 891.

3 Yehoshua Ben Arieh, *Painting the Holy Land in the Nineteenth Century* (Jerusalem, Tel Aviv & New York, 1996).

4 The most important are: F. Wedmore, 'Carl Haag R.W.S.', *The Magazine of Art* (December 1889), 52–61; Friedrich von Boetticher, *Malerwerke des 19. Jahrhunderts* (Hofheim am Taunus, Schmidt & Günther, 1891), p. 461; J.L. Roget, *A History of the Old Water Colour Society* (London, Longmans, 1891), pp. 341–52; L. Göhring, 'Die Beziehungen des Malers Karl Haag zu seiner Vaterstadt Erlangen', *Erlanger Heimatblätter*, 46 (1930), 185–8; U. Thieme and F. Becker, *Allgemeines Lexikon der bildenden Künstler* (Leipzig, Seemann, 1907–50), p. 382.

5 *British Watercolours in the Victoria & Albert Museum, An Illustrated Summary Catalogue* (London, Victoria and Albert Museum, 1980), p. 165. Briony Llewellyn, *The Orient Observed. Images of the Middle East from the Searight Collection* (London, Victoria & Albert Museum, 1989), pp. 42 and 126.

6 In Sotheby's sale of 29 April 1982, 83 lots of Haag's works and some photographs were offered. In 1982, the Mathaf Gallery, London, offered several watercolours in the exhibition 'Carl Haag and his Contemporaries'; information from David Mitchell, Royal Watercolour Society. Single items were sold in other sales in England and Germany and also in antique shops.

7 Cornelia Oelwein, 'Carl Haag (1820–1915). Ein Erlanger Künstler – "well known" in England', *Bayernspiegel*, 4 (Munich, 1995), 18.

8 Stadtarchiv Erlangen.

9 Roget, *op. cit.*, p. 352.

10 Wilfried Rogasch, *Victoria & Albert, Vicky & the Kaiser* (Berlin, Katalog des deutschen historischen Museums, 1997), no. I/41. 'The Terrace of Schloss Reinhardsbrunn' was shown in 1998 in an exhibition in the Kunstsammlungen der Veste Coburg. Delia Millar, *Views of Germany from the Royal Collection at Windsor Castle* (Windsor, Royal Collection, 1998), p. 181, no. 55.

11 Millar (1985), *op. cit.*, p. 125.

12 'Letter to Josef J. Jenkins, 17 February 1859', Archive, Royal Watercolour Society.

13 Three of them are in the Searight Collection at the Victoria and Albert Museum, London.

14 Information from Briony Llewellyn.

15 Cassell, *Saturday Journal*, 786:17 (19 October 1898).

16 *Ibid.*

17 Signed and dated 1859. Millar (1995), *op. cit.*, p. 397.

18 Cornelia Oelwein, *Lady Jane Ellenborough. Eine Frau beeindruckt ihr Jahrhundert* (Munich, Ehrenwirth, 1996), p. 243.

19 Llewellyn, *The Orient Observed, op. cit.*, p. 42.

20 *Ibid.*, p. 42.

21 Emily de Beaufort-Strangford, *Egyptian Sepulchres and Syrian Shrines* (2 vols., London, Macmillan, 1861), vol. 1, p. 343.

22 *Ibid.*, p. 346.

23 'Letter to Josef J. Jenkins, 17 February 1859', Archive, Royal Watercolour Society. RWS,542/6

24 Fani-Maria Tsigakou, *Das wiederentdeckte Griechenland in Reiseberichten und Gemälden der Romantik* (Bergisch Gladbach, Gustav Lübbe, 1982), p. 126; Fani-Maria Tsigakou and Anja Sibylle Dollinger, *Glanz der Ruinen. Die Wiederentdeckung Griechenlands in Gemälden des 19. Jahrhunderts* (Cologne, Rheinland-Verlag, 1995), no. 60 and 61.

25 Evangelisches Kirchenbuchamt, Lüneburg (Reg. Garnisonsgemeinde von 1742–1867, p. 59): marriage between Juliane Margarethe Luise Büttner and Johann Carl Haag on 16 May 1866 in St Michaelis Church, Lüneburg.

26 M. Phipps-Jackson, 'Cairo in London: Carl Haag's Studio', *Art Journal* (1883), 71.

27 For example, Sotheby's London sale on 29 April 1982, lot 35; or Christie's London sale on 15 March 1996, lot 83.

28 Roget, *op. cit.*, p. 351.

29 Papers Stadtarchiv Erlangen.

30 Mary S. Lowell, *A Scandalous Life* (London, Fourth Estate, 1995), p. 288, gives letter of 9 September 1870.

31 Tsigakou and Dollinger, *op. cit.*, no. 60.

32 *Ibid.*, no. 61.

33 Sotheby's London sale 29 April 1982, lot 67.

34 Sotheby's London sale 29 April 1982, lot 74.

35 Lynne Thornton, *Women as portrayed in Orientalist Painting* (Paris, 1988), p. 100.

36 Sotheby's London sale 29 April 1982, lot 72.

37 Llewellyn, *The Orient Observed, op. cit.*, p. 126.

3

John Frederick Lewis:
'In Knowledge of the Orientals
Quite One of Themselves'

Briony Llewellyn and Charles Newton

Bedouin encampments and Cairo bazaars

When J.F. Lewis was created a Royal Academician in 1865, the *Illustrated London News* published a brief résumé of his life to date: 'one of the most strange and adventurous among the many interesting biographies of painters'. After studying with his father, and practising his skills by drawing animals, he had travelled abroad and since then had devoted his life 'to portraying the life and character of the Southern and Oriental races, and delineating the picturesque customs and costumes, architecture, scenery and climatic aspects of Spain, Italy, Greece, Turkey, Egypt and Syria'. While in the East, he had made Cairo his headquarters, and 'ultimately became in knowledge of the Orientals quite one of themselves'.[1]

Contemporary reviewers of his pictures exhibited at the Royal Academy and the Old Water-Colour Society wrote in similar terms of his unique ability to portray Eastern life. Many others recognised the nature of his achievement, but few described this more eloquently than his fellow artist and eastern traveller, Edward Lear. In a letter to Lewis's wife, Marian, Lear lamented the absence of Lewis's work at the Royal Academy exhibition of 1875, the year before he died: 'For besides the exquisite and conscientious workmanship, the subjects painted by J.F. Lewis were perfect as representations of real scenes and people.'[2] More recently, Lewis's images have been seen as manifestations of the nineteenth-century fascination with the exotic, or the Other, rather than as an expression of the artist's own knowledge of and empathy with contemporary Egyptian society. He has been classed as an Orientalist along with the many other European artists who travelled to the Near East during the nineteenth century. These artists depicted many aspects of the area's life and scenery, but few gained more than a superficial knowledge of its culture. Some virtually ignored it, preferring ancient ruins or landscape; others valued it primarily for its evocation of the Bible, or for the structure and decoration of its religious buildings. Most artists interpreted the Orient in terms of sentiments redolent of their own Western society. Lewis's preoccupation with the East was due neither to its antiquities nor to its biblical associations, but to its everyday life. His subjects were its people and their customs: the women in their houses, the traders in the bazaars and the bedouin with their camels in the desert.

The circumstances of Lewis's experience of Egypt help to explain why his attitude towards the country and its inhabitants differed from that of his fellow artists. Unlike his contemporaries, such as David Roberts and William Müller, who passed through the region as tourists, Lewis actually lived for a decade in Cairo from 1841.[3] He established himself there in Ottoman style, in a large, old house in the Azbakiyya district of the city; he adopted local dress, both within and outside his home, and may have learnt some Arabic. He made tours out of the city: to Suez and Sinai in the early 1840s, and possibly after; and to Aswan along the Nile in 1850. In 1847 he was in Alexandria for his marriage to an English girl, Marian Harper. He thus had ample time and opportunity to observe and familiarise himself with contemporary Egyptian society.[4]

No journals or letters home to family or friends appear to survive,[5] so his opinion of his surroundings must be judged from an examination of the sketches that he made in Egypt and the watercolour and oil paintings that he executed later in England. The sketches are both numerous and accurately observed, and clearly indicate that, unlike other Western visitors, many of whom decried Eastern culture, Lewis was sympathetic towards the society in which he had immersed himself.[6] At the same time, his desire to record his surroundings with meticulous care and close attention to detail and his deliberate intention to use them in pictorial images, reveal an attitude that was fundamentally European. In many respects, Lewis's encounter with Egypt is paralleled by that of E.W. Lane, who also lived for many years in Cairo, partly during the 1840s, and also assumed local dress and habits, while at the same time recording his observations for a European market.[7] It is not generally acknowledged that it was this very duality of their lifestyles that enabled both men to produce the successful work for which they later became famous.

On Lewis's return to England in 1851, he was uniquely placed to paint images that, though Western in concept, accurately depicted certain aspects of Eastern life. Whether they are of the desert, a Cairo street or a domestic interior, his compositions do not merely describe a haphazard collection of people, animals and objects, but are of scenes that he could actually have witnessed. They show individuals that he knew – many compositions are clearly portraits – engaged in characteristic activities that often involve interaction and communication.

The most obvious example of this is *A Frank Encampment in the Desert of Mount Sinai 1842 – The Convent of St Catherine in the Distance* (fig. 1).[8] Commissioned by Lord Castlereagh, it records a meeting between the Irish peer and shaykh Hussayn of the Oulad Said tribe, who guided him through the Sinai desert and protected him in 1842. Much has been written about this picture – at the time by John Ruskin and other critics, and also in recent years.[9] Suffice it to note here that it is a complex and fascinating composition that seems to have taken Lewis 14 years to complete, since it was not exhibited until 1856.[10] His difficulties with it may have stemmed from his uneasiness with the concept of the dominant European, arrogantly reclining while the proud Oriental shaykh remains standing before him. In no other image by Lewis is there so clear a confrontation between East and West.

While working on *A Frank Encampment* during the mid-1850s, Lewis exhibited several other scenes of Bedouin life in the Sinai desert. It was as if he needed to focus on the everyday activities of its inhabitants before he could complete his portrayal of a specific and unusual event that involved foreign tourists as well as locals. In 1854, he exhibited two pictures at the Old Water-Colour Society, *A Halt in the Desert* and *Camel & Bedouins. Desert of the Red Sea*, one of which can almost certainly be identified with the watercolour now known as *A Noonday Halt*.[11] In this, two Arabs have recently arrived to confer or make a deal with the men seated in the centre. *A Halt in the Desert*, dated 1855, is a more complex composition, and is probably the same as *The Well in the Desert*, which was exhibited that year at the Old Water-Colour Society.[12] A caravan has halted at an oasis in the Sinai desert: the well and a few palm trees are seen in the left background; in the foreground, merchants reclining beside their richly caparisoned camels are apparently

FIGURE 1
*A Frank Encampment in the Desert of Mount Sinai, 1842 – The Convent
of St Catherine in the Distance* **by John Frederick Lewis**
(*by courtesy of the Yale Center for British Art, New Haven, Connecticut*)

striking a bargain over the textile placed on the ground between them.
Their languid attitudes, as they draw on their pipes and brew coffee, are
seen not as indolence but as the repose due to weary travellers.

In the same year, Lewis exhibited *Greetings in the Desert* at the
Old Water-Colour Society, and showed an oil version at the Royal
Academy the following year, with the subtitle *Selamat Teiyibeen* (fig. 2).[13]
In its review of the picture, *The Art-Journal* described it thus: 'Two men,
perhaps in the condition of merchants, address each other in friendly
terms, grasping each other at the same time by the hand; there are also
camels and a slave introduced. The men do not wear the same costume;
there is a difference in their dress which may define respectively the Arab
of the city and the Arab of the desert, or, some other distinction of
condition or country.'[14] With no detailed explanation from the artist, it
was left to the viewer, then as now, to speculate on the precise meaning
of the picture. Lewis may have intended a deliberate ambiguity in his
depiction of the two men greeting each other in the desert. Both are
extending their right arms as if to shake hands in European fashion, but
the fingers are not yet clasped, and they may be merely touching palms,
as, according to Castlereagh, Bedouin custom demanded.[15]

[38]

FIGURE 2
Greetings in the Desert, Egypt by John Frederick Lewis
(private collection)

The extended narrative contained in *A Frank Encampment* was not repeated, but each of these desert scenes depicts a specific moment in which figures clearly relate to each other in subtle ways, through glances, gestures and objects; through the attitudes in which they sit or stand; even through their camels. In all these representations of Bedouins in the desert, painted at home in his studio, Lewis went to great pains to reconstruct as accurately as possible the scenes that he had observed. Several sketches of men and camels relating to the finished pictures survive, and these were used in conjunction with the many costumes, textiles and artefacts that he had brought back with him to build up his compositions.[16] The individual figures and groups are represented for their own sakes as manifestations of a different contemporary culture, and not as typological symbols of events in biblical history.

By contrast, Frederick Goodall's *Early Morning in the Wilderness of Shur* was just such an image.[17] Described in the 1860 Royal Academy catalogue as 'An Arab Sheikh addressing his tribe on breaking up their encampment at the Wells of Moses', it is placed on the very spot where the Israelites are said to have drunk water after their crossing of the Red Sea, and it deliberately evokes the image of Moses exhorting his people.

Goodall's narrative is explicit, and the associations would have been clearly understood by his public. The meaning of Lewis's desert images, on the other hand, is ambiguous, and they are open to different interpretations. On one level, in their accuracy of observation and sympathetic portrayal of their subjects, they are manifestations of Lewis's close encounter with desert life, as he described it to his friend, William Thackeray: 'under the tents, with still more nothing to do than in Cairo; now smoking, now cantering on Arabs, and no crowds to jostle you; solemn contemplations of the stars at night, as the camels were picketed, and the fires and the pipes were lighted'.[18] On another level, they are a highly accomplished European artist's technically brilliant rendering of the intense light of the desert, and of the forms and colours of the camels, textiles and accoutrements of a foreign culture, designed to astonish and delight his Victorian public through their originality and virtuosity.

The same dual approach may be observed in Lewis's numerous scenes of street life in Cairo, of which several were painted during the last decade of his life. Here, too, where Lewis was specific, other artists generalised. While in Cairo in 1838–9, David Roberts made many drawings of streets and mosques, which were later translated into lithographs that appeared in the third volume of his *Egypt and Nubia* in 1849.[19] These are identified by name and are lively scenes of men and women of varying descriptions coming and going with their goods, their donkeys and their camels, but not participating in a specific event. Many of Lewis's street scenes, by contrast, focus on a particular custom that could typically be observed there. More information about some of these customs can be obtained from descriptions in the published accounts of other British visitors.

The oil painting by Lewis that was exhibited in 1869 as *The Seraff* [money-changer] – *A Doubtful Coin: A Scene in a Cairo Bazaar* is an example of this.[20] Currency was a problem in Egypt in the 1840s, as Lord Castlereagh, writing in 1842, relates. Both Turkish and Egyptian money was in circulation, but since the hostilities between the Ottoman sultan and the Pasha of Egypt, Muhammad Ali, Turkish currency was no longer legal tender. Castlereagh wrote:

The consequence is that every one who pays, endeavours to pass away some Turkish money, and in the old currency it is extremely difficult for a foreigner to tell the difference. Then again, many of the Pasha's pieces of gold have been depreciated, and clipped or split. These the people object to take at their value, and deduct half or a whole piastre, as they think expedient.[21]

Lewis's image clearly shows the dispute between the merchant and the two women who are showing a coin to the seraff for the purposes of arbitration. According to Lane, 'seyrefees', or money-changers, were often Jews and were held in high esteem for their integrity.[22] Hence the disputants' reliance on them for a fair judgment.

Another custom described by Lane is represented in Lewis's *A Cairo Bazaar: the 'Dellal'*.[23] 'In many of the sooks in Cairo, auctions are held on stated days, once or twice a week', wrote Lane.

They are conducted by 'dellals' (or brokers), hired either by private persons who have anything that they wish to sell in this manner, or by shopkeepers; and the purchasers are of both classes. The dellals carry the goods up and down, announcing the sums bidden for them with cries of 'harag'.[24]

Interestingly, this precise extract (very slightly abridged) appeared in the Royal Academy catalogue entry for this painting in 1876.[25] Lewis and Lane undoubtedly knew each other in Cairo in the 1840s, but how much they communicated or whether they discussed their common interests is not yet clear.[26] Lewis's picture displays a rich variety of different individuals – men and women, old and young, dark and pale – all intent on the figure of the broker, whose wares some of them examine. Once again he combines empirical observation with an understanding of the culture he is portraying.

Harem life

Whether the statement that J.F. Lewis was 'in knowledge of the Orientals quite one of themselves' can be applied to Lewis's harem pictures is more contentious, but the case for doing so will be discussed. These harem pictures, far from being pretty images of women and flowers prefiguring the purely aesthetic compositions of Albert Moore, have a type of narrative that is firmly grounded in reality. A better comparison would be with Vermeer, whose pictures have no obvious plot but are intense observations direct from life. The viewer is free to interpret them, yet they contain a subtle and unspoken narrative that is made all the more powerful by the pictures' calm silence.

When Lewis's most famous picture *The Hhareem* was exhibited at the Old Water-Colour Society, in 1852,[27] he did not explain his intentions in the catalogue. For reasons not yet discovered, he decided to include a long description of the painting in the catalogue when it was exhibited again at the Royal Scottish Academy exhibition in 1853.[28] Perhaps he felt that he needed to emphasise that he was painting direct from his observations of everyday life, albeit that of the Cairene daily round rather than the drawing rooms of Kensington. His description is worth quoting in full, as it explicitly denies any element of fantasy in this amazing work, which is a huge watercolour painted as carefully as a miniature right to the corners. The text in the catalogue is as follows:

> The scene is laid in the upper or women's apartments of a house in Cairo, the lower part of the house being always appropriated to the men. The Master (a Bey and a Turk) is habited in the old Mamluke dress of Egypt, now not often worn. Immediately to his left is seated a Georgian, the 'Sit el Gebir' or ruling lady of the Hhareem, having obtained that privilege by being the mother of his eldest son, who is leaning against her knee. The lady stooping forward is a Greek and the one reclining at the Bey's feet, a Circassian. The laughing slave – an old inmate. The girl who is being unveiled by the black guardian is also an Abyssinian, but lately arrived from the upper country, and brought into the Hhareem by the wife of the slave owner, who is a fellah, and is seated in the middle distance, habited in the out-door dress of the common people. The boy to the right is a Nubian, who is bringing in a sheetha or narghile. On the divan and near the boy are gazelles, the frequent indoor and out-door pets of all classes. The windows, which are often of an enormous size, are all covered with the finest carved wood-work, at a distance resembling lace, and which does not prevent the inmates from seeing all that is passing, while it effectively precludes the possibility of being seen from without. The walls of old houses are whitewashed, and only ornamented with borders, often of texts in Arabic from the Koran; the elaborately carved dark wood-work of the ceilings contrasts effectively with the whitewash of the walls. The rooms have

no furniture save the divans, mats or carpets, no tables or chairs, the dinner being served on a round tray of silver or brass, and placed on a stool; as is represented on the right of the picture. Coffee is being brought in by the attendants in the background.[29]

Lewis emphasised the reality of the scene, but there is no denying that what he depicted would seem outlandish in Britain. Yet, instead of regarding his work as fantasy, the challenge should really be to find something in the painting that did not or could not exist. The house, its furnishings and fittings certainly existed; the costumes are real; the situation, although restricted to the wealthy, is perfectly possible. The objection is often made that Lewis could not have seen the interior of a harem and therefore could not have known what one was like. Yet he could have heard first-hand accounts about the interior of harems in Cairo because he had two witnesses whom he could question in his own household: his servant (or slave), Zuleikah, and his wife, Marian. Marian must have visited harems, as did Mrs Lane-Poole, who was living with her brother, Edward Lane, in another part of the city.[30] Lewis also knew of other Europeans, such as Prisse d'Avennes, who lived as he did but who had gone a stage further and had turned Muslim on entering the service of Muhammad Ali.[31] In 1847, Lewis painted the portrait of Madame Linant de Bellefonds, wife of Linant de Bellefonds, Bey and then Pasha in the government service, who lived as a Turk.[32]

Lewis could even be said to have had a modest harem of his own. He painted *The Hhareem* in his own house in Egypt; his new young wife is in the centre of the picture; the 'old inmate' (presumably Zuleikah) is laughing in the background.[33] Did Marian know or care about Zuleikah? Was she still there when Marian arrived? How did Marian feel about being used as a model? Did she enjoy the 'masquerade', dressing in Egyptian clothes and the paradoxical freedom that wearing the veil in the street gave her?

This is strange, for there are other women in the picture, and yet another new one being unwrapped for approval. That he should depict his new young wife in the middle of such a scene would be, on the face of it, an unlikely thing for a Victorian painter to do (and to display it in the Old Water-Colour Society at that), but Lewis was acquitted of prurient intent by reviewers.[34] The only thing we know about Marian is that she and Lewis were devoted to one another. The reason we know nothing else is that she almost certainly loyally destroyed all letters and papers in the traditional manner when Lewis died, and in the process destroyed all evidence about herself. Her views on this picture would now be even more valuable than Lewis's description. Before they were married in 1847, Lewis had not sent back any paintings to England, although he had made hundreds of sketches. Did Marian rouse him out of his lethargy? Did she inspire or persuade him to restart painting in earnest? Did she even suggest the subject?

We do not know where or how Lewis found the models for the other female figures in his painting, but these are manifestly portraits and their expressions speak volumes. The young and eager Bey, who looks rather pathetic in his eagerness, has eyes only for his new purchase. This could be read as a satire at Lewis's own expense, for when this picture was painted Lewis was newly married to a much younger woman. He shows that the callow and wealthy young man is oblivious of the suspicion and disapproval of the other inmates. We are intended to feel that the Bey will eventually regret indulging his desire for novelty at the expense of the feelings of the rest of his household. Is this why Zuleikah is laughing? The picture shows that the fantasy that many males shared (and perhaps still share) has potential difficulties and consequences in reality. In this meticulously recorded scene of everyday life, albeit set in Cairo, his observation of the currents of feeling in all the participants is just as subtle and the standard of painting is even better than most Pre-Raphaelites could manage.

When *The Hhareem* was first exhibited it had no commentary, but it is a narrative picture. Could a narrative be implied in a small and less ambitious painting of a similar subject? At first sight *Life in the Hhareem, Cairo*, of 1858 (fig. 3), has no obvious story.[35] A woman (his wife, Marian, again) in magnificent clothes, is seated holding a posy of flowers in the splendid interior of a Mamluk house, while another woman enters bearing a tray. We know already that, as Thackeray described, Lewis lived like a Turkish bey in every respect except the actual practice of the faith of Islam. The decorous pictures of Marian in her robes in that splendid house are not fantasies at all on one level. So Lewis really was, in that sense, a Pre-Raphaelite.

However, a close examination of the picture reveals an implication that there might be a potential drama unfolding. The woman in the background, holding a tray, is bringing in two coffee cups in the form of

FIGURE 3
Life in the Hhareem, Cairo, by John Frederick Lewis
(by courtesy of the Victoria and Albert Museum)

tiny porcelain bowls, and what looks like two cut glass rose-water flasks
or sweetmeat containers. The posy of flowers held in the lap of the main
figure is a love letter, in the universal language of flowers. Lewis was
fond of this theme, using it in *An Armenian Lady, Cairo – The Love*

Missive, of 1855,[36] and in *The Intercepted Correspondence*, of 1869.[37] We do not know if Lady Mary Wortley Montagu's famous account of the vocabulary of this romantic practice among the Turks still held good for Cairo in the 1840s, but the lady is supposed to be the consort of a Turkish bey.[38] The whole scene could be interpreted as a woman about to take coffee with her confidante to discuss the newly arrived love letter and its implicit offer; they will then read the future in the coffee grounds in the traditional manner (still practised in Cairo), to see how the affair might turn out.

There is a different narrative in *Hhareem Life – Constantinople*, of 1857.[39] On the surface it is a similar scene, with similar models, including the cat, to those used in other pictures, Yet, instead of the peacock feather fan being reflected in the mirror, the head of her companion and, bizarrely, a fragment of the husband in Turkish dress relegated to one corner are reflected. The fan is this time being employed to tease the cat, who has already pulled out a few feathers. The enigmatic smile of Marian and the implied silence of her statuesque companion leave the viewer to speculate about what is happening. It is not merely decorative: there is some unresolved tension in the picture. Could it be the theme of male jealousy again that reaches its full expression in *The Intercepted Correspondence*? Lewis was much older than Marian; was he capable of coolly looking at his own feelings of jealousy? Or is he merely depicting coquettishness? Is he placing the (male) viewer in the fantasy? It could be all or none of these things, but the certainty is that it is a subtle picture and not just a pretty one.

In the past, critics have not thought that there was much content in Lewis's pictures. John Ruskin was one of Lewis's staunchest advocates. Time and again, in his comments on his exhibits at the Old Water-Colour Society and the Royal Academy in the 1850s, he held Lewis's watercolour and oil paintings to be the epitome of technical perfection. Describing *An Armenian Lady, Cairo* in 1855 for example, he wrote: 'no words are strong enough to express the admirable skill and tenderness of pencilling and perception shown in this picture'.[40] Lewis's meticulous attention to detail and his ability to portray people and objects with extreme realism matched exactly Ruskin's earlier instructions to painters:

> [to] go to Nature in all singleness of hearts, and walk with her laboriously and trustingly, having no other thought but how to best

penetrate her meaning, and remember her instruction, rejecting nothing, selecting nothing, and scorning nothing; believing all things to be right and good, and rejoicing always in the truth.[41]

Ruskin's review of *An Armenian Lady, Cairo*, nevertheless, sounds a note of criticism: 'It is only to be regretted that this costly labour should be spent on a subject devoid of interest.'[42] The fact that the painting had been exhibited at the Royal Academy with the subtitle 'the love missive' and a quotation from Byron, 'The token flowers that tell/What words can never speak so well', appears to have escaped his notice. Clearly Lewis intended that a narrative should be attached to this picture, as to many others, but on this there was no comment. Both Ruskin's appreciation of Lewis's brilliant technique as well as his failure to respond to Lewis's subject matter was echoed by other contemporary and later critics. F.G. Stephens, in an article in the *Magazine of Art* in 1896, described the watercolour, *Lilium Auratum*, of 1871,[43] as 'one of the masterpieces of John Frederick Lewis'. He went on: 'As with regard to a very large proportion of Lewis's pictures in oil and drawings in water-colour, it illustrates no story and is possessed of no passion; its subject is the beauty and brilliance of nature set forth by means of the most exquisite execution.'[44]

More recent appraisals of Lewis's work have tended to reiterate this view. The form and construction of his work, as well as the artistic influences on him, have been analysed, notably by Major-General Lewis and Dr Sweetman, but the content and potential meaning of the separate elements that make up his images have not been fully examined, nor has their complexity been fully realised.[45] The sheer intensity and accuracy of Lewis's vision meant that he would often record latent meanings as well as the glorious surface of beautiful things, just as a camera records all types of detail that the photographer did not notice or value at first. Just how conscious Lewis was of what he was doing is now impossible to guess. Yet he did intend his pictures to be read as narratives, hence the epigraphs in the catalogues quoted above. With a better historical knowledge of nineteenth-century Egypt and the objectivity that an interval of a century and a half brings, we can perhaps find a type of narrative that eluded critics at the time.

Ruskin famously (or notoriously) asserted that 'the most beautiful things in the world are the most useless: peacocks and lilies for instance'.[46]

He was, as we now know, wrong, as their beautiful forms have been honed ruthlessly by the blind forces of evolution in order that more peacocks and lilies can be produced. Why the peacock's tail is so efficient in attracting suitable mates and why the lilies' form and scent is so good at attracting pollinating insects are matters of intense scientific research; their beauty is, in fact, very useful. Perhaps in an analogous way, the marvellous surface effect of Lewis's paintings of women had tended to conceal rather than reveal a narrative purpose.

NOTES

1   *Illustrated London News* (25 March 1865), 285.
2   Edward Lear to Marian Lewis, from London, 22 June 1875. Letter in the Lewis family collection.
3   Roberts and Müller were both in Egypt in 1838–9, independently of one another.
4   The most comprehensive account of Lewis's life and work is still the monograph published by his great-great-nephew Major-General J.M.H. Lewis, *John Frederick Lewis, R.A. 1805–1876* (Leigh-on-Sea, F. Lewis, 1978). I am indebted to the late Major-General Lewis for his invaluable help with my research. See also B. Llewellyn, 'The Islamic Inspiration. John Frederick Lewis: Painter of Islamic Egypt', *The Society of Antiquaries of London*, Occasional Paper (New Series), 7 (1985), S. Macready and F.H. Thompson (eds.); and B. Llewellyn, 'J.F. Lewis and Frank Dillon: Two Interpretations of Islamic Domestic Interiors in Cairo' in P. and J. Starkey (eds.), *Travellers in Egypt* (London, I.B. Tauris, 1998), pp. 148–56.
5   The only extensive contemporary account of Lewis's life in Cairo is that of his friend, W.M. Thackeray, in *Notes of a Journey from Cornhill to Grand Cairo* (London, Chapman & Hall, 1846, illustrated reprint Heathfield, Cockbird Press, 1991), pp. 142–6.
6   The sketches were sold in sales after Lewis's death, in 1877 and subsequently; see Lewis, *op. cit.*, pp. 49–50, 82–92.
7   Lane published *An Account of the Manners and Customs of the Modern Egyptians* (1836; repr. 1989 by East-West Publications), [hereinafter *Manners*], and his translation with notes of *The Thousand and One Nights* (3 vols., London, C. Knight, 1839–41). On Lane, see L. Ahmed, *Edward W. Lane* (London, Longman, 1978), and Jason Thompson, 'Edward William Lane in Egypt' *JARCE*, 34 (1997), 243–61; also a forthcoming biography by Jason Thompson.
8   Paul Mellon Collection, the Yale Center for British Art, New Haven.
9   John Ruskin, 'Academy Notes on some of the Principal Pictures' (1856), repr. in E.T. Cook and A. Wedderburn, (eds.), *The Works of John Ruskin* (London, George Allen, 1903–12), pp. 73–8; K. Bendiner, 'The Portrayal of the Middle East in British Painting 1833–61', Ph.D. thesis, Columbia University, 1979, p. 213; Mary Anne Stevens (ed.), *The Orientalists: Delacroix to Matisse* (London, Royal Academy of Arts, Washington, National Gallery of Art, 1984), cat. no. 89.

10 London, The Old Water-Colour Society, no. 134.

11 The Fitzwilliam Museum, Cambridge.

12 Victoria and Albert Museum, London.

13 Watercolour sold at Sotheby's, New York, 23 May 1989, lot 49; oil at Christie's, London, 20 June 1986, lot 92.

14 *The Art-Journal* (1856), 164.

15 Frederick William Stewart (Fourth Marquis of Londonderry and Lord Castlereagh), *A Journey to Damascus through Egypt, Nubia, Arabia Petraea, Palestine and Syria* (2 vols., London, 1847), p. 284.

16 A fine example recently on the art market is *Study of Camels and Bedouin in the Desert of Sinai* in The Fine Art Society, London, Spring 1997, cat. no. 7. See also note 6 above. On the last day of the sale, held five months after the artist's death, 57 lots of Eastern dresses, robes, head-dresses, weapons etc. were sold, Christie's, 7 May 1877.

17 Guildhall Art Gallery, Corporation of London. See also review in the *Art-Journal* (1860), 163.

18 Thackeray, *op. cit.*, p. 146.

19 This was the last volume of David Roberts's massive and highly successful series of lithographs, *The Holy Land, Syria, Idumea, Arabia, Egypt & Nubia* (London, F.G. Moon, 1842–9).

20 Royal Academy, 1869, no. 97, now in Birmingham Museum and Art Gallery. A watercolour variant is in the Forbes Magazine Collection, New York.

21 Castlereagh, *op. cit.*, pp. 39–40.

22 *Manners, op. cit.*, p. 539.

23 Oil painting sold at Sotheby's, London, 30 March 1994, lot 180; watercolour at Sotheby's, London, 10 July 1997, lot 172. Both dated 1875.

24 *Manners, op. cit.*, pp. 319–20.

25 A. Graves, *The Royal Academy Exhibitors*, 5 (1906).

26 Jason Thompson is working on connections between Lane and Lewis as part of his forthcoming biography of Lane.

27 No. 147.

28 No. 494.

29 This passage reads like something out of Edward Lane's *Manners, op. cit.*, but although they lived in Cairo at the same time and in the same way, and possibly in the same district, we do not know how much contact they had with one another.

30 See Sophia Poole, *The English Woman in Egypt: Letters from Cairo* (3 vols., London, Charles Knight & Co, 1844–6).

31 See E.M. [Emile Prisse d'Avennes fils], *Notice biographique sur Émile Prisse d'Avennes, voyageur français archéologue, égyptologue et publiciste* (Paris, 1896).

32 See Lewis, *op. cit.*, 50, and J. Mazuel, *L'Œuvre géographique de Linant de Bellefonds* (Cairo, Publications de la Société Royale de Géographie d'Égypte, 1937).

33 Thackeray calls Lewis's servant, 'Zuleikah', and describes her as having 'two of the most beautiful, enormous, ogling, black eyes in the world . . .' but 'upon his honour she was only the black cook . . .', Thackeray, *op. cit.*, pp. 143–4.

34 For example, '[this painting gives] no offence to Western feelings of decorum', *Athenaeum*, 1175 (4 May 1850), 480.

35 Victoria and Albert Museum, London, no. 679–1893.

36 Exhibited Royal Academy, London, 1855, no. 90; sold at Sotheby's, *Victorian Pictures*, 5 November 1997, lot 184.

37 Private collection.

38 See Lady Mary Wortley Montagu, 'Letter to Lady . . ., Pera of Constantinople 10 March 1718', *Complete Letters*, ed. Robert Halsband (2 vols., Oxford, Clarendon Press, 1967).

39 Laing Art Gallery, Newcastle, no. 45–16.

40 John Ruskin, *Notes on some of the Principal Paintings exhibited in the Rooms of the Royal Academy* (London, 1855), p. 13.

41 John Ruskin, 'Modern Painters' in Cook and Wedderburn, *op. cit.*, p. 624.

42 John Ruskin (1855).

43 Sold at Sotheby's (20 November 1997), lot 252, now in a private collection.

44 *Magazine of Art*, 20 (1896), 260, and illustration facing.

45 Lewis, *op. cit.*; John Sweetman, *The Oriental Obsession: Islamic Inspiration in British and American Art and Architecture, 1500–1920* (Cambridge University Press, 1988), pp. 132–44.

46 John Ruskin, *The Stones of Venice* (3 vols., London, 1851–1853), vol. 1, ch. 2.

4

William Holman Hunt's Visits to Egypt: Passion, Prejudice and Truth to Nature*

Judith Bronkhurst

On 22 September 1852, William Holman Hunt, then at Fairlight, near Hastings in Sussex, wrote to the young Rosaline Orme, niece of Coventry Patmore, enclosing a small pen and ink sketch (fig. 1) inscribed *Grand Cairo*. He described it as a painting in the East:

> The lady in black is the daughter of a Greek merchant, lately dead, who has come with her cousin, the fair lady, to have her portrait painted with the gazelle, into which she believes her lover to have changed after his murder by her father. What do you think of the plot? You will allow that it has the merit of originality.[1]

The wry tone leads us to interpret the sketch as a consciously unrealistic projection of a fantasy – the artist at the easel is definitely a self-portrait. Fantasy was indeed an essential component of Hunt's response to the East. His deeply-felt beliefs as a Protestant Englishman inform many of the images he produced in Egypt, even those that appear to show this Pre-Raphaelite at his most literal.

At Fairlight, Hunt read *Eōthen* and *The Crescent and the Cross*,[2] and shared Clive Vale Farm with Edward Lear, who in early 1849 had travelled to Cairo, Suez and Sinai. There is no doubt that his example was of the greatest importance to Hunt. The artist also consulted Sir Austen Henry Layard, who, to quote Hunt's letter of 15 August 1853 to his travelling companion, Thomas Seddon, 'gives me every encouragement, assuring me that there will be no insurmountable difficulties in the way of making use of the wonderful materials to be found for our Art labours . . . in the East'.[3]

---

* First published in *Apollo* magazine, London, in November 1998.

FIGURE 1
***Painting in the East, Grand Cairo* by William Holman Hunt**
(by courtesy of the Courtauld Institute of Art)

'The East' for Hunt meant, above all, the Holy Land. Indeed, he wrote to Seddon on 27 October 1853, excusing his delay in starting:

> Had I thought it probable that Syria would have been approachable this season I should not have began [*sic*] the modern picture ['The Awakening Conscience'] . . . I quite see the advantage of Egypt as a place of sojourn for the winter months. Had Syria been open however I should have wished only to go through it as a tourist unless we saw something which recommended it as a superior place to remain in.[4]

In the event, Hunt agreed to travel to Egypt even though it was unclear whether the political situation would make a visit to Syria practicable. He finally reached Cairo by 11 February 1854, Seddon having arrived there the previous December.[5] We find him writing to his Oxford patron, Thomas Combe, on 12 February:

> Last night was the most brilliant and calmest moonlight night I ever saw – after dinner we all went into the garden and sat for an hour and more smoking our hookahs and admiring the beauty of

the scene. In truth I believe this country would suit me much better than any other in the world and I think if I could have a few friends with me I should stop in the East altogether.[6]

The only watercolour Hunt executed of Cairo reflects this initial enchantment. It was first exhibited in the group Pre-Raphaelite exhibition at 4 Russell Place, Bloomsbury, London, in 1857 as *Sketch from a house in New Ca[iro] looking towards the Gebel Mokattum*, which suggests that it was not executed from Hunt's base, Williams's Indian Family Hotel on the Esbekiya. Perhaps the house was that of the British Consul, the Hon. Frederick Bruce. Hunt and Seddon dined with him on 11 February, and he was responsible for introducing them to various Cairene dignitaries.[7]

Hunt's choice of subject may have been influenced by Warburton's lyrical description of his first view of Cairo in *The Crescent and the Cross*:

> The bold range of the Mokattum mountains is purpled by the rising sun, its craggy summits are cut clearly out against the glowing sky . . . Just where the mountain sinks upon the plain, the citadel stands upon its last eminence, and widely spread beneath it lies the city, a forest of minarets with palm trees intermingled, and the domes of innumerable mosques rising, like enormous bubbles, over the sea of houses.[8]

Hunt has, however, omitted the Citadel, and the mosques and minarets are overshadowed by the prominent Christian belfry in the right foreground.[9] It is tempting to interpret this as the artist's way of asserting the superiority, for him, of Christianity to Islam.

The frame of *Cairo: Sunset on the Gebel Mokattum* (the title by which it is usually known) and that of four Syrian watercolours were designed by the artist, probably in 1861 prior to the ensemble being shown that spring at Gambart's German Gallery, 168 New Bond Street, London. The intricate patterning of the medallions on the gilt cuff is copied from Plate XXXIV of Owen Jones's 1856 sourcebook, *The Grammar of Ornament*, example no. 2, 'from a copy of the Koran', while the black on gold pattern of the outer flat is based on Plate XXXV, example no. 14, 'taken from Pavements and Walls in Private Houses and Mosques in Cairo'. Hunt used the same frame design for another watercolour begun in Egypt in 1854, *The Wilderness of Gizeh* (fig. 2).

FIGURE 2
The Wilderness of Gizeh **by William Holman Hunt**
(by courtesy of the Courtauld Institute of Art)

The lyricism of *Cairo: Sunset* conveys nothing of Hunt's negative reaction to the city, as relayed in his letter to Combe of February 1854: 'It is the horrible state of dilapidation in which one finds every thing that disgusts so much.' However, he continued, 'many of the people seem cleaner than the English in many respects, for instance the shop keepers keep their hands and naked feet in the most unexceptionable state.'[10] The only oil Hunt began in the city (fig. 3) focuses on a Cairene bazaar, but *A Street Scene in Cairo: The Lantern-Maker's Courtship* – unlike J.F. Lewis's similar subjects, which convey an insider's point of view – generates a certain amount of disquiet in a contemporary viewer since the spectator is cast in the role of voyeur. Hunt himself had no such problem, writing in his memoirs:

> One day in the town, while I was mooning about the bazaars, I had my attention attracted to a young tradesman evidently courting a girl; she had come duly veiled . . . In an unlit corner I could watch the growth of his natural curiosity, and his pleadings to be allowed to satisfy his eyes as to the features hidden under the black *burko*. To raise up the veil was an act for which there could be no toleration; to press it close so as to see the outline of the face, the mouth, and the chin, was the utmost that propriety could allow. There was more than

FIGURE 3
The Lantern Maker's Courtship by William Holman Hunt
(by courtesy of the Manchester Art Galleries)

a superficial custom in the incident, it symbolized human interest in the unknown.[11]

At the time he was much more censorious, writing of his subject to Combe on 27 April, 'I hope it may have some value as an illustration of an unwise state of society which as it appears is fast falling to pieces as I trust with all the more serious deceptions of the Mohomadden world.'[12]

At first glance one might think that Hunt has failed to convey this attitude in the painting, which in many respects functions as an attempt to convey a good deal of information about contemporary Cairo to a western audience. However, the top-hatted European riding on a donkey at the far right was added in London in 1856.[13] His whip is poised to strike a cowering Egyptian whose laden camel is blocking the thoroughfare.[14] In *Eōthen* Kinglake had stated, 'You will find, I think, that one of the greatest drawbacks to the pleasure of travelling in Asia, is the being obliged more or less to make your way by bullying',[15] but Hunt seems to have regarded this as his prerogative, writing to Combe shortly after his arrival: 'You would be astonished at their want of courage; when we in walking come upon a party of natives who do not at once get out of our way, at our expostulation with them, we raise our sticks, and lay about on ten or twenty altogether.'[16] The artist's letter of 12 March to Dante Gabriel Rossetti well describes the press of people in a Cairo street, adding:

> Through all this breaks the frank . . . (not wantonly rude for I believe, despite the desire to a different conviction, that no stranger can have peace in the East unless he become the dictator of his own terms – and certainly the reception of his conditions hard and selfish as they are would seem to establish this rule . . .) It is not an insignificant thing to see his course down a street – here is a running footman he is to make way in the narrow and crowded place for his master's carriage, with a strong coorbash he scourges old and young who in their lameness age or indolence have not escaped from the way at his 'ho-ah! hoah!' but with the sight of a black coat and a saucy look all his courage goes as the frank walks composedly past him, and compels his master's coachmen to slacken their pace as he takes his own time to go his own way by virtue of a reserve of power in his right hand which is used on whomever should by accident or design attempt to impede him. and this is called forth not infrequently.[17]

Thankfully, racial tensions are not apparent in Hunt's major painting, begun in April 1854 at Giza, *The Afterglow in Egypt* (fig. 4). He would have been prepared for greater cooperation from the fellahin than he had experienced in Cairo, having read in *Eōthen* that Bedouin women 'are not treasured up like the wives and daughters of other Orientals' (1844, p. 248). Moreover, E.W. Lane had indicated that the peasant women of Upper Egypt rarely concealed their faces with a head veil.[18] The sketch of the head of the model for the painting in Hunt's letter of 2 May 1854 to his sister, Elizabeth, demonstrates that he was able to study her features in detail. Indeed, the artist, who was working in the open air, became a great tourist attraction, and wrote tongue-in-cheek to his sister:

> I must . . . not complain of a want of favour for several Egyptians have asked me to become a Mahommedan and accept their daughter or sister in marriage. One young lady in fact was so gracious as to offer herself. I am afraid however that you would disapprove of her complexion . . . I subjoin a portrait of the young lady, to enable you to hold a council with mother and the others . . . and send me notice of your decision. She is very liberal I must tell you, agreeing to allow me to take three other wives beside herself.[19]

Although the figure in 'The Afterglow' is posed from life, the idea of depicting her balancing a sheaf of corn on her head may owe something to an illustration in Lane's *Manners and Customs* (vol. 1, p. 58), while the positioning of the arms and the way in which the water-pot is balanced on the palm of her right hand may be indebted to the female figure in David Roberts's 'Entrance of the Temple of Amun, Thebes' from his *Egypt and Nubia* (1849).[20] Hunt could never sublimate the artist into pure ethnographer, and we find him writing to the critic Ernest Chesneau on 3 December 1882:

> The title . . . comes from my choice of the hour which seemed most picturesque for the figure of a girl, one of very many now seen in Egypt with a singular resemblance to the old sculpturesque type.[21]

This ability to see life imitating art is again apparent in a drawing of fellah children engaged by Auguste Mariette to help excavate the Sphinx. Here the frieze-like composition suggests classical precedents, an attempt to portray the timelessness of, to quote Hunt's memoirs, 'the ancient national type'.[22]

FIGURE 4
Afterglow in Egypt by William Holman Hunt
(by courtesy of the Bridgeman Art Gallery)

In 1886 Hunt stated that the title of *The Afterglow in Egypt* was intended 'to express nothing but that the light is not that of the sun, and although the meridian glory of ancient Egypt has passed away, there is still a poetic reflection of this in the aspect of life there'.[23] Hints of death are included in the overall image: not only the poppies in the sheaf of corn but also the pomegranates in the hexagonal motifs on the frame at the level of the girl's hips, pomegranate seeds having been consumed in the underworld by Persephone, daughter of Demeter, the Greek goddess of the harvest. The pomegranates are the only non-Egyptian decoration on the frame, which was again based on 'Arabian' motifs from *The Grammar of Ornament*; the inscription 'Plate 34' on Hunt's sketch for the frame[24] refers to this illustration in Owen Jones, where the source for the interweaving frets in the cusped top is to be found. The wave-like scroll patterns between the frets are similar to Plate XXXXIII, example no. 22.

Apart from *The Afterglow*, Hunt's visits to Giza of February–March and April–May 1854 resulted in relatively straightforward works on paper, such as *The Wilderness of Gizeh* (fig. 2), *The Haunt of the Gazelle* and *Arab Reclining by a Stream*,[25] as well as more complex watercolours, as his response to the landscape and light flowered in a great outburst of creative energy. In *The Great Pyramid* (fig. 4) the monument is relegated to the background, reflecting Hunt's desire to avoid a topographical approach to what he considered a hackneyed subject. Indeed, he described the Pyramids in his letter to Millais of 16 March 1854, as 'extremely ugly blocks, as one always knew, and arranged with the most unpicturesque taste'. He felt, nevertheless, that 'while they are at hand it is as well to make a sketch of them with some effect and circumstance, to satisfy curiosity and one's own love of past experiences. It may be possible to gain some poetical feeling to repay for the patience one must exert.'[26]

Hunt left visiting the monuments until 6 May, and two days later graphically recounted the experience in an illustrated letter to Millais. Although he still regarded 'the big blocks' as 'merely colossal tombs of pride', he was deeply affected by his adventure. On penetrating the central chamber of the Great Pyramid, he mused on:

The intention of such a huge work, it was impossible to feel that there was no other than the human design . . . but here I rebuked

FIGURE 5
The Great Pyramid **by William Holman Hunt**
(by courtesy of the Prudence Cuming Association Ltd)

myself as a dreamer and thinking a work of folly would never be an acceptable servant of God the words came into my mouth and I chanted out 'The dead praise thee not, O Lord: neither all they that go down into silence. But we will praise the Lord: from this time forth for evermore'.[27]

This passage reminds us that Hunt's primary purpose in going to the East was to reach the Holy Land, 'to use my powers to make more tangible Jesus Christ's history and teaching'.[28] But the letter to Millais indicates that his convictions as an Anglo-Saxon Protestant were, at the Pyramids, in danger of being undermined by the scene itself. In general, on this first visit to Egypt, he kept his distance from the Arabs, and thus his prejudices, intact. He strongly disapproved of any show of solidarity, as a caricature of Thomas Seddon in his letter of 12 March 1854 to Rossetti makes clear:

I never knew such an extraordinary combination of ability &c and absurdity &c as he is – his devout admiration of the Arabs is perfectly exasperating – they are the meanest sneaks in the world and yet he never tires in praising them. His adoption of the costume is simply amusing in the result for somehow the wind and other little circumstances disturb the arrangement with a familiarity never assumed towards a native.[29]

In perhaps Hunt's most striking Egyptian watercolour of this period, *The Sphinx, Gizeh, looking towards the Pyramids of Sakhara* (fig. 6), the Pyramids are relegated to the left background, while the Sphinx is observed from behind. This unconventional viewpoint enabled the artist to concentrate on the striations of the Sphinx as if it were a geological phenomenon, rather than a monumental sculpture with a human aspect.

FIGURE 6
The Sphinx, Gizeh, looking towards the Pyramids of Sakhara
(by courtesy of the Harris Museum and Art Gallery at Preston)

The most vibrant colour is reserved for the enormous snake in the foreground. Its presence may be a comment on the ménage at Giza: Seddon's servant, Hippo, was a noted snake charmer whose exploits fascinated his master, and Hunt's letter to Millais of 16 March 1854 contains a sketch of him entwined by a huge serpent. More importantly, it relates to Hunt's own encounter during an evening walk 'round the Great Pyramid' on 27 April:

> There, within two paces was an enormous serpent writhing about and rearing itself up most fearfully. There was no time and no necessity for consideration . . . so I retired some twenty feet, lowered my gun, and fired and fortunately hit the beast in the throat and breast; he twirled about considerably but was too much hurt to be dangerous so I brought him home on the barrell of my gun: he is between six and seven feet long, of the most deadly kind . . . I find the feat has increased my reputation with the Arabs.

By this date Hunt's knowledge of Egyptian attacks on Christians in Cairo and its environs had led him to 'regard these people as the most detestable in existence',[30] and one can perhaps view the serpent as a symbol of Hunt's belief in English racial superiority.

The snake in *The Sphinx, Gizeh* has been stoned rather than shot, and this may refer to the prophecy in Genesis 3:15 that the seed of Eve will bruise the serpent's head. It thus becomes an image of the triumph of good over evil. Hunt was avidly reading the Bible at this period, and his decision to adopt a position facing east, like the Sphinx, may have been partly motivated by religious considerations. According to his record of a conversation with Dickens in 1860, Hunt at that time viewed the Sphinx as some sort of precursor of Christianity: 'the whole idea connected with this "Watchful One" may be that it is lifting up its head to look always towards the rising sun for that Great Day in which the reign of absolute righteousness and happiness shall come'.[31]

Reading the artist's letters from his first visit to the Near East, one is struck by the way in which he operates on two levels, responding to the landscape for its religious associations while keenly observing it as an artist/traveller. This was true even before he reached Syria: for example, during his May 1854 visit to the Great Pyramid he wrote:

> looking over the flat reach of sand divided by the fat Nile I had almost seen Abraham and Sarah stealing into the land with below the poor workmen driven like cattle to rear the huge collection of stone, and with the patriarchs departure I could think of how at the time the revelation of God was being lost altogether and how idolatry was spreading itself about the whole earth, as a comforting substitute for the truth of Gods omnipotence and eternity.[32]

[62]

This deeply-felt response on an aesthetic as well as a religious level resulted in works that, in my opinion, have far more bite than if Hunt had been able to adopt objectively the role of artist/explorer, an aim he elucidated on 12 August 1855 in a letter to William Michael Rossetti:

> I have a notion that painters should go out, two by two, like merchants of nature, and bring home precious merchandize in faithful pictures of scenes interesting from historical consideration, or from the strangeness of the subject itself. Only call to mind the principal names in your memory, and consider how absolutely nothing Art has done, even where quite easy to illustrate the idea connected therewith to give you a truer notion of the thing. In landscape this is an idea which Lear has had for some time – it naturally suggests itself to a painter in travelling unless he be entirely thoughtless – and he has done some good things in the work but it must be done by every painter and this most religiously, in fact with something like the spirit of the Apostles, fearing nothing, going amongst robbers, and in deserts with impunity as men without anything to lose, and every thing must be painted even the pebbles of the foreground from the place itself, unless on trial this prove *impossible*. . . . I think this must be the next stage of PRB indoctrination and it has been this conviction which brought me out here, and which keeps me away in patience until the experiment has been fairly tried.[33]

Hunt's first visit to Egypt lasted only just over three months,[34] but in 1857, the year after he came back from the East, he designed, in collaboration with J.G. Crace, a couple of justly celebrated Egyptian chairs based on the Thebes stool in the British Museum.[35] One of these can be seen in the drawing-room of the artist's home at Draycott Lodge, Fulham, in a photograph published in the *Art Annual* of 1893.[36] In 1892 the elderly Hunt had returned to Egypt, by which date his reputation as the greatest religious painter of the age was assured. His attitude was now that of a relaxed tourist, and in a letter of 9 February to Sir Henry Cunynghame he rejoiced that he and his wife Edith had decided to go by boat from Cairo to Asyut,

> for I scarcely ever in the same time had such a succession of delightful sights as those we have witnessed on the Nile. One of my principal frets has been that I brought so little sketching material. My idea was that it would not do for me to get involved in pictures of

Egyptian Temples which I doubt not the poetry of, but which could scarcely fail to appear to have been anticipated by previous artists – who had done them by sunset, and sunrise, without even thus making them very inexhaustible in interest. I still entertain the same conviction but what has been a surprise to me have been the beauty and paintability of simple scenes on the Nile itself – without Temple, or other point, to mark the special locality. . . . Each day goes by wonderfully quickly – for the succession of delights is an incredibly perfect *pastime*, of the only kind that I could ever be satisfied with.[37]

A couple of watercolours derive from this trip, and one sketchbook survives.

The Nile certainly appears to have been executed from the deck of a ship, and is on a large enough scale to have come from 'the one large sketch book' mentioned in Hunt's letter to Cunynghame. The drawing is uncharacteristically uncluttered, conveying the artist's fascination with the river itself. On 25 February he wrote from Cairo to his artist friend Frederic Shields that the Nile 'sometimes is disturbed as the sea but at others it is like a mirror in reflectiveness, and boats sail along with sheets large enough to carry them into the sky'. He added:

> Every day rather each hour shewed us some new wonder of beauty, it is really a mercy to be allowed to see such delights – and I feel – if at the beginning of life it would be enough to inspire one for the imaginative work of a long career.

What is more, Hunt's attitude towards the Egyptians was no longer conditioned by the extent to which they cooperated in furthering his aims. Referring to the people of the Nile, he wrote to Shields:

> [they] ply their trade and they get bronzed to a perfect silky purple, every muscle is playing about under their polished skins, and their forms are magnificent. Buffaloes, camels, apes, cows, and horses go along the banks led by young naked boys, and sometimes these ride the beasts, making perfect groups for a sculptor.[38]

Such sights were to remain word pictures, but Hunt did execute one figure subject derived from this trip (fig. 7). It was described in the catalogue of his 1907 retrospective exhibition thus:

A postman carrying the letters down to the Nile post boat. The fire is the signal to the boat to expect them. A native is warming his hands at the blaze.

'The subject struck Mr. Holman Hunt as a very beautiful one from the fact that the flames of the signal fire seemed to echo the forms of the wheat-sheaves standing beside it, and the varying glow of the fire and the moon upon the golden sheaf was of poetic suggestion.'[39]

FIGURE 7

The Nile Postman by William Holman Hunt

(by courtesy of the Courtauld Institute of Art)

'Poetic suggestion' also characterises many of the works from Hunt's 1854 trip to Egypt. These derive their force from the artist's complex response to the East, a blend of passion, prejudice and truth to nature, as well as a fierce awareness of artistic precedent and a determination to forge a new path. 1854 was to be the artist's most prolific year, surely justifying what Hunt himself called his 'Oriental mania'.[40]

NOTES

1 Flora Masson, 'Holman Hunt and the Story of a Butterfly', *Cornhill Magazine*, n.s., 39:173 (November 1910), 644, published in Mary Bennett, 'Footnotes to the Holman Hunt Exhibition', *Liverpool Bulletin*, 13 (1968–70), 33, sketch reproduced Fig. 9, 33. Quotations from Holman Hunt's letters have been edited as little as possible. The transliteration from Arabic in the titles of works of art follows his spelling rather than modern usage.

2 Hunt to Miss Orme (1 October 1852), published in Masson, *op. cit.*, p. 646.

3 MS. E.J. Seddon coll., on loan to John Rylands Library, University of Manchester, published in George P. Landow, 'William Holman Hunt's Letters to Thomas Seddon', *Bulletin of The John Rylands University Library of Manchester*, 66 (1983–1984), 152. [Hereinafter, Landow (1984).]

4 Landow (1984), *op. cit.*, 156.

5 John Pollard Seddon, *Memoir and Letters of the late Thomas Seddon, Artist. By his brother* (London, James Nisbet, 1858), pp. 43, 30. [Hereinafter, Seddon (1858).]

6 MS. 1 February 1854 and Cairo February [11/12], Bodleian Library, MS. Eng. lett. c. 296 fol. 25.

7 Seddon (1858), *op. cit.*, pp. 43–44, 46.

8 Eliot Warburton, *The Crescent and the Cross; or, Romance and Realities of Eastern Travel* (London, Henry Colburn, 1845), vol. 1, p. 63.

9 I am grateful to Peter Stocks for discussing the topography with me.

10 MS. Bodleian Library, MS. Eng. lett. c. 296, fol. 25.

11 William Holman Hunt, *Pre-Raphaelitism and the Pre-Raphaelite Brotherhood* (London, Macmillan, 1905), vol. 1, pp. 385–6. [Hereinafter, Hunt (1905).]

12 MS. 26/7 April 1854, Arizona State University Library.

13 Hunt (1905), *op. cit.*, vol. 2, p. 105.

14 The whip is more clearly elucidated in the small version of the picture, which I reproduce. Hunt, in a letter of 4 December 1857 to Ford Madox Brown, described this as a sketch 'of the Cairo picture' (MS. National Art Library, Victoria & Albert Museum Library, Brown Papers). The large version, Birmingham Museums and Art Gallery, is reproduced in *The Pre-Raphaelites*, ed. Leslie Parris (London, Tate Gallery/Penguin Books, 1984), no. 86, p. 160. [Hereinafter, Tate (1984).].

15 Alexander Kinglake, *Eōthen, or Traces of Travel Brought Home From the East* (London, John Ollivier, 1844), p. 242. In 1858 Hunt was approached with a commission to illustrate *Eōthen*. The artist considered this 'too difficult a task to undertake', partly because he felt that Kinglake regarded 'places of great interest without feeling' (Hunt to unidentified correspondent, [28 January 1858], MS. Archives of the History of Art, The Getty Center for the History of Art and the Humanities, Los Angeles.) [Hereinafter, Getty.]

16 MS. February, Bodleian MS. Eng. lett. c. 296 fol. 25.

17 MS. Henry E. Huntington Library, San Marino, California, published in Mary Lutyens (ed.), 'Letters from Sir John Everett Millais, Bart, P.R.A. (1829–96) and William Holman Hunt, O.M. (1827–1910) in the Henry E. Huntington Library, San Marino, California', *Walpole Society*, 44 (1972–4), 56. [Hereinafter, Lutyens (1974).]

18 E.W. Lane, *An Account of the Manners and Customs of the Modern Egyptians, Written in Egypt during the Years 1833–1835* (2 vols., London, Charles Knight, 1846), vol. 1, p. 78. Hunt published an extract from Lane in the 1861 Royal Academy catalogue entry on 'A Street Scene in Cairo'.

19 MS. Rylands Eng. MS.1215/67, partly published in Tate (1984), p. 162.

20 David Roberts, 'Entrance of the Temple of Amun, Thebes' in *Egypt and Nubia* (London, 1849), pl. 53.

21 MS. Huntington, published in Lutyens (1984), p. 87.

22 Hunt (1905), *op. cit.*, vol. 1, p. 382.

23 William Holman Hunt, 'The Pre-Raphaelite Brotherhood: A Fight for Art', *Contemporary Review*, 49 (June 1886), 828.

24 Pen and Indian ink over pencil, 38.1 x 19.7 cm. (15 x 7¾ ins.) size of image, on sheet size 51 x 35 cm. (20 x 13 ¾ ins.). Dating from *c*. 1863, this drawing is in the collection of Peter J. Batkin Esq. It is reproduced in Paul Mitchell and Lynn Roberts, *A History of European Picture Frames* (London, Paul Mitchell in association with Merrell Holberton, 1996), fig. 3, p. 11.

25 *The Haunt of the Gazelle*, watercolour heightened with white, with traces of pencil, 14.5 x 20.1 cm. (5¾ x 8¼ ins.), National Museums and Galleries on Merseyside (Walker Art Gallery), reproduced in colour in Mary Bennett, *Artists of the Pre-Raphaelite Circle: The First Generation. Catalogue of Works in the Walker Art Gallery, Lady Lever Art Gallery and Sudley Art Gallery* (London, Lund Humphries, 1988), pl. 10. 'Arab Reclining by a Stream', watercolour heightened with white, with traces of pencil, 25.4 x 35.3 cm. (10 x 13⅞ ins.), Sheffield City Art Galleries, reproduced in colour in *The Orientalists: Delacroix to Matisse. European Painters in North Africa and the Near East*, Royal Academy exhibition catalogue (1984), p. 167. [Hereinafter, RA (1984).]

26 MS. Arizona State University Library, partly published in RA (1984), *op. cit.*, p. 186. Many of Hunt's letters to Millais of this period are written tongue-in-cheek.

27 MS. Rylands Eng. MS. 1216/9, partly published in Hunt (1905), *op. cit.*, vol. 1, n. 1, p. 386, sketches reproduced pp. 384, 385.

28 Hunt (1905), *op. cit.*, vol. 1, p. 349.

29 MS. Huntington, published Lutyens (1974), *op. cit.*, p. 58. The caricature is reproduced pl. 10b, facing p. 147.

30 Hunt to Combe, 26/7 April 1854, MS. Arizona State University Library, published in Tate (1984), *op. cit.*, p. 269.

31 Hunt (1905), *op. cit.*, vol. 2, p. 217.

32 Hunt to Millais, 8 May 1854, MS. Rylands Eng. MS. 1216/9.

33 MS. Huntington, published in Judith Bronkhurst, '"An Interesting Series of Adventures to Look Back Upon": William Holman Hunt's Visit to the Dead Sea in November 1854' in *Pre-Raphaelite Papers*, ed. Leslie Parris (London, Tate Gallery/Allen Lane, 1984), p. 123. Hunt's programme may well have been inspired also by a passage lauding the importance of objective artistic recording in Ruskin's 1851 pamphlet *Pre-Raphaelitism* reproduced in *The Works of John Ruskin: Library Edition*, ed. E.T. Cook and A.D.O. Wedderburn (London, George Allen, 1903–1912, vol. 12, pp. 349–50).

34 Seddon's last letter from this trip to Egypt is dated 24 May 1854 (Seddon (1858), *op. cit.*, pp. 74–83).

35 See Judith Bronkhurst, 'Holman Hunt's Picture Frames, Sculpture and Applied Art' in *Re-Framing the Pre-Raphaelites: Historical and Theoretical Essays*, ed. Ellen Harding (Aldershot and Brookfield, Vermont, Scolar Press, 1996), p. 246, reproduced Fig. 62, p. 247.

36 Alice Meynell, 'William Holman Hunt. Part III. The Artist's Home and Studio', *Art Annual* (1893), 28.

37 Getty, *op. cit.* Edith Holman Hunt's watercolours of the trip are in a private collection.

38 MS. Rylands Library, Eng. MS. 1239/15, partly published in Ernestine Mills (ed.), *The Life and Letters of Frederic Shields* (London, Longman, Green and Co., 1912), pp. 317–18.

39 *Collective Exhibition of the Art of W. Holman Hunt, O.M., D.C.L.* (Liverpool, Walker Art Gallery, 1907), p. 39. The watercolour is reproduced in colour in Christie's sale catalogue of 3 June 1994, lot 79.

40 In his letter to W. Bell Scott of 11 February 1860, MS. Princeton University Library, published in George P. Landow, 'William Holman Hunt's "Oriental Mania" and his Uffizi *Self-Portrait*', *Art Bulletin*, 64 (December 1982), 648.

5

David Urquhart and the Role of Travel Literature in the Introduction of Turkish Baths to Victorian England

Nebahat Avcioğlu

I have brought him [the reader] in presence of the most trivial practices. I have not described as a stranger would, a different manner of life; but endeavoured, as a native, to explain matters from which we might derive benefits in health, comfort, happiness, or taste from their old experience . . . I have no expectation that my suggestions will modify the lappet of a coat, or the leavening of a loaf; but there is one subject in which I am not without hope of having placed a profitable habit more within the chance of adoption than it has hitherto been – I mean the bath.[1]

In this chapter I argue for the importance of travel literature as a means of transporting the architecture (both the style and function) of one culture to another. I show that the promoter of Turkish baths in Britain, David Urquhart, a diplomat and traveller, regarded them, with the political context of Britain in mind, as a foreign model that embodied progress. By examining Urquhart's political motivations and the role of his travel writings in promoting his views on domestic architecture and social order, I try to place the subject of travel literature within the history of Oriental architecture in Britain.

The relationship between architecture and travel literature is crucial to an understanding of how Turkish baths came to be built in Britain. Urquhart's travel accounts, *The Spirit of the East* (1838) and *The Pillars of Hercules* (1850), were the means of disseminating his knowledge and views of the East. He intended them to be studied rather than read as the memoirs of an adventurer.[2] He positioned himself carefully with respect to other travel writings on the East. On the one hand, he wished to use his work as a vehicle for his views and, on the other, he wanted to distance it from those of other travel writers by pleading with his readers to dismiss any previous knowledge obtained from 'other travellers' accounts', so as to start with a fresh mind.[3] Although he did not name any particular travellers, he was convinced that most of their accounts had been formed before the actual journeys to the East. He thought that these opinions 'became obstacles to his [the traveller's] investigation'. It is worth quoting Urquhart in full, because he makes an argument about Orientalism similar to that of Edward Said's:

> Arrived [the English traveller] in the midst of habits and institutions so completely at variance with those of his country, and struck, of course, immediately with all those things which are worse and inferior to his own country, whether that inferiority exist in reality or in his previous opinion respecting excellence, his eyes naturally revert homewards, with a feeling of satisfaction and exultation; and, from the position on which he stands, where smaller objects are confounded or lost, he takes a more comprehensive view of his country's greatness;[4]

Urquhart's meticulous studies on 'man, manners and institutions' of the Turks indeed distinguished him from those made during other study trips, which concentrated merely on aspects of government for the purposes of espionage or condescension. His two books were ultimately a vehicle for promoting his views on domestic architecture and social order, which were underpinned by his radical politics and inextricably linked with his political background. He was born in 1805 into an aristocratic family of Scottish highlanders and educated at the Dominican school at Sorèze in France and at St John's College in Oxford, where in 1821 he met the ageing utilitarian, Jeremy Bentham. Urquhart, much the younger man, was captivated by Bentham's philosophy and his ideas about laws and morals.

Urquhart's travels to the East started at an early age in the company of Lord Cochrane, a notorious political radical of his time. While Cochrane was fighting against the Turks during the Greek War of Independence, Urquhart chose to spend a year in Istanbul. The trip made a lifelong impact on his career and also on the future of the relationship between England and Turkey. On his return to England in 1830, he published his observations on the Russian dominance of Turkey, Persia and the Caucasus, in a series of letters published in the *Courier*. As a consequence, he was brought to the attention of the King, William

IV, and sent to Albania in 1831 on a secret mission under the orders of Sir Stratford Canning, the then ambassador in Istanbul. After the completion of this mission, he decided to stay in Istanbul in order to find a way to rehabilitate the relationship between England and Turkey that had been hindered by the refusal of the English Government to support the Ottomans in their war against the Russians.[5]

Urquhart's prolific writing and publishing played a central role in the development of his political thinking. His major book on the 'Eastern Question', *Turkey and its Resources* (1833), earned him the reputation among his contemporaries of being the foremost expert on the topic.[6] He founded his own political journal, *The Portfolio; or, a Collection of State Papers, etc., Illustrative of the History of our Own Times*, in 1835. Throughout his career, he placed great emphasis on the value of having a first-hand knowledge of Turkey. His various publications on the 'Eastern Question' brought him to the attention of the newly appointed ambassador to Istanbul, Lord Ponsonby, who was in position from 1832 to 1837 and recommended Urquhart for a diplomatic position there. The appointment was made by Lord Palmerston, who later became a political opponent of Urquhart's over the question of Russia's role in the Middle East, despite their belonging to the same political party.[7] Urquhart was eventually assigned a position at the British embassy in Istanbul as First Secretary in 1835. His political philosophy, shaped by Bentham, manifested itself in his proposal to draw up a commercial treaty between Turkey and England in 1836, an idea that he had been nurturing for several years. For him, economics and politics were the inseparable bonds that united peoples. He observed that the Turkish economy was under the control of the Russians, which left the Turks in a relatively weak position to fight their wars. Urquhart argued that if Turkey could have a better market outside Russia – for example, in England – the Russian government's economic bondage could be overcome. Turkey and England eventually came to an agreement to sign the Commercial Treaty in 1838. Although Urquhart drafted the treaty, he subsequently disowned his role in it. He argued that the modifications imposed by the Palmerston government left Turkish traders, and English traders in Turkey, in a much less competitive position than the Russians because of the retention of high import and export duties.[8] At the end of this controversy, Urquhart was recalled from Istanbul, bringing his official position as a diplomat to an end.

Once back in England, he took up the causes of political reform and philanthropy. He joined the Chartists, the association of working men, in their demand for reform. But the kind of reform he suggested was to have access to diplomatic papers and to study the statistics of Anglo-Turkish trade – a very radical thought for his time.[9] Elected as a Member of Parliament for Stafford in 1847, he set up Working Men's Foreign Affairs Committees soon afterwards to study Russian crimes.[10]

Urquhart's philanthropic efforts included not only encouraging the working classes to read diplomatic papers but also improving the conditions in which they lived. This activity went hand in hand with Edwin Chadwick's reports of 1842 on the conditions of sanitation for the labouring population. Seen in this light, it was not surprising that, in 1847, Urquhart gave his first public lecture on the benefits of Turkish baths to the Working Men's Club in Stafford, less than a year after the Hygiene Reform Bill, which also resulted in the Public Baths and Washhouses Act of 1846. The Act was preceded by the establishment of public baths and washhouses in 1844, sponsored by the Society for Obtaining Baths and Washhouses for the Labouring Classes. Like Bentham's *Panopticon*, the public bath, as conceived by Urquhart, was an embodiment of utilitarian principles aimed at improving the social conditions of the poor and the working classes through the control of their physical environment – one that manifested itself in a special architectural form. The argument used to promote bathing was that cleanliness was linked to happiness and mental health, and that regular washing as an act of self-improvement would result in a more productive labour force. Bentham's credo, 'the greatest happiness of the greatest number',[11] gave the outline for Urquhart's endeavours in promoting Turkish baths. Urquhart believed that the habits of the East could be seen as models to 'derive benefits in health, comfort, happiness, or taste'.[12]

Urquhart's attempt to introduce Turkish baths into Victorian society was not, however, a simple act of seeing the Other as a way of defining the Self by contrast. Urquhart believed that the habits of the East could be seen as models from which 'benefits in health, comfort, happiness, or taste' could be derived. This belief was realised through his introduction of Turkish baths in Britain. Urquhart placed his faith in the baths as the means of providing 'the comforts of life within the reach of the whole mass of the population',[13] and not only for the improvement of working-class conditions, for he believed in the wholeness of society as opposed to the Benthamian hierarchy of classes. Although Urquhart had adopted utilitarian principles as a result of his friendship with Bentham, he envisaged the need for philanthropy to bridge the gap between the classes. He wanted to create such an occasion and the Turkish baths were to be the vehicle.[14]

Because decoration, comfort and luxury are often associated with Turkish baths, it might seem strange to link them with utilitarian baths. Indeed, architecturally they were very different and, with this distinction in mind, Urquhart had hoped that Turkish baths would lead to a very different kind of social reform from utilitarian baths.

Urquhart was critical of the conventions that governed relationships between classes and in particular, the lack of dialogue between the classes. In his view, this dialogue was 'broken off by there being no settled occasion on which we are in contact with them [the lower orders]'. His first-hand experience in Istanbul convinced him that the baths, by virtue of the social habit of washing, provided the opportunity for the different classes to mix. He observed that 'the classes are constantly brought together into the presence of each other' and concluded that, as a result, 'they know one another'.[15]

Turkey, for Urquhart, was a kind of enlightened utopia. In his view, it was no accident that Turkey appeared to be more advanced than England in certain respects. In both of his travel accounts, he advocated studying and imitating Turkish architecture because it embodied the culture's economic, political and religious achievements. He studied the architecture of both nations and outlined the differences in *The Spirit of the East* and *The Pillars of Hercules*. He used this comparative knowledge of architecture as a means of criticising British society and imposing his socio-political ideas.

Unlike most of his contemporaries, monumental architecture was not his priority. On the contrary, he believed that profound use of space was best illustrated in the form of a simple room as this, he argued, was where the interaction of a whole society could be understood. He discussed his observations on the subject in *The Spirit of the East*, in which he argued that Turkish architecture was 'meaningful' and thereby offered a critique of the conventional English approach to architecture and its inherent hostility to the Turks.

Being a Turcophile was a precarious business at the time of the Crimean War, in 1853–6. Russia's desire for mastery over the Dardanelles and the Black Sea polarised the British public into two separate groups, 'Turcophiles' and 'Anti-Turks'. Urquhart's promotion of an Islamic institution such as the baths was an unconventional type of political adventure. But he strongly believed that architecture played a crucial role in Turkey's social and political structure.

Urquhart insisted that Turkish 'domestic architecture ought to be understood by whoever seeks to become acquainted with their [the Turks'] ideas and manners'.[16] He perceived the Turkish room to be the 'principle of all architecture' in Turkey and he claimed that 'the Room is the first step to acquaintance with the East'. To support his views he included a one-page engraving in *The Spirit of the East*, showing a very simple plan of 'a typical' Turkish room. This must have surprised British readers accustomed to images of Eastern art and architecture always taking the most ornamental forms. It must also have been a calculated act, as he strongly criticised Western ideas of forms and proportions in architecture. Arguing that English architecture was founded on false principles, he wrote 'we build our houses with reference not to the inside, but to the out'.[17] English architecture was, in his view, a sign of England's political incompetence. He argued that:

> Our apartments are regulated by no intelligible principles, and cannot be rendered subservient to the social purposes of a people between whom laws have not established broad lines of demarcation, and who, therefore, in the adjustment of the grades of society, preserve the natural inequality of men.[18]

Clearly Urquhart believed that architecture should serve society and social purposes and overcome class divisions.[19] For him the contemporary debate behind the search for a national style in England was the result of England not having subtle characters of architecture of her own, unlike Turkey. Urquhart perceived the Turkish room to be a display of the public character of the state, where people of all classes come together and 'where each individual's grade may be known by the place he occupies'. The architectural rules and principles in Turkey, he said, were fixed not in the 'details and decorations of the stone' but in its culture, politics and religion.

Urquhart compared Turkish and English culture in terms of three political and historical categories: kings or sultans, proprietors and the people. He argued that 'the people' in Turkey were 'free in principle and in feeling' because, unlike in England, the feudal aristocracy had not taken possession of the lands that they governed and converted the people into serfs.[20] He also blamed the English aristocracy for being the main cause of a breakdown in communications between the people and the king. His Turkish experience shaped his belief in the political importance of a monarch or sultan being in close contact with his people. As an analogy, he idealised the Turkish sultan as an 'architect' – as someone who would act with the interests of a 'proprietor', and as a person for whom the just proportions of a room in a house came before the considerations of profit.[21] From this point of view, his political activities designed to promote Turkish values in Britain can be seen as the construction of Turkish baths.

Urquhart needed to justify the introduction of Turkish baths in Britain. He used a conservative strategy to argue for the continuation of tradition, claiming that different nations in antiquity had shared similar bathing practices, such as the Greeks and Romans. His real point was that these habits or practices had only survived in Turkey. In his speech to the Society of Arts, in 1862, he explained that 'the Turks have preserved the bath from ancient times; they have also the habits and manners belonging to it; and, therefore, when you say "Turkish bath", you confess that you have to go to the Turks for it'.[22] However, he recognised the animosity towards the Turks among the British that existed not only as a result of the Russo-Turkish wars but also because of the anti-Muslim tradition dating back to the capture of Istanbul in 1453. He also realised that British 'self-love' had to be overcome before the people could learn from the experiences of the Turks. Urquhart believed that the habit of washing had to be acquired and maintained by means of experience. Habits, however, could never travel disembodied from their architectural settings. The social activity of washing in Islamic society and Turkish baths were mutually dependent on each other for their existence, and this in turn affected their capacity to be translated into England.

Nineteenth-century conventions of travel writing placed a high premium on narratives of personal experiences. Travellers described mosques and palaces mainly because to do so was part of a literary tradition, whereas describing baths involved a novel physical experience.[23] Washing in the same places as the natives was the closest that the traveller came to participating in their culture. Such experiences resulted in a changing relationship between the roles of architects and travellers when it came to the construction of buildings in the Oriental style in Britain in the nineteenth century; the authority of the travellers' observations mattered more than the architects' knowledge of construction.

This was precisely the case when the first Turkish bath was built in Britain. When a physician from Cork, Dr Richard Barter, approached Urquhart to build one in his hospital at Blarney, near Cork, he also asked Urquhart to oversee the architectural construction.[24] Barter had already been interested in 'water-cure' projects before reading *The Pillars of Hercules*, but it was this book that prompted him to establish a Turkish bath in his institution. In a letter to Urquhart, he wrote, '. . . your description of the Turkish bath has electrified me. If you will come down there and superintend the erection of one, men, money and materials shall be at your disposal.'[25]

Urquhart responded promptly, and took responsibility for overseeing the architecture and construction of the bath at Cork. Soon after it had been built, Urquhart and Barter toured England and Ireland lecturing about the benefits of Turkish baths. A year later, Urquhart built his own at his residence in Rickmansworth, Hertfordshire. As part of his philanthropy, he opened the baths to the poor and the working classes free of charge.[26] Many users of the bath wrote enthusiastic letters to newspapers praising Urquhart's generosity and concern. One person wrote, 'Mr. Urquhart . . . has kindly permitted the public to use [the bath], which I, with many others, have done.'[27] Although Urquhart's bath was accessible to the working class, *The Pillars of Hercules*, with its detailed discussion of the construction and medical uses of the bath, was affordable for, and therefore read mostly by, the middle and upper classes. Members of the working class wanting this information wrote to Urquhart directly. For example, a certain B. Morrell wrote:

> Excuse me for troubling you with a few questions on the use of 'the Turkish Baths' . . . I am desired to ascertain if the said work can be accessible to our Committee; and if so, how? and where? Perhaps I ought to state that we have already gone pretty near the extent of our means, so if the work be an expensive one, possibly we may not be able to secure a copy.[28]

Others followed Dr Barter's example and consulted Urquhart and his travel writings in order to construct Turkish baths. William Potter, who claimed to have re-introduced public Turkish baths into Britain, also drew his knowledge of them from Urquhart's *The Pillars of Hercules*.[29] In the strict sense of the word the first 'public' Turkish bath in England was indeed built by him in Manchester in 1859. Potter summarised the importance of this work in shaping the future of England by stating that 'he [Urquhart] could have had but a faint idea of what that interesting and brilliant work was destined to do for his fellow-countrymen'.[30] It is not true that Urquhart had not predicted the consequences of his work, rather that he had not been sure who would take up his suggestions.

In order to spread the habit of washing and increase awareness of its medical importance, one part of Urquhart's strategy was to convince like-minded philanthropists and physicians to construct their own private baths, as they were potentially significant allies.[31] Two of his medical friends, George Witt and William Erasmus, welcomed the idea and acted upon his suggestion.[32] Urquhart intended his own private bath to be a paradigm – a model whose aim was to show the benefits and the method of construction for others to follow. Some members of the wealthier classes responded by visiting Urquhart's bath and obtaining plans from him.

Although Urquhart was trying to encourage people to build private baths he was eager to find the opportunity to establish a genuine public Turkish bath in London, where he was in regular contact with the physician members of the Royal Society and the Medical Society of London. In one of their meetings at Riverside (Rickmansworth) on 27 July 1860, he made his proposal:[33]

> If the bath is to be introduced, we must have a model institution. The capital must be raised, not for dividends; and there must be no pandering to the public taste or to common notions. I should be quite prepared to undertake – on condition of not being interfered with – not only for the architectural part, but also to instruct men in shampooing, so that the double and heavy expense and delay would be saved of sending out an architect to Constantinople, and bringing from Constantinople a staff of shampooers, &c.[34]

The model for the establishment had to be taken from Istanbul because that was where Urquhart gained his experience in washing. He insisted that anyone who undertook the design process should be familiar with the baths in Istanbul, which meant that the architect had to be sent there to gather first-hand experience. Urquhart was prepared to take on the duties of architect, because he felt that only he had the authority, the knowledge, and the experience. With these points in mind, he began working on the first genuine public Turkish bath, at Jermyn Street Hammam, in London.[35]

As a traveller, Urquhart's knowledge of the baths in Istanbul, as well as his scholarly knowledge of the Turkish language, was anything but superficial.[36] During his tenure as First Secretary at the British Embassy, he carried out 'three years of diligent statistical inquiries'.[37] Urquhart's Orientalism provided the key not only to his philanthropic principles, but also to the design and construction of Turkish baths in England.

Travel has long been a means of changing the Self, a method of altering social status. With Urquhart, the transformation of social being through travel literature was no longer a cliché. What he tried to achieve demonstrated the possibility not only of social mobility, in the sense of movement from one social place to another, but also of cultural mobility from East to West. His travel writings and his political views were the means of this transmission of culture. Scholars of travel literature have agreed that when one writes about the Other, one reinterprets the Other for one's own audience. In effect, this act of cultural appropriation is not only a familiarisation with the Other but in the case of some travellers in the past it was a way of changing one's own habits. In the case of Turkish baths, Urquhart sought to inculcate a habit of washing among all classes, using his own experiences together with travel literature as a vehicle for this social reform.

NOTES

1 David Urquhart, *The Pillars of Hercules or a Narrative of Travels in Spain and Morocco in 1848* (2 vols., London, 1850), vol. 1, p. v.

2 David Urquhart, *The Spirit of the East* (2 vols., London, 1838).

3 *Ibid.*, vol. 1, p. xi.

4 *Ibid.*, vol. 1, p. 51.

5 For a detailed historical account of this war see Edmund Ollier, *Cassell's Illustrated History of the Russo-Turkish War* (2 vols., London, Paris, New York, Cassell, 1885–1886).

6 See Gertrude Robinson, *David Urquhart: Some Chapters in the Life of a Victorian Knight-errant of Justice and Liberty* (Oxford, Basil Blackwell, 1920); and Lord Alexander Lamington, *In the Days of the Dandies* (London, 1906). The popularity

of the book is difficult to gauge without further research into readership response. There were five editions in two years, although this evidence must be evaluated cautiously.

7　See M. Taylor's 'The Old Radicalism and the New: David Urquhart and the Politics of Opposition, 1832–1867' in Eugenio F. Biagnini and Alastair J. Reid (eds.), *Currents of Radicalism. Popular Radicalism, Organised Labour and Party Politics in Britain, 1850–1914* (Cambridge, Cambridge University Press, 1991), pp. 23–44.

8　Robinson, *op. cit.*, pp. 58–60.

9　A. Briggs, *The Age of Improvement 1763–1867*, 2nd edn (London, Longman, 1960), p. 434.

10　*Ibid.*, p. 380. This contributed to the dispute between 'Anti-Turks' and 'Turcophiles', which ignited the animosity between Urquhart and Palmerston.

11　J. Dinwiddy, *Bentham* (Oxford, Oxford University Press, 1989), p. 26.

12　Urquhart (1850), *op. cit.*, vol. 1, p. 49.

13　Urquhart (1838), *op. cit.*, vol. 1, p. 49.

14　Urquhart (1850), *op. cit.*, vol. 1, p. 64.

15　*Ibid.*

16　Urquhart (1838), *op. cit.*, vol. 2, pp. 336–7.

17　*Ibid.*

18　*Ibid.*

19　*Ibid.*, *op. cit.*, vol. 2, p. 373.

20　*Ibid.*, *op. cit.*, vol. 2, p.14.

21　*Ibid.*, *op. cit.*, vol. 2, pp. 14, 373.

22　D. Urquhart, 'On the Art of Constructing a Turkish Bath', a paper read before the Society of Art in February 1862; see Sir John Fife (ed.), *Manual of the Turkish Bath* (London, 1865), p. 164.

23　See Nebahat Avcioğlu, 'Peripatetics of Style: Travel Literature and the Political Appropriations of Turkish Architecture, 1737–1862', Ph.D. dissertation, University of Cambridge (1997).

24　This date coincided with a competition for British architects to design a memorial church in Istanbul to commemorate the loss of British lives in the Crimean War. While Urquhart was promoting Turkish architecture in England, England was reciprocating by sending architects to introduce English architecture to Istanbul.

25　E. Wilson, *The Eastern or Turkish Bath* (London, 1861), p. 52.

26　*St Alban's Times* (3 May 1860), 'The Baths at Riverside. – We are happy to record the fact, that Mr. Urquhart, who resides at Rickmansworth, has with his accustomed liberality, thrown his beautiful baths open for the use of the public, and that many are now taking advantage of his kindness. Amongst them are some invalids who are recovering their health and strength by the use of these baths, which must be a great boon to the neighbourhood'; for another note from a user see *St Alban's Times* (19 May 1860). Newspaper cuttings collected by David Urquhart now in the Wellcome Institute, Urquhart papers, MS. 6236.

27　'An Inhabitant of Rickmansworth' (19 May 1860), *St Alban's Times*, Wellcome Institute, Urquhart papers, MS. 6236.

28　B. Morrell, letter to D. Urquhart, 29 April 1858, Wellcome Institute, Urquhart papers. Correspondence on Turkish Baths, MS. 6236 letter no. 14.

29 W. Potter to the Editor of the *Examiner and Times*, 'The Roman or Turkish Bath' (15 November 1858), Wellcome Institute, Urquhart papers, MS. 6236. In Urquhart's annotated copy of the article, he underlined this claim.

30 W. Potter (proprietor of the Turkish Bath, Manchester), *The Roman or Turkish Bath: Its Hygienic and Curative Properties* (Manchester and London, 1859), p. 5.

31 Fife, *op. cit.*, pp. 204–205.

32 Wilson, *op. cit.*

33 'First Dialogue. Heat: How Useful for Man, and How Used by Him' (27 July 1860). There were about 40 medical and professional people at the meeting. It was in the form of a question and answer session with Urquhart being on the receiving end. Fife, *op. cit.*, pp. 1–48.

34 *Ibid.*, p. 27.

35 For a more detailed discussion of the construction of the Jermyn Street Hammam, see N. Avcıoğlu, 'Constructions of Turkish Baths as a Social Reform for Victorian Society: the Case of the Jermyn Street Hammam' in Colin Cunningham and James Anderson (eds.), *The Hidden Iceberg of Architectural History*, Papers from the Annual Symposium of the Society of Architectural Historians of Great Britain (1998).

36 Robinson, *op. cit.* See also the section on 'Turkish Literature' in David Urquhart (1938), *op. cit.*, vol. 2, pp. 272–97.

37 Urquhart (1838), *op. cit.*, vol. 1, p. xii.

6

J. Wolff and H. Stern: Missionaries in Yemen[1]

Aviva Klein-Franke

The Middle East enchanted many people from many countries and nations: travellers, scholars, traders, adventurers, antiquity plunderers, wanderers and missionaries. The motivation of many scholars and others in travelling to the Orient was to discover the past by exploring inscriptions on stones and ruins, for the Orient 'delivered some messages to them and fascinated their mind and heart' – as is engraved on the gravestone of the Austrian scholar, Mueller.[2]

Karsten Niebuhr visited Yemen in 1763 as part of a delegation commissioned by the King of Denmark. After his account was published, many more scholars dared to visit Arabia and the Near East. Many of them published their experiences, which further motivated others to do the same.

Travellers from Western Europe either travelled individually or belonged to societies. Trade societies encouraged governments to open a dialogue with local authorities in the Middle East to develop diplomatic relationships to benefit their businesses. Consequently their governments became interested in the region because of its strategic importance. Therefore the governments supported all travellers to the Orient and ensured that they had protection against the threat of piracy at sea and of robbers on land.

The Church Missionary Society

The work of English missionaries in the Orient was conducted by the Church Missionary Society (CMS). The foundation document of the CMS, in March 1809, stated that it was created to help the Jews. The motivation was religious: to help the Jews in their fight against anti-Semitism by bringing them redemption through Christianisation.

The CMS was reformed and changed its name in 1815, becoming the sole representative of the Society for Promoting Christianity among the Jews (SPCJ). Sir Thomas Baring was nominated as the president of the Society.[3] The CMS was involved in missionary work in England as well as in Eastern Europe; it was also active in the Orient and sent missionaries to Christianise Jews living under Islam. The CMS also established the *Jewish Intelligence* newspaper to report the activities of the society and its missionaries.[4]

J. Wolff and H.A. Stern

Joseph Wolff and Henry Stern were sent by the CMS to work in Yemen and had much in common. Both were born in Germany into Jewish rabbinical families;[5] both were well-educated in Jewish thought and tradition; both spoke Hebrew fluently and were educated in Oriental languages. From an early age both of them were convinced that they wanted to embrace Christianity, and it was on their own initiative that they were baptised. They were denounced by their families at a young age, but devoted themselves to Christian missionary work among the Jews. As devoted Christians they worked as members of the SPCJ for many years.

Wolff and Stern were sent to Yemen at different times to try to aid suffering and needy Jews. It was not an easy task, and at many times on their journeys they were ill or in danger of their lives. More than once they had to escape from prison or, even worse, from the death penalty. Their families had to sacrifice their happiness, with the head of the family absent on duty in remote areas each year for many months. However, they were convinced that Christianity, which was for them the chosen way of life, would bring salvation to the Jewish people wherever they lived. Their education in Jewish studies and Hebrew was an advantage during this work.

Wolff and Stern's way of life was not unique. There were many German converted Jews working in England for the SPCJ. It was often debated as to whether converted Jews were the best agents through whom the Christian Gospels should be conveyed to their brethren. Certainly, converted Jews from Germany were most successful missionaries and a blessing for the church, since they were energetic in their efforts on its behalf.

Joseph Wolff

Joseph Wolff was born in 1796 to Sara and Rabbi David Wolff, in the small village of Weilersbach, near Bamberg, which had a population of fifty Catholic and 15 Jewish families. The family moved to Halle shortly after his birth. When Joseph was four years old, his father began to teach him all the Jewish ceremonies and practised the Talmud with him daily; he began to read Hebrew from the age of six. Throughout his childhood he heard that the Jews expected the Messiah and that this event could not be far off. However, although his father considered Christians worshippers of a cross of wood, he sent his son to a public Christian school, in order to learn German. The Wolff family moved many times from one town to another. At the age of seven and a half, the family left Halle to move to a small village near Bamberg.

When Wolff was eight he discussed the coming of the Messiah with the village milkman, as every evening he bought milk for the family from him. The milkman listened to him, then said, 'My dear child, you do not know the true Messiah, Jesus Christ . . . your ancestors always expected an earthly kingdom and not a heavenly one, and therefore they killed him; they did likewise to the prophets. If you read your own prophets critically, you would be convinced.'[6] Two days after this conversation with the milkman, Wolff went to a Lutheran clergyman to explain that he knew he would like to become a Christian, but when the clergyman heard how old he was, he told him to come back a few years later. When he was ten the family moved again and his father sent him to Frankfurt to study Latin. There he met 'enlightened' Jewish youths and heard them stating that both Jews and Christians have the same moral principles.

A few months later, Wolff was sent to Bamberg to stay with his uncle and attend school, studying Latin and history. One day he heard his teacher saying, 'It is an impossible thing to be a moral man without God and without Christ', and this teacher read the Gospel to Wolff. After this lesson, Wolff told his uncle that he wanted to embrace the Christian faith but his uncle cursed him and made him leave his house. Wolff then moved from place to place, earning his living by teaching Hebrew. It was not for many years that Wolff found a home amongst the warm family of the SPCJ.[7]

Wolff studied in Prague, Vienna, Heidelberg and in Weimar, where he became acquainted with Goethe. In Vienna he wanted to be converted but was told that 'by the law of the Austrian empire it is forbidden to baptise a Jew without the permission of his parents if he is still under 18 years of age'.[8] Wolff moved to Munich and found a teacher who explained to him the distinction between Protestants and Catholics. In Switzerland, he met a Franciscan friar with whom Wolff prepared for baptism.[9] On 13 September 1812, at the age of 17, he was baptised in Prague.[10]

It was in Rome in 1816 at a Christian seminar that Wolff became acquainted with Lord Henry Drommend, who was active in the CMS in London. He invited Wolff to come to London to work for the Society.[11] Wolff's first mission was to go to Jerusalem. He travelled via Gibraltar, Malta and Alexandria and reached Jerusalem in 1821.[12] He then travelled throughout the Orient and visited Jews in Persia, Afghanistan, Syria, Palestine, Egypt, Ethiopia, India, Bukhara and Yemen. On 15 November 1836, Wolff arrived at the port of Mocha with Joseph al-Nadaf, a Jew, and reached Sanaa in December 1836.[13] At the end of that month he left Mocha for Aden.[14]

Henry Stern

Henry Stern was born on 11 April 1820 in Unterreichennach, a small town near Gelsenhausen. He was the son of Hanna and Ahron Stern and the youngest of seven children. He spent a happy childhood with his family. At the age of twelve, he was sent to Frankfurt-am-Main to continue his studies. His father then sent him to Hamburg to study medicine. In Hamburg Stern met Dr Moritz, a converted German Jew, and a most devoted and successful missionary who was working with the SPCJ.[15] Stern became close to Moritz and, through him, to Christian literature. He was convinced that the creed of the Christians was far more rational than the burdensome rituals imposed by the rabbis.

In 1839, Henry Stern accepted a good position in a private company in London, but on his arrival found that his job had fallen through. He had no money and no job. He knew no one in London and was too ashamed to ask his family for money to pay for the journey back to Germany. However, in London he eventually met another converted German Jew, Dr Reichardt, who was, at that time, the superintendent of the Operative Jewish Convert Institutions, which had been established to employ converts and potential converts.[16] Stern discussed the Messiah with him.

On 15 March 1840, at the age of twenty, Stern received the rite of baptism in the chapel of the CMS, where he had first heard the message of salvation.[17] He was then sent to study Oriental languages at Cambridge and, after less than two years, with a knowledge of German, English, French, Latin, Greek, Hebrew and Arabic, he was presented to the committee of the CMS as being fully qualified to begin Jewish missionary work.[18] He served the CMS with devotion for the next 45 years.

Stern began his missionary work one generation after Wolff. His mission was among the Jews of Kurdistan; in Hamdan, Isfahan, Tehran and Mosul; along the Nile, in Khartoum, with the Karaites in Egypt; among the Falasha in Ethiopia and Yemen.[19] About ten years after his first mission to the Arabian Gulf, Stern was appointed as director of CMS activities in Constantinople, and it was there that his family joined him. While there, Stern received a message from the CMS to the effect that the Jews of Yemen were subjects of oppression and persecution and that the Muslim rulers in Yemen were of a most fanatical character. Stern was asked to take a mission to Yemen, which he was willing to do as he had a deep sympathy with his suffering brethren in Arabia. He knew that his mission was dangerous and the CMS was not sure he would return safely, so his family was sent back to England. Stern received a *firman* (edict) from the Sultan and sailed from Constantinople in July 1856 on this uncertain mission, wearing local dress and calling himself Dervish Abdallah. He entered Yemen at the port of al-Hudayda,[20] having shaved his hair, beard and moustache.[21] Although he looked like an Arab, he lived amongst the Jews, and prayed in their synagogues until he arrived in Sanaa, when his true faith was discovered. Subsequently he was not allowed to stay in the Jewish quarter and resided in the Samsam *khan* (caravansary).[22] His companion during his travels in Yemen was a Jew called Eliyahu.[23] He returned to Europe via Mocha, arriving in Aden on 6 December 1856 and in Constantinople on 1 January 1857.[24] He died in England on 13 May 1885.[25]

The significance of Wolff's and Stern's missions to Yemen

Wolff's and Stern's missions to Yemen took place at a time of political instability. Economic collapse and messianic expectations occupied the minds of Yemeni Muslims and Jews alike. Uncertainty increased when civil war broke out; one Yemeni tribe fought another in order to gain the upper hand and rule the country. In addition to this unstable situation, the presence of the British in Aden (before the occupation), brought tensions on the border with Yemen. After the occupation of Aden by the British,[26] Southern Arabia became a battlefield between the British forces, the Ottomans (who occupied the shore between Mocha and al-Hudayda) and the Yemenis, who fought against both the British and the Ottoman forces to free their country from invaders.

Wolff and Stern were well prepared when they set off on their journeys, having access to many pamphlets and essays written by converted Jews and published by the CMS, with instructions and advice about missionary work among the Jews.[27] They both shipped a heavy load of hundreds of books with them, mostly volumes of the Bible, the New and Old Testaments, in Hebrew and English, and also Arabic copies of *Pilgrim's Progress* and *Robinson Crusoe*.[28]

The two missionaries were not only interested in missionary work among the Jews of Yemen but also in searching for descendants of the ten missing tribes of Israel.[29] Wolff had met Yemeni Jews eleven years before he began his mission to Yemen: in 1825 he met Yemeni Jews in Basra and Bushire and was impressed with their behaviour and appearance. He was convinced that they were descendants of B'ne Israel (sons of Israel) who settled in Arabia after the expulsion from Eretz Yisrael by Nebuchadnezzar at the time of the first temple (sixth century BC).[30]

Wherever Wolff went in Yemen he felt a great expectation of the coming of the Messiah on the part of both Jews and Muslims.[31] The chief rabbi, Joseph ben Salem al-Qareh, told Wolff about Jews who expected the arrival of the Messiah within 1,290 days.[32] Wolff was told that one of the gates of Sanaa, Bab al-Astran, would remain locked until the Messiah appeared.[33] Wolff, who dressed like a Muslim, could recite from the Bible in Hebrew as well as from the Holy Quran in Arabic. In this atmosphere it was also easy for Wolff to preach about the Christian Messiah.[34]

An appearance by preachers of the Gospel in Jewish communities was an unusual event, not only because many of the communities heard about Jesus for the first time, but also because in most places they had never before met Christians who spoke and preached in Hebrew to Jews. It took them some time to realise that they had to listen with care and not take for granted that anyone who spoke Hebrew was necessarily a Jew.[35] Nevertheless, the Jews welcomed Wolff warmly, as he wrote to

Baring, 'They are frank and unreserved in their intercourse with me, in fact the very idea that I had crossed deserts and seas to seek their good produced a feeling of gratitude.' The aim of his mission was not the only reason for their politeness to Wolff, as he mentioned, 'I believe it was more owing to the few Hebrew sentences I addressed them than other reasons.'[36]

Wherever Wolff arrived he first looked for the head of the Jewish community and talked to him in Hebrew. He spoke of harmony and unity between the Old and New Testaments. He wrote to Baring about the Jewish reaction to his preaching:

> They the Jews felt the truth of my words and their own hearts responded to the declaration, that sin had driven them from their country and God had reduced them to the suffering and misery which has been their lot for so long a period, these striking facts not only appealed to their understanding but, as I could feel, also awakened and touched their souls.[37]

Wolff distributed the New Testaments to his audience, read to them from the book and discussed it with them. He was impressed by their intelligence, as he wrote to Baring:

> They had many questions to ask and some of them considerably important such as 'whether those who had never heard of Christ could be blamed or charged with unbelief', 'whether the Bible was the only revelation from God'; and 'whether a pious and devoted life could not procure pardon and forgiveness of sin.'[38]

Wolff described the institutions and social structure of the Jewish communities. He reported the battle between Ottoman forces and Yemenis in Mocha, and mentioned that 'Bilmas [the *wali* of Mocha] had plundered the Jewish quarter and burnt their houses.'[39] During the Ottoman invasion, a major synagogue was burnt. According to Wolff, fifty families lived in the city in 1836; twenty years later, by the time of Stern's visit, there were only ten families. Wolff heard from the Jews of Mocha that their city was called Diqlah in biblical times.[40] He described urban and rural daily life and mentioned a large palace in Sanaa, which, by the time of Stern's visit to the city, had already been destroyed. According to Wolff's description, it was a beautiful building with an impressive interior. Wolff and Stern mentioned that in the Jewish quarter in Sanaa there were 18 synagogues. They described the houses and crafts of the Jews, 'monopolisers of every useful art and every branch of trade'.

From Wolff's letters to Baring, we learn about the connections between the Yemeni Jews and the Indian Jews. The Yemeni Jews obtained books from Yoseph Zemach in Calcutta; they also had connections with Jewish communities in Baghdad and Basra,[41] and there were families in Yemen who had relatives in Bukhara.[42] Wolff enriched the knowledge of Yemeni Jews about other Jewish communities outside Yemen; he told them about the rich Jewish families of Rothschild and Goldman, and about the Jews of England, Germany and Gibraltar, as well as general history and Napoleon.[43] He also discussed Jewish subjects with them: Maimonides and Saadja al-Faumi; the Jews of Spain and their expulsion; the Karaites; Mount Sinai; Mecca; Jerusalem and its antiquities; and the Druze and Samaritans of Palestine.

Wolff always enquired about the Jews he visited and about their life in the diaspora but it seemed that not all the Jewish communities in Yemen kept in touch with each other. The head of the Jewish community, Salem al-Qareh, gave Wolff a present of the precious manuscript of Maimonides from the fifteenth century. Wolff also bought old manuscripts and sent them to Baring in England. He used to ask the local Jewish communities to write him an essay about their history.[44] When Wolff asked the head of the community in Yarim, Abraham ben Yahya, how many Jews there were in Yemen his answer was: in Sanaa 2,000 families, Aden 100, Djibla 150, Yarim 80; altogether 2,658 Jewish families.[45] Wolff himself estimated the Jewish population in Yemen to be ten times this figure – approximately 200,000.[46]

Wolff asked about the ancient civilisation of Yemen and collected information about the settlements of the Jews, their numbers and how many synagogues they had, and about the living conditions in Yemen. He reported that some Jews in Yemen lived in bigamous marriages. He gathered their oral traditions and was the first to acknowledge the legend of their arrival in Yemen and the reason why, in their eyes, their time in the diaspora was cursed: in the sixth century BC, when Esra the Scribe asked them to come to Jerusalem to help to rebuild the temple, they refused. Esra cursed them to stay in the diaspora for the next 2,500 years.[47]

Wolff met tribes in southern and northern Yemen who, according to their tradition, were the children of the Jews of Khaibar who had embraced Islam at the time of the Prophet Muhammad. He met others who claimed to be the children of Hobab, called the Rechabites, who lived in the region of Arhab, and others who claimed to be *nasara*, Christians, before embracing Islam.[48] Wolff also met Arabs who claimed that they became Jews under the Himyarite king, Dhu Nuwas, and later became Muslims. Jews in Sanaa also told Stern they were descended from B'nei Djedad (the tribe of Gad).[49]

Before Wolff left Yemen, he wanted to bless the Jews, to place water on their heads and mention their names.[50] In his eyes he had performed the act of baptism, but the Jews did not recall this act. The Christian faith among the Jews of Yemen was not practised after Wolff left the country, and each boy born went through the circumcision ceremony as before.

Stern also mentioned success in his labours but he wrote that because of the political and religious situation in the country he did not dare to baptise many:

> I have now been twelve days in the city, and during the whole of that time, with the exception of a few hours rest by night, every minute was occupied in preaching the Gospel to Jews and Mahomedans. Among the former, besides the two converts already adverted to, there were several more who felt the converting power of the Gospel, and even desired to be baptized, a request with which their peculiar position forbade me to comply, and among the latter [Muslims] the impression produced had evidently shaken the faith of many, though perhaps their understanding was not quite convinced.[51]

Stern stated in his account that, when the Jews heard in the villages that a stranger came and spoke Hebrew:

> It was rapidly circulated among the Jews and numbers came on the following day to see this unexpected friend of their nation. I had lengthy conversations with the majority of them and through every word I said, every truth I urged was opposed to their religious prejudices. Still they all eagerly listened to the foreign teacher, and readily inclined to the doctrines he pressed upon them.

He also mentioned:

> In passing through the market where numerous Jews exposed their scanty wares, I was agreeably surprised to see some of them reading

our book and others quietly discussing the merits of our faith. Poor despised people, my heart bleeds when I think on the anguish to which you are doomed, and the sufferings to which you must submit.[52]

Stern, too, mentioned in his account that, 'Arabia Felix was waiting for the message of salvation.'[53] Stern mentioned that the questions the Jews asked him about his preaching were not easy to answer; he admired their way of thinking, when the Jews came to him and told him:

> Everything that you have told us we can believe; thus we will admit that Jesus was born of a virgin – that he performed many miracles – that he taught excellent doctrines – that he toiled, suffered and died, all this we can believe, but that the deity should make atonement for man, this is an enigma which it is impossible for us to understand.[54]

Stern spread the New Testament among the Jews of the rural regions. He saw them reading it in their shops in the markets. It seemed to him that the Yemeni Jews became confused when trying to analyse his preachings and looking for the differences between what was written in the New Testament and what their own religion demanded. In Sanaa, Stern's books were rejected by the Jews because the *qadi* (judge) ordered a two hundred dollar tax on Stern's books.[55]

Stern discussed their faith with both Jews and Muslims. During his weeks of stay in Sanaa, he did not meet the chief rabbi, who was in Qaryat al-Qabel at the time as many learned families lived temporarily outside Sanaa because of the civil war. Stern mentioned that he met Mori Said Mansoora, 'one of the principal rabbis'.[56] At this time Sanaa was not ruled by an Imam, that is, a religious authority, but by a civil governor: according to Stern this was the reason for the worsening conditions of the Jews.[57]

Stern was presented to the governor of Sanaa as a visitor to the Jews. He discussed religious issues common to the three religions with shaykh Ahmad al-Qeimah. Stern complained to the governor that the Jews rejected him, although he had come a long distance to help them. The shaykh called a few learned Jews to appear before him, and ask them if Stern's books were like their Torah. According to Stern, their answer was: 'The Torah of the Christians is the same as the Torah of the

Jews.'[58] The governor of Sanaa disagreed with the Jews and argued with them about the content of Stern's books. Stern preached about his belief, 'our book teaches us the knowledge of sin, of corruption of mankind and the necessity of an atonement'.[59] The rumour was spread rapidly from town to town that a 'Nazarene had arrived with books and money to upset the religion of the country'. A crowd of people gathered before the governor's palace.[60] All this was very unusual in Yemen and caused much trouble and turbulence. Stern's behaviour was confusing, not only for the Jews but also for the Muslims. Both groups said that the visitor was either a *yahudi* (Jew) or *nasrani* (Christian) or he was a *nasrani* (in faith) but *yahudi* (in origin).[61] After this discussion the Jews distanced themselves from Stern and wanted him to leave the country as quickly as possible. Not only was Stern's life in danger in Yemen, but the Jews also feared riots because of his discussions. Stern had to escape and Jews helped him find his way out of the country via Mocha.

The missionaries and Jacob Saphir

The Jewish records in Yemen do not mention these visits. However, we learn from a third source what the Jews thought and what happened during Stern's visit. Two years after Stern left Yemen, Jacob Saphir, a traveller from Jerusalem, arrived in 1858, to sell Hebrew books and to buy old manuscripts. Saphir advised the chief rabbi to ask the Sultan in Constantinople for help to improve the Jews' situation or to write to the British government. Rabbi al-Qareh opposed any interference from an outsider, as they had been punished in the past for making contact with foreign organisations or governments. Two years previously they had been accused of cooperation with the Ottoman forces in al-Hudayda because of Stern, and been punished as a result.[62] Their version differs from that of Stern: the Jews of Sanaa realised that Stern did not belong to the Jewish faith, therefore they rejected him. When the Jews realised what he was preaching, they refused to rent him an apartment in the Jewish quarter and he was forced to stay in the Muslim town but he came every day to the *Qaʿ al-Yahud*.[63] Stern complained to the governor of Sanaa, saying that he had come from a great distance to help the Jews but they hindered his preaching and rejected him. The governor of Sanaa called the Jewish leaders to explain their behaviour and asked why they rejected a man who came to visit them armed with a *firman* from the Sultan, with letters of recommendation from the Ottoman governor in al-Hudayda and from Mr T., an important merchant in al-Hudayda,[64] as well as from the British political agent in Aden. When the Jews answered that they could not accept his message because Stern was not one of them, the governor punished them with a fine of 200 *riyals*.[65]

Saphir found that the Jews, especially in the villages, still had Stern's copies of the New Testament. The Jews told Saphir that they could not pray from these books, but because they were written in Hebrew characters they hesitated to throw them away, and therefore used the text for amulets for the Muslims. In each place that Saphir visited, he explained the message of the missionaries. The result was that the Jews burned the books in his presence.[66]

Conclusion

Stern had a charismatic personality. He caused a sensation, but gave rise to fear among the Jews of Yemen since he spoke Hebrew yet dressed like a Muslim. Even worse, he was not Jewish but a Christian who dared to despise the Holy Quran in front of the Jews.[67] With Muslims, Stern discussed Moses and the prophets.[68]

The accounts by Wolff and Stern of their work in Yemen are unusual, in that they managed, as devoted Christians, to discuss the religious issues of the three religions openly, separately and together with both Jews and Muslims.

The visit of these two missionaries in Yemen differed from those of other travellers. Their aim was to contact minority groups, especially Jews, and to convert them to Christianity. Before they arrived, no one had come to Arabia specifically to seek out the Jews, to visit them and live amongst them, particularly with this aim. They also collected information about the minority groups and published it.

However, while Wolff and Stern only wrote about the positive aspects of their missions, Saphir's account gives a different story, at least about Stern's visit, which shows us how important it is not to rely on one source.

Wolff and Stern claimed that their visit was a success and that they had managed to baptise Yemeni Jews. They even mentioned the names of the baptised families.[69] It might be that their accounts were tendentious: the missionaries wanted to show that they had been a success. This, in itself, leads us to be sceptical when we read their accounts. Nevertheless, their descriptions of the life of Jews in a nineteenth-century Islamic country before the Ottomans invaded Yemen, and their statistical data, as well as the historical events they mentioned in their accounts, are important sources of information. In contrast, not a single local community chronicle records anything about the missionaries' visits, although they stayed many weeks among the Jews.

Wolff recorded his account of Yemen in a series of letters to Sir Thomas Baring that he published shortly after his arrival back in England. Before Stern's account of his visit to Yemen was published as a book, he first published chapters from it in the *Jewish Intelligence*, the *Jewish Chronicle* and in other newspapers in England.[70] Many chapters from Stern's account were published in the *Jewish Chronicle* in the second half of the nineteenth century, and through this many Jewish communities in Europe learned about the history and culture of the Jews of Yemen.[71] Indeed, most information on the Jews of Yemen which was published in nineteenth-century English, German and Hebrew newspapers was taken either from Wolff's or Stern's accounts.[72] The information about the countries and societies where the missionaries worked and the knowledge that is revealed from the missionaries' accounts of Jews living in Islamic countries are important in many cases as they are the only source we have.

NOTES

1 Transcription from Hebrew has been done simply, as heard and pronounced. Names are given as the authors themselves used them; thus the same name can appear in different forms.

2 R. Meissner, 'One Hundred Years of Austrian Scholarly Interest and Research in Yemen', *Tema* 83, Nethanya (1993), p. 115.

3 CMS Archives, Wolff file, CMJ. e. 50, 5.

4 W.T. Gidney, *The History of the London Society for Promoting Christianity among the Jews* (London, 1908), p. 84; Josef Tobi, *Yehudei Teiman ba-Me'ah ha-Yod-Tet* (Tel Aviv, 1979), p. 47.

5 Joseph Wolff, *Journal of the Rev. Joseph Wolff in a Series of Letters to Sir Thomas Baring, Bart. Account of his Missionary Labours from the Years 1827 to 1831; and from the years 1835 to 1838* (London, 1839), p. 1.

6 *Ibid.*, p. 8.

7 *Ibid.*, p. 25.

8 *Ibid.*, p. 8.
9 Hugh Hopkins, *The Life of Joseph Wolff: Missionary Extraordinary* (Worthing, Churchman, 1984), p. 1.
10 *Ibid.*, p. 7.
11 *Ibid.*, p. 16.
12 Joseph Wolff, *Missionary Journal of the Rev. Joseph Wolff, Mission to the Jews* (London, 1829), p. 65.
13 Wolff (1839), *op. cit.*, p. 390.
14 *Ibid.*, pp. 372, 382, 396.
15 Henry A. Stern, *Journal of a Missionary Journey into Arabia Felix, Undertaken in 1856* (London, 1858), p. 16.
16 *Ibid.*, p. 18.
17 *Ibid.*, p. 19.
18 *Ibid.*
19 *Ibid.*, p. 23. The Yemeni coast was partly occupied by the Ottomans at that time.
20 Albert Augustus Isaac, *Biography of the Rev. Henry Aron Stern, for more than Forty Years a Missionary among the Jews, containing his Account of his Labours and Travel in Mesopotamia, Persia, Arabia, Turkey, Abyssinia and England* (London, 1886), p. 101; Stern, *op. cit.*, p. 8.
21 Isaac, *op. cit.*
22 Stern, *op. cit.*, pp. 10–11, 29–30.
23 *Ibid.*, p. 12.
24 *Ibid.*, p. 55.
25 Isaac, *op. cit.*, p. 479.
26 The British invaded Aden on 19 January 1839 and it remained under British rule until 1967.
27 For example, 'Attempts for the instruction and conversion of the Jews' (London, 1836) [Bodleian Library, CMS Dep. 147/4], and also the essay by Rev. Andrew Fuller, 'Jesus and the true Messiah: a sermon' [Bodleian Library, CMS Dep. 147/1].
28 Tim Mackintosh-Smith, *Yemen: Travels in Dictionary Land* (London, John Murray, 1997), p. 90.
29 Erich Brauer, *Ethnologie der jemenitischen Juden* (Heidelberg, 1934), p. 5.
30 Gidney, *op. cit.*, p. 184.
31 Bat-Zion Eraqi-Kloreman, 'Jewish and Muslim Messianism in Yemen', *IJMES*, 22 (1990), 201–28.
32 Wolff (1839), *op. cit.*, p. 391.
33 *Ibid.*
34 Joseph Wolff, *Researches and Missionary Labours among the Jews, Mohammedans and other Sects* (London, 1835; Philadelphia, 1837), p. 501; see Yehuda Nini, *Teiman ve-Zion* (Jerusalem, 1982), p. 142.
35 Wolff (1839), *op. cit.*, p. 18.
36 *Ibid.*, p. 391. The same was also said by Stern, *op. cit.*, p. 10.
37 *Ibid.*
38 *Ibid.*
39 Wolff (1837), p. 501; Nini, *op. cit.*, p. 64.
40 Wolff (1837), *op. cit.*, p. 501; Jacob Saphir, *Sefer Masa 'Teiman*, ed. Avraham Ya'ari (Tel Aviv, 1941), p. 220. [Abridged from Saphir's account, *Even Saphir* (2 vols., Lyck, 1866; Mainz, 1874).] Saphir heard another version from the

Jews of Yemen, that Diqlah is identical with the city of Saada, see also Nini, *op. cit.*, p. 64.

41 Wolff (1839), *op. cit.*, p. 391.
42 *Ibid.*, p. 394.
43 Wolff (1829), *op. cit.*, p. 343.
44 He sent his account as a letter to Baring in England. Unfortunately some of his letters were lost, but when he returned to England he recalled the missing information.
45 Wolff (1839), *op. cit.*, pp. 16–17.
46 *Ibid.*, pp. 16–17, 393.
47 *Ibid.*, pp. 391, 394; see also Brauer, *op. cit.*, p. 305.
48 *Ibid.*, pp. 17, 385ff.
49 Stern, *op. cit.*, p. 30.
50 Wolff (1839), *op. cit.*, p. 394.
51 Stern, *op. cit.*, p. 42.
52 *Ibid.*, p. 97.
53 *Ibid.*, p. 5. See also Nini, *op. cit.*, p. 51 and 'Eraqi-Kloreman, *op. cit.*, 201ff on the messianic expectation in Yemen at the time of Stern's visit.
54 Stern, *op. cit.*, p. 23.
55 *Ibid.*, p. 33.
56 *Ibid.*, p. 19.
57 *Ibid.*, p. 24; Nini, *op. cit.*, p. 51.
58 *Ibid.*, p. 36.
59 *Ibid.*, p. 37.
60 *Ibid.*, p. 15.
61 *Ibid.*, p. 28.
62 Stern, *op. cit.*, p. 34; Nini, *op. cit.*, p. 525.
63 Saphir, *op. cit.*, p. 120.
64 Stern, *op. cit.*, p. 6.
65 *Ibid.*, p. 34.
66 Saphir, *op. cit.*, pp. 119–20.
67 *Ibid.*, p. 10.
68 Stern, *op. cit.*, p. 22.
69 Joseph Halévy, 'Voyage au Nedjran', *Bulletin de la Société de Géographie de Paris*, 6 (1873), 27, did not appreciate Wolff's report and thought it incredible.
70 Brauer, *op. cit.*, p. 6; Tobi, *op. cit.*, p. 47.
71 Halévy, *op. cit.*, pp. 5–31, 249–73, 581–606.
72 The representative of the newspaper *Juedische Presse* in Alexandria sent an article about Stern to Germany; see Tobi, *op. cit.*, pp. 298ff.

7

The Copts of Egypt:
Neither Christian nor Egyptian?

Hoda Gindi

When Europe conceptualises the Orient, Egypt's Christian past and present is invisible. Egypt's Biblical connotations were obvious, and 'the Biblical record was employed to support [Egypt's] representation as a land of despotism, barbarity and injustice',[1] but the Christian or Coptic era was, in Stanley Lane-Poole's words, in 1898, a 'vast chasm of history'[2] into which the Copts sank into oblivion. It was 'the dark period . . . between the extinction of the worship of Isis and the Muslim call to prayer'.[3] The European travel narrative of the nineteenth century, therefore, virtually ignored both the historical Coptic era and the modern Copt, the perception and imagination of the traveller seemingly unable to conceive of the plurality – Ancient, Coptic and Muslim – of Egypt. Ancient and Modern Muslim Egypt were sufficiently removed in time and, conceivably, inherently alien in presence, respectively, as to be contained within the Occidental abstraction of the Orient; the Copts, on the other hand, both ancient and modern, strange but not entirely alien because of their purported Christianity, seemed to escape inclusion within the constituted idea of the Orient.

As a result, nineteenth-century European travellers' accounts of the Copts are relegated to a few lines, or sometimes a chapter, of their tomes about Egypt, and are mostly critical of Coptic Christianity, heritage and people. Even the claim of the Copts to Christianity is debatable. Edward Lane describes them as, 'Christians of the sect called Jacobites, Eutychians, Monophysites, and Monothalites, whose creed was condemned by the Council of Chalcedon', who had seceded 'from what was generally considered the orthodox Church'.[4] Though Lane does not openly condemn the Copts as heretics, Lane-Poole does not hesitate to represent them as 'separated by the adoption of the heresy of

[97]

Eutyches'.[5] Georg Ebers, a noted German novelist of his day, who visited Egypt in the late 1870s, makes a clear comparison, 'Verily, as this unclean fluid [water] is to pure wine so is Koptic [sic] Christianity to the other creeds of Christendom.'[6] Such descriptions are indicative of the attitude of Western Christianity to the Copts – at best one of disapproval, at worst an accusation of heresy. Both are a manifestation of Edward Said's view of the 'doctrine of European superiority' – of 'the idea of European identity as a superior one in comparison with all the non-European peoples and cultures'.[7] In other words, Western Christendom 'othered' the Copts who, unlike the Byzantines, were not Europeans, and were thus 'described as a schismatic eastern Christian minority',[8] and 'an implacable enmity' arose 'between them and the Greeks, under whom they suffered much persecution'.[9] Paradoxically and censoriously, the 'othering process' and therefore, the persecution, is often considered the responsibility of the Copts themselves, since 'this enmity was, *of course* [my emphasis] more bitter on the part of the Copts'.[10] Like his great uncle, Lane-Poole writes that it was 'the Copts who *subjected themselves* [my emphasis] to persecution and isolation'.[11]

'*It is well known* [my emphasis] [that the Copts were] one of the sects which the Roman church condemns as heretical', Sonnini, the French naturalist wrote in the year 1800,[12] and 'their interpretation of truth is partial and ignorant'.[13] As a result, many nineteenth-century travellers thought it incumbent upon them to recommend, and in the event of it occurring, to commend, the conversion of these heretics to true Christianity – the European version! In 1848, Eliot Warburton pronounced that as the missionaries have failed with the Muslims – 'for among the Moslems their efforts are admitted to be all but hopeless' – they should 'labour upon the Copts' very indifferent character':

> Such is the material upon which our Missionaries have to labour, . . .
> Mr Lieder and Mr Kruse have made persevering and exemplary efforts in their calling, and, . . . their labours have been . . . successful.
> The Coptic Patriarch is on the best terms with Mr Lieder, calls him his 'father', allows and encourages the Coptic children to attend the Missionary schools, and sanctions the circulation of the Scriptures and Church of England tracts amongst his flock.[14]

The irony of the Patriarch, the Father of one of the most ancient Churches in Christendom, calling a missionary 'his father' is entirely lost on Warburton, in his unconscious superiority. Further, the Patriarch is in Said's terms 'seen to *require* and beseech domination'.[15] More importantly, the children at the missionary schools are 'allowed to imbibe truth, for the first and, perhaps, for the last time, in their lives'.[16]

Sophia Poole writes of the necessity for missionaries in Egypt not to convert Muslims but to teach the Copts, and she answers those who have the temerity to ask why:

> Much are they mistaken who say, 'What need is there of missionaries here to instruct the Copts, who are a Christian people?' . . . their moral state is far worse than that of the Muslims; that in the *conduct* of the latter there is much more Christianity than is exhibited in that of the former.[17]

The Hon. Mrs Georgina Damer records in her *Diary* (1841) her appreciation of the zeal of the missionaries and her hope that the 'next generation' of 'young Copts' will be better people because of the 'knowledge' imparted to them by the missionaries through the 'establishing of schools.' Such instruction will succeed 'in reforming the gross errors that have gradually deformed the original Christian creed', and she ends on a triumphant note: 'A Protestant service in the Coptic language is regularly performed.'[18] In the same vein, A.A. Paton bestows 'much praise . . . on the German missionaries, who, chiefly with English funds, have been most active in educating Copts'.[19]

Ebers is concerned that 'these communities', the Copts, 'have retained little of Christianity but the name' and 'the true spirit of their faith is wholly wanting'. He continues approvingly:

> Therefore it is not surprising that, . . . all the noblest and best elements of the Koptic [*sic*] community have been diverted and absorbed into other confessions. The American Missionary Society – a Presbyterian body from the United States – has been particularly active and successful among them, and there is hardly a town in Upper Egypt where they have not succeeded in winning over many Monophisite Christians to evangelical orthodoxy.[20]

Ebers had obviously not heard 'the rhetorical question' asked by the 'Coptic Archbishop of Asiut', one of these towns in Upper Egypt, to which the Presbyterian mission had addressed itself, 'We have been living with Christ for more than 1800 years, how long have you been living with Him?'[21]

The church services of these 'heretics' are delineated. That they are not really 'divine services' is clear from the language used to describe them and the attitude of the Europeans to them: they go, not to take part in a 'divine service' but to watch the goings-on; the discourse therefore is that of the theatre and not of theology. It is a performance they are attending. To Paton, a Palm Sunday service is a complete theatrical event: the stage with its lighting is 'the temple . . . an oblong square, and lighted from above'; the curtain is 'a screen of inlaid chips' which separates the stage from the audience, the latter being the congregation. Then come the actors whose various costumes are described and the delivery of their lines discussed:

> The patriarch and his deacons made their appearance, the former in a dress of purple and gold . . . The deacons were dressed in simple white robes of linen and gold . . . The patriarch was so infirm, and coughed so often, that when . . . he rose to read a passage in the Coptic Gospel, his voice did not rise above a whisper. A grey-bearded priest then came to a desk, and putting on a pair of spectacles – which being without ear-joints, and simply fastened to his nose by elastic compression, gave him a strong nasal twang . . .'[22]

Lucie Duff Gordon, who attempts a dialogic encounter with Egypt, records her fascination with a ritual she witnesses, but 'Of what is this symbolical? I am at a loss to divine',[23] 'wunderlich', though it was.[24] 'Up' in 'the women's gallery', she 'was looking down on the strange scene below':

> I believe they celebrated the ancient mysteries still. The clashing of cymbals, the chanting or humming unlike any sound I ever heard, the strange yellow copes covered with stranger devices;[25]

The music is not church music but 'a jig-tune'; and the whole play ends with 'Then an old man gave a little round cake of bread, with a cabalistic-looking pattern on it.'[26] The emphasis is on drama and magic but certainly not on sacrament. Lane-Poole, too, dramatises the service:

> During the celebration the central folding doors are thrown back, the silver-embroidered curtain is withdrawn, and the higher altar is displayed.[27]

But, as in a bad play, the scenery is gorgeous but the drama is poor, for what all these preliminaries lead to is only 'the nearly cubical plastered brick or stone altar'.[28] Sonnini sees no drama but merely comedy, for the 'ceremonies' are 'comic scenes' that excite laughter. His mirth, he unrepentantly says, is 'to the great offence of the community'.[29]

Ebers categorically denies that a Coptic service is a divine service: he is forced to endure 'the odious medley of gossip, singing, and bell-tinkling, which the Kopts [sic] call divine service'.[30] He continues, castigating priests and congregations alike for the loud 'chattering and squabbling' that goes on during the service, to which the congregation 'pay so little heed . . . that they eagerly discuss all sorts of worldly business'.[31] Richard Pococke, whose 'careful scholarly volumes were the definitive eighteenth-century English work on the Near East',[32] did not mince his words: 'the Coptis [sic] of all the Easterns, seem to be the most irreverent and careless in their devotions',[33] and Paton makes a direct comparison with the West when he states austerely that in the Coptic service 'there was certainly a want of that reverence and absorption which is visible in our own service . . . but here there was much general conversation and whispering, and at one moment a most audible discussion between the deacons as to the forms of the service'.[34] Edward Lane says decorously and damningly that 'the form of service in itself struck me as not much characterized by solemnity' but his excoriation is reserved for the priests:

> The priests . . . are often guilty of excessive indecorum in their public worship. I heard a priest, standing before the door of the sanctuary in the patriarchal church in Cairo, exclaim to a young acolyte . . . 'May a blow corrode your heart!' And a friend of mine once witnessed, in the same place, a complete uproar. A priest from a village . . . was loudly cursed and forcibly expelled by the regular officiating ministers;[35]

According to Sonnini, utter chaos reigns in services conducted by monks in the monastery of Zaïdi el Baramous:

> It is impossible to give an idea of the confusion that sometimes prevails in their church: they often know not what they are to sing; one would have a particular anthem or psalm, and another a different one; they then dispute and come to blows: in the mean time a third chants a prayer, which is followed by the choir, and

thus the quarrel is terminated. Their singing consists of Turkish and Arabic airs, accompanied by cymbals, the noise of which mixed with squalling voices, and their discordant music, makes the church re-echo with a medley of jarring sounds.[36]

Ignorance abounds. Not only are the priests and the people ignorant of the form of the service, but the Copt knows nothing, according to Lane-Poole, about the history of his church, its traditions, and language.[37] He adds, patronisingly, 'there is something truly heroic in the constancy of these ignorant people – for the Coptic priesthood was never famous for learning – to the faith of their forefathers'.[38] Pococke, in one terse sentence, sums up the Copts: 'They are all exceedingly ignorant, both priests and people.'[39] Lucie Duff Gordon gives an example of the ignorance of a bishop that almost cost him his life and was harmful to the well-being of his people. This came about because the said bishop would not listen to Duff Gordon's wise advice about the follies of fasting. According to her the Bishop is duly punished for not listening to her exhortations: 'he fell down, and cannot speak or move'.[40]

Lane-Poole confidently asserts that 'Coptic literature . . . enshrines only religious books, and does not contain a single historical record.'[41] And, worse, 'we have very little to go upon in the way of literary documents' because the Copts themselves destroyed them:

> There are gaps and dark places that will probably never be filled and illumined; unless, among the manuscript treasures that have survived their Coptic possessors' passion for kindling fires with codices, may some day be discovered the long-sought annals of the Church of Egypt.[42]

In the event of these ignorant barbarians having left anything salvageable, it is apparently the European who rescues the Coptic heritage. Paton tells the story of 'an intelligent German missionary' as follows:

> he had seen a magnificent copy of the Gospels, with much of the text and beautiful Arabic poetry, and a Coptic commentary. Five leaves being wanting, he went to the patriarch, expecting to be able to find five analogous leaves in [his] library . . . but was astonished at being told that the patriarch had never seen any copy of the Gospels so beautiful, and did not even know of the existence of such a manuscript.[43]

Lane-Poole mentions, in passing, that in 'the group of convents in the Nitrian valley' 'Curzon found *his* [my emphasis] precious store of manuscripts',[44] the inference being that the monks were too ignorant to be aware of the value of their heritage.

If 'history itself' is 'made by men'[45] then Coptic history, according to the nineteenth-century European traveller, is made by European men, and sometimes, women; their supreme confidence that they have made a history for a people without a history goes beyond even Fanon's contention:

> Colonialism has made the . . . effort to plant deep in the minds of
> the native population the idea that before the advent of colonialism
> their history was one which was dominated by barbarism.[46]

To many of the nineteenth-century European travellers, the Copts were a people without a history and without culture.

Duff Gordon attributes the ignorance of the Copts to 'stupid bigotry',[47] which is another of their failings. She is aggrieved to discover that, in spite of her condescension, the Copts 'did not seem to acknowledge me at all as a *coréligionnaire*'.[48] To Lane, one of the most remarkable traits in the character of the Copts is their bigotry.[49] Lane-Poole speaks of the Copts' 'implacable hatred' of other churches[50] and connects, like Duff Gordon, ignorance with bigotry: 'with all his ignorance and degradation the Coptic scribe is conceited and bigoted to an extent that none but those who have seen him . . . can imagine'.[51] St John who in his *Egypt and Mohamed Ali* pointedly writes of 'their religion' (as does Lane-Poole, when discussing the 'rites' of 'their religion')[52] – thereby disclaiming all possible kinship between Christianity and the Copts – despises the latter for being 'bigotly tenacious of their ancient customs'.[53]

Bigotry is allied to ignorance and spawns traitors. Lane-Poole declares emphatically that the Copts are tarred with the taint of treachery because their 'implacable enmity' to, and their 'implacable hatred' of the 'Greeks . . . induced the Copts or Jacobites to throw themselves into the arms of the Arab conqueror' which was an act of 'shameful surrender'.[54] Further, such treachery was 'out of mere sectarian spite'.[55] Lane writes with unconcealed glee that, though the Copts' 'revenge was gratified when they gladly received the Arab invaders of their country, and united with them to expel the Greeks', it was short-lived, and 'they were made to bow their necks to a heavier yoke'.[56]

The emotive language – 'shameful surrender', 'revenge' and 'Arab invaders' – is symptomatic of 'imperialist culture'[57] and illustrative of the European attitude to the Orient: the Copts had the temerity to prefer the Arab to the European, the Muslim to Christian Byzantium, the second of which binary oppositions had persecuted them and discredited their faith.

It is worth speculating as to whether this belief that the Copts betrayed Europe and Christianity by opening the gates to 'Amr ibn al-As became an unconscious 'inherited idea'[58] that caused the Copts to be branded as despicable and abject in the eyes of European travellers. For, with monotonous regularity, unanimous opprobrium is directed against their character. Sonnini uses both 'traitor' and 'treachery' to express his horror at the perfidy of the Copts. He gives the example of a Copt, whom he had earlier in his book extolled because he had become a Catholic, but who is now to be castigated because he is:

> like all the men of his nation, no better than a traitor, so much the more dangerous from his being, by long habit, completely versed in the arts of treachery and dissimulation.[59]

He continues, generalising:

> the Copt, brutish and gloomy, insinuating and deceitful, was distinguished for the cringing and insidious deportment of the most abject slave.[60]

St John merely states as fact, that the Copts are 'a cunning, scheming and thrifty people';[61] Lane disparages them with aplomb, for not only does he give an account of the Copts' base character himself, but triumphantly produces 'a respectable Copt' who testifies to 'his nation's' 'unfavourable character'.[62] Lane depicts the Copts as being 'of a sullen temper, extremely avaricious, and abominable dissemblers, cringing or domineering according to circumstances'.[63] And the Coptic acquaintance, whom he quotes with satisfaction, 'avows them to be generally ignorant, deceitful, faithless, and abandoned to the pursuit of worldly gain, and to indulge in sensual pleasure'.[64] To Warburton, 'the Copts have a very indifferent character . . .; they are considered deceitful, sensual, and avaricious.'[65] Sophia Poole tells two gruesome stories of men beating women to death, dramatically ending each story with the chorus 'This is a Copt, by profession and a Christian' and 'This man also is of the same profession!'[66]

Paton comments sardonically on the servility of the Copts, contrasting their demeanour in church with their behaviour when with a Pasha: the Copts are 'disorderly worshippers' but 'nothing can exceed the reverence and humility of a Copt in the presence of a Pasha'.[67] Lane-Poole at the end of the nineteenth century sums it all up:

> The Copt is servile, too often venal . . . he truckles to the great and domineers over the helpless, and in the art of lying stands supreme. His manner is sullen and reserved, and this is not improved by his devotion to date-spirit . . . while in bribery, or rather in the taking of bribes, the Coptic secretary is without peer.[68]

As their contemptible character is denounced, so the professions and skills of the Copts are denigrated. All the travellers agree that the Copts are merchants and traders, scribes, accountants and tax-collectors, none of which they consider very creditable, and, as for the last, positively evil. In this connection Duff Gordon preens herself:

> A very pious Scotch gentleman wondered that I could think of entering a Copt's house; adding, that they were the publicans (tax-gatherers) of this country, – which is true. I felt inclined to mention that better company than he or I had dined with publicans, and even sinners.[69]

Neither their faith nor their character, therefore, entitles the Copts to membership in Christendom according to nineteenth-century travellers. There remains the question of race and nationality of the Copts. The Ancient Egyptians, though the tyrants of the Ancient World, were admired for their tremendous achievements; how, therefore, could these universally and justifiably vilified uncultured Copts be their descendants? Warburton is uncertain, 'The Copts *claim* [my emphasis], and are generally admitted, to be descendants of the ancient Egyptians.'[70] Yet, they were, in Paton's words,

> undistinguished by any architectural decoration, – a truly remarkable lapse in the external circumstances of a nation, when we think of the colossal magnificence of the Pharaonic and the elegance of the Greek periods of Egyptian architecture.[71]

A partial solution is offered: the Copts are descended from the Ancient Egyptians but they are 'degenerate descendants' and are 'so different from their ancestors'.[72]

To Lane, 'the Copts are undoubtedly descendants of the ancient Egyptians, but not an unmixed race – their ancestors in the earlier ages of Christianity having intermarried with the Greeks, Nubians, Abyssinians, and other foreigners'. So, 'with respect to their personal characteristics, we observe some striking points of resemblance, and yet, upon the whole, a considerable difference, between the Copts and the ancient Egyptians'.[73] Being so racially mixed, casts doubt on the very Egyptianness of the Copts. Lane-Poole is categoric: the Copts may be the inheritors of Ancient Egypt yet are not really Egyptians as their blood has been adulterated by their experiences: 'The modern Copt, despite the inheritance of ethnical, linguistic, and religious memories that has descended upon him, possesses the defects of a subject race.'[74]

The perfunctory discussion of the origin of the Copt is reductionistic, in so far as it centres almost exclusively on the history, the church monuments and services and the professions of the Copts – the professions themselves having been inherited because of historical circumstances. A nineteenth-century Copt as a human being in a time contemporaneous with the nineteenth-century European in a space that may be designated his native ground disappears from view. Lane-Poole says as much when he writes, after having listed what he reckons to be the vices of the Copts, that 'Whatever may be thought of the Copts individually, there can be no question that historically they possess a peculiar fascination.'[75] And he blames the Copts who have 'been losing [their] character for so many centuries' for this state of affairs:

> At present, there is no doubt that the coldness with which travellers like Lane and Klunzinger have looked upon the Copts is natural, and the neglect which has befallen [them] is not so surprising.[76]

Lane's example is indeed of pivotal importance, for, in Paton's words, Lane 'has done more than any other individual to acquaint Europe with the genuine native Egyptian'.[77] His was the authoritative work; he was supposed to have acquired and disseminated 'information both authentic and perfectly correct'.[78] Lane's *Modern Egyptians* has one chapter on 'The Copts', but the reason for their inclusion is only because of 'The fame of that great nation from which the Copts mainly derive their origin.'[79]

However, 'gaining an insight into their religious, moral and social state' was well nigh impossible, and Lane had 'almost despaired' when 'a Copt of a liberal as well as an intelligent mind . . . a character of which I had doubted the existence'[!] came to his rescue.[80] 'To his kindness' Lane is 'indebted for the knowledge of most of the facts' in this chapter. It is a little difficult to believe that Lane, a man who, with infinite resource and consummate acting, assumed 'an Arabic name' and 'lived among the people as one of them'[81] and who made Cairenes 'even forget that he was not an Arab',[82] could not have devised some means of finding out about the Copts himself. The inference to be drawn is that Lane was not particularly interested in the Copts and was reluctant to include them in his *Modern Egyptians*. He does not include them in the mainstream of his narrative; he relegates them to and isolates them in a chapter and doubly marginalises them by depending on hearsay rather than observation. Apart from depending on the Copt's acquaintance – not a friend – the chapter abounds with 'I am informed', 'I am told', 'It appears', and the last few pages of the chapter are 'derived from El-Makreezee's celebrated work'.[83]

Lane, the doyen of travellers, the acclaimed authority on Egypt, has done more perhaps than any traveller to deprive the Copts of their nationhood for he does not even allow them a voice with which to speak; through his representation, taken at third hand, he has formulated the Copts as 'objects'.[84] Thus, not only are they neither Christians nor Egyptians, their very humanity is suspect.

The Orient conceived in binary oppositions of threat and promise, evil and exotic, is presently so widespread that the concept itself, para-doxically, has become a stereotype as well as paradigm. However, what is significant is that the Copt is singularly missing from the ranks of 'the Orient and the Oriental, Arab, Islamic, Indian, Chinese or whatever'.[85] This is true, not only of the nineteenth-century European traveller whose narratives marginalise the Copts, but, even more tellingly, of the creator/critic of the discourse of Orientalism, Edward W. Said. Neither do the Copts have a presence in the suggestively titled *Europe's Myths of the Orient* by Rana Kabbani, or even in Leila Ahmed's book explicitly concerned with Lane, *Edward W. Lane*. To a Europe that 'was able to manage – and even produce – the Orient politically, socially, militarily, ideologically, scientifically, and imaginatively'[86] the Copts are conspicuous by their absence.

It is precisely because a stereotype rejects what it cannot subsume, that the Copts are excluded by the 'Western consumer of Orientalism'.[87] The Copt is not a Muslim, therefore he cannot, reluctantly, be branded as Satanic and evil; however, as an Oriental he has all the vices pertaining to the Muslim without his exoticism. Paton puts it succinctly:

> The Coptic quarter [has] passages dark, dismal, gloomy, and noisome. Here are neither arabesques, nor covered mustabahs, nor effendies with pipe-bearers, nor ulama in their white turbans and smooth chins, and the bazaar itself is shabby and out of repair . . .[88]

His Christianity doubly disadvantages him because he is neither a Muslim, and, therefore, not a modern Egyptian, nor is he a Western Christian; he is an Eastern Christian of non-European extraction and thus as a heretic he cannot be accepted as belonging to the Universal Church. The Copt, therefore, is in the unenviable position of being neither an outsider nor an insider; without having the power to inform and inflame the imagination of the West, he has no role to play on the Oriental 'theatrical stage'[89] created by Europe on which are enacted the representations of power and fantasy.

NOTES

1 Sahar S. Abdel-Hakim, 'British Women Writers in Egypt in the Middle Decades of the Nineteenth Century: Sophia Poole, Harriet Martineau and Lucie Duff Gordon', unpublished doctoral thesis, University of Cairo, 1996, p. 105.
2 Stanley Lane-Poole, *Cairo: Sketches of its History, Monuments and Social Life* (1898; repr. New York, Arno Press, 1973), p. 202.
3 *Ibid.*, p. 203.
4 Edward W. Lane, *Manners and Customs of the Modern Egyptians Written in Egypt during the Years 1833–1835* (London, 1836; repr. The Hague and London, East–West Publications; also Cairo, Egypt, Livres de France, 1978), p. 524.
5 Lane-Poole, *op. cit.*, p. 204.
6 Georg Ebers, *Egypt: Descriptive, Historical and Picturesque*, trans. Clare Bell (2 vols., London, Cassell, 1878, repr. 1887), p. 202.
7 Edward W. Said, *Orientalism* (New York, Pantheon, 1978), p. 8.
8 Aziz S. Atiya, *The Copts and Christian Civilization* (Salt Lake City, University of Utah Press, 1979), p. 1.
9 Lane, *op. cit.*, p. 524.
10 *Ibid.*, p. 534.

11 Lane-Poole, *op. cit.*, p. 204.
12 C.S. Sonnini de Manoncourt, *Travels in Upper and Lower Egypt*, trans. Henry Hunter (London, J. Debrett, 1800; repr. 1972), p. 556.
13 Stanley Lane-Poole, *op. cit.*, p. 220.
14 Eliot Warburton, *The Crescent and the Cross: Romance and Realities of Eastern Travel* (1848; repr. London, Maclaren, 1908), p. 70.
15 Edward W. Said, *Culture and Imperialism* (1993, repr. London, Vintage, 1994), p. 8.
16 Warburton, *op. cit.*, p. 71.
17 Sophia Poole, *The Englishwoman in Egypt: Letters From Cairo Written during a Residence there in 1842, 3 & 4* (2 vols., London, Charles Knight, 1844), p. 96.
18 Hon. M.G.E. Dawson Damer, *Diary of a Tour in Greece, Turkey, Egypt and the Holy Land* (2 vols., London, Colburn, 1841), vol. 1, pp. 170–1.
19 A.A. Paton, *A History of the Egyptian Revolution from the Period of the Mamelukes to the Death of Mohamed Ali*, 2nd edn, enlarged (2 vols., 1863, repr. London, Truebner, 1870), vol. 2, p. 281.
20 Ebers, *op. cit.*, p. 202.
21 Quoted in Atiya, *op. cit.*, p. 1.
22 Paton, *op. cit.*, pp. 282–3.
23 Lucie Duff Gordon, *Letters from Egypt, 1863–1865* (London, Macmillan, 1865), p. 107.
24 *Ibid.*, p. 106.
25 *Ibid.*
26 *Ibid.*, p. 107.
27 Lane-Poole, *op. cit.*, p. 217.
28 *Ibid.*
29 Sonnini de Manoncourt, *op. cit.*, p. 354.
30 Ebers, *op. cit.*, p. 202.
31 *Ibid.*
32 Richard Bevis (ed.), *Bibliotheca Cisorientalia: An Annotated Checklist of Early English Travel Books on the Near and Middle East* (Boston, J.K. Hall, 1973), p. 23; see also Leila Ahmed, *Edward W. Lane: A Study of His Life and Works and of British Ideas of the Middle East in the Nineteenth Century* (London & New York, Longman, 1978), p. 50.
33 Richard Pococke, *A Description of the East and Some Other Countries* (2 vols., London, J & R. Knapton, 1743–5), vol. 1, p. 176.
34 Paton, *op. cit.*, p. 283.
35 Edward W. Lane, *op. cit.*, p. 531.
36 Sonnini, *op. cit.*, p. 354.
37 Lane-Poole, *op. cit.*, p. 208.
38 *Ibid.*, p. 205.
39 Pococke, *op. cit.*, p. 170.
40 Duff Gordon, *op. cit.*, pp. 262–3.
41 Lane-Poole, *op. cit.*, p. 209.
42 *Ibid.*
43 Paton, *op. cit.*, pp. 280–1.
44 Lane-Poole, *op. cit.*, p. 210.
45 Said, *Orientalism, op. cit.*, p. 54.

46 Frantz Fanon, *The Wretched of the Earth*, trans. Constance Farrington (1961; repr. Harmondsworth, Penguin, 1967), p. 170.
47 Duff Gordon, *op. cit.*, p. 262.
48 *Ibid.*, p. 33.
49 Lane, *op. cit.*, p. 539.
50 Lane-Poole, *op. cit.*, p. 204.
51 *Ibid.*, p. 208.
52 *Ibid.*, p. 205.
53 James A. St John, *Egypt and Mohammed Ali or Travels in the Valley of the Nile* (2 vols., London, Longman, 1834), vol. 1, p. 381.
54 Lane-Poole, *op. cit.*, p. 204.
55 *Ibid.*, p. 214.
56 Lane, *op. cit.*, p. 524.
57 Said, *Culture and Imperialsim*, *op. cit.*, p. 11.
58 Rana Kabbani, *Europe's Myths of Orient: Devise and Rule* (London, Macmillan, 1986), p. 10.
59 Sonnini, *op. cit.*, p. 642.
60 *Ibid.*, p. 643.
61 St John, *op. cit.*, vol. 2, p. 32.
62 Lane, *op. cit.*, p. 539.
63 *Ibid.*
64 *Ibid.*
65 Warburton, *op. cit.*, p. 70.
66 Sophia Poole, *op. cit.*, p. 97.
67 Paton, *op. cit.*, p. 283.
68 Lane-Poole, *op. cit.*, pp. 206 and 208.
69 Duff Gordon, *op. cit.*, p. 60.
70 Warburton, *op. cit.*, p. 51.
71 Paton, *op. cit.*, p. 282.
72 Sonnini de Manoncourt, *op. cit.*, pp. 157 and 632.
73 Lane, *op. cit.*, p. 522.
74 Lane-Poole, *op. cit.*, p. 206.
75 *Ibid.*, pp. 208–9.
76 *Ibid.*, p. 208.
77 Paton, *op. cit.*, p. 285.
78 Said, *Orientalism*, *op. cit.*, p. 159.
79 Lane, *op. cit.*, p. 521.
80 *Ibid.*
81 *Ibid.*, p. 8.
82 *Ibid.*, p. 9.
83 *Ibid.*, p. 541.
84 *Ibid.*, p. 521.
85 Said, *Orientalism*, *op. cit.*, p. 62.
86 *Ibid.*, p. 3.
87 *Ibid.*, p. 67.
88 Paton, *op. cit.*, p. 280; see also Warburton, *op. cit.*, pp. 52–3.
89 Said, *Orientalism*, *op. cit.*, p. 63.

8

Gender Politics in a Colonial Context: Victorian Women's Accounts of Egypt

Sahar Sobhi Abdel-Hakim

The phrase 'gendering Orientalism' has recently been in frequent use. However, it is usually used in reference to the analysis of Western women's representations of Oriental women. This has two disturbing implications: first, that Orientalism was not otherwise 'gendered'; and, second, that gender may be reduced to femaleness. Orientalism addresses the question of gender, but in its own way. Said was attacked by feminist critics for not including women's writings in his analysis.[1] Ever since then there has been a contest between those who focus on the gender of the writer and those who are preoccupied with the gender of the topic. Sara Mills' *Discourses of Difference*[2] draws a clear-cut division between the positions that Western women occupied as oppressed females and as oppressing colonialists. Mary Louis Pratt's *Imperial Eyes*,[3] by contrast, overlooks the gender axis (although she reveals an insightful awareness of it) and rightly groups male and female colonialist discourses as pointing in a monolithic direction. Her focus, as a result, is on colonial relations and representations rather than on the gender question. Reina Lewis' *Gendering Orientalism*[4] is about Western women's representations of Oriental women, and so addresses a gender-specific Orientalist discourse. Despite the fact that many critics today claim to analyse more than one of the axes along which the politics of domination were constructed, current analyses reveal an unbalanced oscillation between the two polarities of race-culture and gender.

Edward Said addresses the question of gender in his own way, or rather from the position from which he is speaking. Said traces the orthodox male/female paradigm in the West/East construct, pointing to a basic similarity between the politics of domination at home and abroad. G.C. Spivak[5] adds a gender dimension from a feminist perspective that complements Said's theory and attempts to resolve the binary lock. Spivak changes critical positions without losing sight of any of the axes of polarisation. She is equally interested in race-culture, gender and class politics. She attempts to depolarise oppositions by fusing them, challenging the simple binaries by depicting more than one position of marginalisation. Accordingly, Spivak produces texts that demonstrate the intricate relations of power between (among) the diverse categories producing a web of the politics of oppression and their opposition to dominant power (a term equally diversified in the process) occupied by both whiteness and indigenous masculinity.

Robert Young's *Colonial Desire: Hybridity in Theory, Culture and Race* is also important in our context for two main reasons: first, it addresses the case of Egypt; second, it relates both the economic and the sexual aspects that can rightly be said to have conditioned the colonisers' perception. Young argues that colonialism was generated by, and itself generated, a fantasy of desire that was collectively shared and that mechanically operated over space. He deprecates the dialectic of inclusion/exclusion in favour of centrality and deviation:

> [Colonialism] worked not only according to a paradigm of the Hegelian dialectic of the same and the other but also according to the norm/deviance model of diversity and inequality. . . . [It] operated both according to the Same-Other model and through the 'computation of normalities' and 'degrees of deviance' from the white norm.[6]

Young's paradigm illustrates the centrality of white (middle class, male) power and supplies a matrix on which a number of positions can be identified without obliterating the differential dialectic. Nevertheless, there are two difficulties with this theoretic model. First, it does not address native reaction to colonial politics, which varied not only geographically according to the diverse cultures of the various peoples but also historically within the one locale. *Colonial Desire* assumes a process of Western writing over vacant, 'virgin' land. The second problem is his organic reading of colonial mechanical expansion, which rightly explains masculine fantasy but excludes white women's contribution in this area and perpetuates the assumed feminisation of the colonised.

Writing the place, writing the self

Between the 1840s and 1860s, Sophia Poole, Harriet Martineau and Lucie Duff Gordon visited Egypt and produced three popular narratives of their experience of the country. On Edward William Lane's second visit to Egypt the author, who had by then achieved renown for *Manners and Customs of the Modern Egyptians*, persuaded his sister, Sophia Poole, to join him for a long stay in the country for the explicit purpose of supplying a complementary account to his own, which would describe harem life and customs. The outcome of the visit is *The Englishwoman in Egypt (1844–1851)*, a pioneering account of Egyptian women. Poole was brought to Egypt to report both as an English observer and as a woman. In compliance with the strategy of the vanguard scholars, and particularly the advice of her authorial brother, she had to live as an Oriental, adopting Oriental dress and way of life. Poole's Orientalisation was, however, devised as one of the accessories that completed Lane's disguise. It supplied Lane with a harem but disadvantaged Poole, for the domain of the Englishwoman was that of unveiled interiors in which, devoid of her veil of privilege, resuming her identity as an Englishwoman but one coated with an Oriental underdress, she was metamorphosed into a hybrid creature and disturbingly placed on equal footing with the inmates she visited. Although the acceptant Poole echoed the 'necessity' of adopting Oriental dress, she found it 'stifling to a degree not to be forgotten'.[7] Lane deeply disturbed Poole by suggesting her similarity to the women she visited. His privilege was her loss.

The harem, her specialisation, is represented in a series of sketches that borrow from Lane and add to his representations, keeping her confined within the interests and discursive strategy of the Arabist. Walking in Lane's footsteps, she minutely graphed the interior decoration and architectural plan of the place, moving to Oriental dress and ornament, and reproducing Lane's descriptions but dressing them on female bodies so that the bodies simultaneously embellish and degrade the ornaments and the whole becomes a sign that reads a culture. Her account focuses on the two male attractions, namely, the women's bodies and Oriental ornament and dress. The walls and the women internally reciprocate, forming a divided whole in which 'chaste and beautiful' decorations complement and oppositionally define the 'costly' bodies bedecked with jewellery.[8]

However, aware of her topical confinement, Poole converted her disadvantage to a privilege. She repeatedly stressed the inaccessibility of the harem to Western males, marking her importance as a 'valuable helpmate'.[9] She repetitively reminded everyone that the harem curtain is an 'impassable barrier to men'.[10] Disturbed by the duality of her identity as elevated Englishness and degraded femininity, she constructed herself as a functional woman among her nation. Reclining on the cultural polarity, she divided womanhood, 'othering' Oriental women for her emergence as an Englishwoman. With a feminine euphemism, indicated by redundant references to the unutterable and interspersed with ellipses and blanks, *The Englishwoman in Egypt* passively allows a reconstruction of the harem in the reader's imagination. With such rhetorical strategies she delineated the difference between these women and their illicit deeds, and herself as a representative of Victorian female propriety. It is through such references that she both contributed to the association of Oriental women and promiscuity and adopted a self-protective measure in compliance with patriarchal laws. Terrified of exclusion on account of her gender, Poole took to a narcissistic reconstruction of her identity as European, consolidating and protecting herself by differentiating within the then unbreachable boundaries of gender specificity. This allowed the Englishwoman a space within which she subverted her femininity in compliance with Victorian patriarchy. It allowed her to incorporate herself as a functional Briton among her nation and, in the words of a male authority, 'gained for her . . . a place in literature'.[11]

Having divided and hierarchised womanhood along the cultural axis, and having created a precedent, Poole speculated on the pathological status and hence the ensuing death of native culture, both Muslim and Coptic, therefore evacuating a space that demanded re-culturation through the fusion of 'Western' Christianity. The native figures in her text are pathological figures that relate more to death than to life and whose ensuing death is represented as a welcome termination to their miserable lives. These diseased figures are infected by Muslim superstition and custom which are voiced in ceremonies ranging from fasting[12] to marital 'predestination' and 'assassinating' weddings[13] to the burial of Oriental ornament and dress (culture) with the dead.[14] Death, especially of children, is in her text a welcome solution to the degenerative cultural condition. On the death of a little child she commented:

> I heard it with feelings of unmixed thankfulness to God. What had been his prospect here? Of Muslim parents, he would have been

educated in a false religion, mentally and physically dark, to grope his way in poverty through childhood, with life's struggle before him, the child of oppressed parents who could rarely afford to lighten his burden by their presence; lonely, blind, and miserable. When I hear of the death of children under circumstances such as these, I always rejoice.[15]

Along with her desire for evacuating the country, her text is replete with calls for rehabilitating the vacant space, 'There is one thing alone which can revise such a state of things – one holy influence – it is, and must be, Christianity.'[16]

In 1846–7, Harriet Martineau went on an Oriental tour, in the course of which she visited Egypt, Palestine and Syria. She recorded her reflections in a text that is not merely a descriptive travel book but a reconstruction of the history of the East. *Eastern Life: Present and Past*, of 1848, is a narrative of Oriental history in which it comprises an early chapter in the history of humanity. In it Martineau advocates a theory of the birth of civilisation. She writes the history of civilisation as the product of 'heroes' and 'great men', whom she racially defines in a way that affiliates them to Asia. Through emigration to African nations, they gave birth to civilisation. She posited that Egypt's ancient civilisation was born of the union of emigrant Aryans who settled in north Egypt and maintained relations of marriage and trade with the Ethiopians, and therefore gave birth to the world's first-born civilisation. This Egyptian civilisation eventually gave birth to two children, the Greek and the Oriental civilisations. The Greek child grew up in an invigorating environment in which it developed mentally, whereas the Oriental child, roaming eternally in the desert, developed piety, spirituality, passion and a whole set of feminine attributes. Martineau did not simply gender the races, but also pointed out the historic precedence of the fruitfulness of their union through intermarriage and trade.

Building on social evolutionary philosophy, Martineau also maintained that with each successive generation civilisation became more mature and advanced. She related the model of the individual's life to that of the nation: 'it is with races of men as with individuals'.[17] Her history is constructed around the metaphor of the temporal development of Oriental civilisation from its infantile materialistic Egyptian phase, to the femininely juvenile spirituality of the topographically rugged Palestine and Syria. The growth of human civilisation is subdivided into three phases: the 'organic' phase, which she relates to ancient Egypt; the 'critical' phase of Oriental theosophy; and the 'Golden Age' of positive Western 'scientific thought'. Building on the then popular recapitulation theory, she traced the progressive phases of Oriental history from infant Egypt to childish Palestine to juvenile Syria, inscribing a linear progressive paradigm of Oriental civilisation that geographically ran parallel to her itinerary but stopped short with the termination of her tour while she progressed further to her Western, mature destination. Moving within the framework of the body metaphor, yet switching the gender definition from the sexual to the racial, Martineau advocated a synthetic theory that is a call for the re-unification of the two races (or the two sexes) in order to perpetuate humanity and civilisation. She proposed to wed East and West so that 'the reflective and substantiating powers which characterise the Western Mind be brought into union with the Perceptive, Imaginative, and Aspiring faculty of the East, so as to originate a new order of knowledge and wisdom'.[18] Martineau's fantasy was not merely one of copulation; rather it was a femininely appropriated desire for respectable child-giving and family rearing in a pre-Freudian construct of an Oedipal family as a model for the expression of a desire for paternal domination and exploitation. Hers was a female proposal for legitimate matrimony devised for the termination of backward Oriental culture as an inevitable consequence of the development of a new, more advanced synthesis.

The predominance of interest in Oriental males in her text is counterbalanced and foregrounded by the inclusion of a chapter on the Oriental harem, one that bridges her evolutionary paradigm of Oriental history, suggesting sociocultural stagnation and oneness among the female component of populations that are otherwise subdivided and classified as constituting successive phases of Oriental history. Throughout *Eastern Life*, time and space are related in a consolidating, doubly emphatic paradigm that narrates a pre-given history. It is only in the chapter describing two harems in Egypt and Syria that the construct is broken, privileging social staticity over progressive evolutionism. In this chapter, the geographic specificity of each country as the birthplace of a given civilisation and the evolutionary history of Oriental temporal space are obstructed and substituted by a homogenising timeless Orient. This is achieved through a strategy of combining that comprises the infantile Egyptians and the juvenile Syrians. Syria, Martineau's sign for Oriental present, and Egypt, the human nursery, are both related through a gendered space that relates the East throughout history. Gazing at the women she noted:

> I saw no trace of mind in any one. . . . How should it be otherwise, when the only idea of their whole lives is that which, with all our interests and engagements, we consider too prominent with us? There cannot be a woman of them all who is not dwarfed and withered in mind and soul by being kept wholly engrossed with that one interest, – detained at that stage in existence which, though most important in its place, is so as a means to ulterior ends.[19]

'Dwarfed' and 'withered' as bodily signs of the degeneration of mind and soul are conditioned by these women's detention in the physical phase of humanity, with its preoccupation with the body here exclusively written as a sexualised confinement: a confinement of the body in a given sexed space and the confinement of the women's existence in the female body as exclusively sexual objects. She also argued that their detention in the physical phase of humanity could not be helped, for 'here humanity is wholly and hopelessly baulked' by their fleshly bodies.[20] She was left with one solution. She wrote that the working of the Oriental institution 'is such as to make one almost wish that the Nile would rise to cover the tops of the hills, and sweep away the whole abomination'.[21] Along with her desire for exploiting the physically stronger portion of the population, she wished for female elimination. The women's extermination would be carried out by a flood of the life-giving principle, the purifying waters of 'Father Nile', that would drown them and prevail, filling their geo-space.[22]

In accordance with an evolutionary theory that constructed a relation of causality between confinement and extermination, and building on her fantasy of the unisexuality of the Orientals and, therefore, their non-procreativity, the political economist Martineau reproduced Egypt as a depopulated land but one of economic plenty, hence constructing a rift between the people and their land:

> Of the progressive depopulation of Egypt for many years past, I am fully convinced; but I am confident that the deficiency of food is not the cause, nor, as yet, a consequence. While I believe that Egypt might again, as formerly, support four times its present population, I see no reason to suppose, amidst all the misgovernment and

oppression that the people suffer, that they do not still raise food enough to support life and health. I have seen more emaciated, and stunted, and depressed men, women, and children in a single walk in England, than I observed from end to end of the land of Egypt. – So much for the mere food question. No one will suppose that in Egypt a sufficiency of food implies, as with us, a sufficiency of some other things scarcely less important to welfare than food.[23]

The rift between the people and the land is exacerbated by the oppositional 'progress' of an excess of agricultural produce, and a declining population. The economic balance is tipped just as it is diametrically opposed in the case of England which is analogously but antithetically recalled for the economic play. Historically and economically 'Egypt might again, as formerly, support four times its present population' but this does not 'as with us' imply a sufficiency of 'welfare'. Rather, it is a sign of deficiency that needed to be addressed.

In 1862, on the advice of her doctors, Lucie Duff Gordon headed for Egypt in pursuit of its dry weather. She lived in Luxor, and published her family correspondence in two volumes entitled *Letters from Egypt*, in 1865, and *Last Letters from Egypt*, in 1875. Unlike other women writers, Gordon does not report on the harem. As a result, she moved farther from the sex-same to the racially different, but maintained the sexual metaphor. Her text was, and still is, celebrated as the first penetration of Upper Egypt. Many contemporary feminist critics have argued that Gordon's stay in Upper Egypt is a sign of her possession of 'manly' courage and 'masculine' reason, a perception that relates to Gordon's self-representation.[24] Her biographer points out that ever since her childhood, Gordon had expressed a yearning for manliness,[25] and was pronounced by George Meredith, among others, as being 'manfully minded'.[26] Indeed, Gordon constructed her identity as male, opposing herself simultaneously to Englishwomen and to the Egyptians she encountered. Writing from that position, she sexually homogenised the Egyptians, opposing them to herself. The few Egyptian women in her text are sexed bodies represented as attractive and desirable.[27] After the male fashion, Gordon celebrates a chance to visit a Bedouin woman, 'I think it will be pleasant, as the Bedouin women don't veil or shut up, and to judge by the men ought to be very handsome.'[28] She relates the male and female physique of the Bedouins and celebrates the women's physical exposure to her. The celebration is in effect an acclamation of a fantasised penetration, of a transgressive voyeurism that was not prohibited in the first place but perceived as an effect of her masculinity. After all, Oriental women were never veiled from other women.

During her stay Gordon socialised mainly with the male, 'pure blood', educated Arabs whom she regarded as the elite of the country. They are represented as docile, delicate, imaginative, sensual and irrational. These attributes she reads in their smiles, laughter, blushes, weeping, soft voices, supple bodies and delicate limbs. A prominent figure in her text is Shaykh Yoosuf, with whom, Hatem suggests, Gordon had a liaison: 'he is lovely to behold and has the prettiest and merriest laugh possible . . . Yoosuf quietly came round and sat below me on the mat, leaned his elbow on my cushion, and made more demonstrations of regard for me than ever.'[29] Yoosuf's posture is that of a docile and contentedly submissive devoted lover. The romantic tableau is not merely demonstrative of the feminised body that it paints, but of the relation between two sexed figures, one of which acquires sexual identity by its very physical absence and its oppositional relation to the represented figure.

Gordon's texts are now applauded for their philanthropic representation of the fellahin and their condemnation of the atrocities committed by their domineering masters.[30] Her solicitation of the rights of the fellahin revolves mainly around the question of their utilisation as forced labour by both the government, which conscripted males to carry out the public works needed for the regulation of agriculture and the cultivation of new land, as well as by the French for building the much-dreaded Suez Canal. Her attack reflected English politics before the British takeover. The British attack on the corvée (unpaid, forced labour) was designed to evoke public opinion against the French with the hope of stopping the Canal project by depriving the French of the labour force needed for the construction work.[31] Furthermore, it was in the interest of the British to keep the fellahin as an agricultural labour force for the cultivation of cotton, especially after the outbreak of the American Civil War and the ensuing decline of imports from America of that strategic crop to the British factories. Gordon's argument against the corvée was basically an argument for the preservation of 'hands to till the soil'.[32] Her attack on the Turkish government was devised to support the call for substituting colonial masters of what she saw as an inherently submissive people, for 'The English domineers as a free man and a Briton, which is different, and that is why the Arabs wish for English rule.'[33]

A politics of gender: a gender for politics

Victorian women writers did not (could not) challenge male discursive strategies. They adopted male gender politics and pursued the sexual metaphor in their perception and representation of themselves and the Egyptians, acceding to rather than subverting male fantasy. The sexual division of the natives that was obliterated and substituted by racial-cultural difference in male discourses was equally suspended in female writing, either by ignoring the native males and focusing on the domestic, constructing less problematic gender-specific, racial-cultural divisions, or by perpetuating the white male politics of the natives' metaphorical castration and domestication. With a stable acceptance of gender division, white women's reaction shifted with the individualised self-genderisation of the speaking subject. They reacted to the encounter by taking up one of three positions. The spouses and the spinsters alike confirmed genderisation by its affirmation (Poole), coupling (Martineau), and negation (Gordon).[34] For dependent feminine spouses, writing was a process of rewriting the masculinely encoded space, a process of reproducing, regenerating and textually multiplying.[35] In this sense, they played a crucial role in authenticating and prolonging masculine imperialism, inscribing the charted plan and acquiescing in their own and their companions' subjugation. The Anglo-female encounter with the Egyptians also generated phallic texts wherein the independent spinsters reproduced male sexual-economic desire, with its double movement of aggressive attraction and aggressive repulsion and single target of exploitation and violent control over land and people.[36] Martineau's paradigm of the importance of femaleness to cultural-economic generation is a dialectic of male domination and female ratification dynamically repeating itself over white women and over the desired land and people. Yet, in the one case it racially-culturally preserves, in the other, exterminates primitivity by transplanting the seeds of civilisation. Gordon's domestication of the natives is an articulation of a simultaneous attraction to the feminised body and to resplendent white masculinity, the latter being a legitimating paradigm of liberation that allows the enunciation of white female desire. Her politics pays service to gender hierarchisation by its reactionary negation of her femaleness as well as by its geo-racial translation.

Victorian women played a crucial role in the promotion of colonialism. The avant-garde feminine spouses supplied the information on the human resources of the country that were inaccessible to males and made them available for exploitation. Poole surveyed the harem and economically split it, producing it as a space of excessive wealth and excessive consumption that was contemporaneous with the British 'diplomatic' efforts for the increase of cotton cultivation and the cessation of Egyptian industrial enterprises. Martineau partitioned the natives and their land and called for exploitation in an aggressive articulation of colonial economy as settlement and extermination. Gordon's philanthropy is an articulation of the Anglo-French struggle over the Egyptians' bodies and land: whether they should be utilised in cultivation or communication, grow raw material for the British imperial factories or dig the Canal to enhance communication, serve industry or trade and administration. In compliance with British politics, she was arguing for tilling rather than digging the soil. Victorian women writers followed, rather than constructed, a politics and a discourse that were gendered from the outset. Their re-emergence in a global context allowed those entrapped in these confining limitations a space for subversive self-definition.

NOTES

1 The only female-authored text that Said refers to in *Orientalism* is Gertrude Bell's *The Desert and the Sown* (1907; repr. London, Virago, 1985).

2 Sara Mills, *Discourses of Difference: An Analysis of Women's Travel Writing and Colonialism* (London, Routledge, 1991).

3 Mary Louise Pratt, *Imperial Eyes: Travel Writing and Transculturation* (London, Routledge, 1992).

4 Reina Lewis, *Gendering Orientalism: Race, Femininity and Representation* (London, Routledge, 1996).

5 G.C. Spivak, 'Can the Subaltern Speak?' in P. Williams and L. Chrisman (eds.), *Colonial Discourse and Post-Colonial Theory* (New York and London, Wheatsheaf and Harvester, 1993); *In Other Worlds: Essays in Cultural Politics* (London, Routledge, 1988); *The Post Colonial Critic* (London, Routledge, 1990).

6 Robert J.C. Young, *Colonial Desire: Hybridity in Theory, Culture and Race* (London, Routledge, 1995), p. 180.

7 Sophia Poole, *The Englishwoman in Egypt* (3 vols., London, Charles Knight, 1844; 1851 edition), vol. 1, p. 63. [Hereinafter Poole (1851).]

8 Poole (1851), *op. cit.*, vol. 3, p. 82.

9 Poole (1851), *op. cit.*, vol. 2, p. 18.

10 Poole (1851), *op. cit.*, vol. 3, p. 80.

11 Stanley Lane Poole, *Life of Edward William Lane* (London, Williams & Norgate, 1877), p. 121.

12 Poole (1851), *op. cit.*, vol. 1, p. 108.

13 Volume 3 of Poole (1851), *op. cit.*, is exclusively descriptive of the wedding of Muhammad Ali's daughter.

14 See, for example, her description of the funeral of Muhammad Ali's wife in Poole (1851), *op. cit.*, vol. 3.

15 Poole (1851), *op. cit.*, vol. 3, p. 43.

16 Poole (1851), *op. cit.*, vol. 3, p. 17.

17 Harriet Martineau, *Eastern Life: present and past* (Philadelphia, Lee, 1848), p. 148.

18 *Ibid.*, p. 488.

19 Martineau, *op. cit.*, p. 239.

20 Martineau, *op. cit.*, p. 240.

21 Martineau, *op. cit.*, p. 241.

22 Elsewhere in the text she genders paternal Nile and maternal desert and points out their joint responsibility for the birth of the Egyptian (human) civilisation.

23 Martineau, *op. cit.*, p. 6.

24 Harisse Gendron, 'Lucie Duff Gordon's *Letters from Egypt*', *Ariel*, 17 (1986), 51.

25 Katherine Frank, *Lucie Duff Gordon: A Passage to Egypt* (London, Hamish Hamilton, 1994), pp. 60–62.

26 George Meredith, 'Introduction', *Letters from Egypt 1863–1865*, by Lucie Duff Gordon (London, Virago, 1986), p. xxiii. (Introduction by Sarah Searight in 1983 edition.)

27 See also Mervat Hatem, 'Through Each Other's Eyes' in N. Chaudhuri and M. Strobel (eds.), *Western Women and Imperialism* (Bloomington, Indiana University Press, 1992), p. 51.

28 Lucie Duff Gordon, *Letters from Egypt 1863–1865* (London, Macmillan, 1865), p. 171. [Hereinafter Duff Gordon (1865).] *Last Letters from Egypt* (London, Macmillan, 1875) [Hereinafter Duff Gordon (1875).]

29 Duff Gordon (1865), *op. cit.*, pp. 255, 288. Emphasis in the original.

30 See, for example, Catherine B. Stevenson, *Victorian Women Travel Writers in Africa* (Boston, Twayne, 1982), p. 40.

31 See Abdel-Aziz M. al-Shenawy, *Qanat al-Suways* (Cairo, Ma'had al-Buhuth wa-al-Dirasat al-Arabiyya, 1971), p. 580.

32 Duff Gordon (1865), *op. cit.*, p. 105.

33 Duff Gordon (1875), *op. cit.*, p. 106.

34 'Spouses' and 'spinsters' are here not used to indicate the women's marital status as such but their social status in relation to white males during their time in Egypt.

35 This equally applies to Sophia Poole, Sara Belzoni and Georgiana Dawson Damer.

36 This can fairly be said of Amelia Edwards, Lucie Duff Gordon, Emmeline Lott, Harriet Martineau, Florence Nightingale and Isabella Romer.

9

The Image of Nineteenth-Century Cairo as a Medieval City in Kinglake's *Eōthen*

Loubna A. Youssef

For obvious strategic reasons, the capital of Egypt has been situated at the head of the Delta between Lower Egypt and Upper Egypt, for more than 6,000 years, though under different names. Today's Cairo is a conglomeration of different historic sites from different eras of the history of Egypt: Memphis, founded by Mena, the first king of the Old Kingdom of Ancient Egypt; *Fustat* (the tent), founded by the Muslim leader 'Amr ibn al-As in AD 641; *al-'Askar* (the camp), founded in AD 751 by the Abbasid caliphs; *al-Katai* (the wards), founded by Ahmad ibn Tulun in AD 870; and *al-Qahira* (the victorious), founded by Gawhar al-Sikili in 969. Until then, 'the city was not even thought to be a single unit, but a group of communities which happened to share the same location and a few common interests',[1] but the founding of the University of al-Azhar in AD 970 established Cairo as the centre of the Muslim world. With such a long history behind Cairo, this grand city has attracted ancient and modern archaeologists, travellers and writers of different nationalities and interests. The focus of this chapter is on the image of Cairo in Kinglake's *Eōthen*.[2]

Unlike Edward Lane,[3] who is detailed, accurate and objective, and unlike Burton and Thackeray, who both generally portray scenes from Cairo as ones 'which imprint themselves upon Memory, and which endure as long as Memory lasts'[4] – that is, as a city with the 'mystic grandeur'[5] of *The Arabian Nights* – Kinglake 'can't dissociate' Cairo and the Plague.[6] With the eye of a painter and engraver, Lane produced a picture of a real city, whereas Burton, Thackeray and Kinglake did not. Cairo is beauty incarnate for Burton and Thackeray, but an image of hell for Kinglake. And although as a first-person narrator Kinglake should be more moved by tragic events, he plays a game to keep his distance from them. Pritchett explains that Kinglake's game involved 'betting on whether he will be bumped into or not' and adds, 'He often loses, but the game cheers him up.'[7] Kinglake at one point says that he wants to 'escape' from Cairo and at another he says:

> I took it into my pleasant head that all the European notions about contagion were thoroughly unfounded, – that the Plague should not alter my habits and amusements in any respect.[8]

This is definitely not true as will be shown later. In his 'Introduction' to *Eōthen*, J. Raban comments on 'the absurd distance that the narrator is able to put between himself and his appalling subject'. He adds: 'There's no natural piety in his account: it is snobbish, pitiless, monstrously comic.'[9]

This is applicable to the Cairene experience, but it is not the case with the long detailed account of his journey in the desert. True, this long interval, that will lead him to his destination, Cairo, starts off as an ordeal that requires a 'contract' with an agent;[10] it is conveyed to show that for Kinglake the desert is not simply a dry, sandy wasteland. It has a life and a character of its own and is peopled with interesting creatures: Arabs whom he equates with Bedouins, Bedouin women, camels and other travellers like him.

Kinglake and the desert

For Kinglake, the desert seems more inspiring than Cairo and his description of the desert involves the reader who actually goes through the journey with him:

> As long as you are journeying in the interior of the Desert you have no particular point to make for as your resting place. The endless sands yield nothing but small stunted shrubs – even these fail after the first two or three days, and from that time you pass over broad plains – you pass over newly reared hills – you pass through valleys that the storm of the last week has dug, and the hills, and the valleys are sand, sand, sand, still sand, and only sand, and sand, and sand, again. The earth is so samely, that your eyes turn towards heaven

> – towards heaven, I mean, in the sense of sky. You look to the Sun,
> for he is your task-master, and by him you know the measure of the
> work that you have done, and the measure of the work that remains
> for you to do . . . No words are spoken, but your Arabs moan, your
> camels sigh, your skin glows, your shoulders ache, and for sights
> you see the pattern, and the web of the silk that veils your eyes, and
> the glare of the outer light.[11]

The parallel structures, the incremental repetition, images of the earth,
the heaven, the sky, the sun and Time all merge to create a sense of the
sublime and the beautiful. Kinglake does not describe anything with
such vividness or lyricism in his section on Cairo. It is also tempting
here to quote part of his vivid description of the camel to show how he
manages to convey to the English reader an experience that is altogether
unusual, yet enjoyable and real. He writes:

> The camel kneels to receive her load, and for a while she will allow
> the packing to go on with silent resignation, but when she begins
> to suspect that her master is putting more than a just burthen upon
> her poor hump, she turns round her supple neck, and looks sadly
> upon the increasing load, and then gently remonstrates against the
> wrong with the sigh of a patient wife; if sighs will not move you,
> she can weep; you soon learn to pity, and soon to love her for the
> sake of her gentle and womanish ways.[12]

And a few lines later, Kinglake gives an accurate and vivid description
of Bedouin men followed by another of Bedouin women. With the
dexterity of a capable observer and writer, he brings the Bedouins to life.
Knowing how foreign and different this race is to the British reader, he
draws a picture that can be seen and heard.

Now that the reader has met the Bedouins in person, Kinglake
introduces them in action. He narrates an episode that in a way echoes
an incident that happened earlier, just before he and his party started the
journey in the desert. On both occasions, the Arabs are portrayed as
guileful, cunning, theatrical and unscrupulous opportunists resorting to
various stratagems to 'strike terror, and inspire respect'[13] and to obtain
free food. Kinglake, who on the other hand, represents the British, in
particular, and Europeans, in general, is straightforward, sympathetic,
considerate and altogether credulous. He cannot help introducing this
interesting comparison:

The Arabs were busily cooking their bread! Their pretense of having brought no food was false, and was only invented for the purpose of saving it. They had a good bag of meal, which they had contrived to stow away under the baggage, upon one of the camels, in such a way as to escape notice. In Europe the detection of a scheme like this would have occasioned a disagreeable feeling between the master, and the delinquent, but you would no more recoil from an Oriental, on account of a matter of this sort, than in England you would reject a horse that had tried, and failed to throw you.[14]

Having learnt a lesson, Kinglake adopts this wily attitude when he gives the reader a glimpse of his eagerness to reach Cairo:

My poor Arabs being on foot would sometimes moan with fatigue, and pray for rest, but I was anxious to enable them to perform their contract for bringing me to Cairo within the stipulated time, and I did not therefore allow a halt until the evening came.[15]

On the fifth day of his journey in the desert, Kinglake runs into a caravan of Cairenes and a British traveller. Is this an attempt to break the monotony of life in the desert? Is he whetting the reader's appetite for Cairo? Is he introducing Cairenes in preparation for meeting others and being in Cairo? Is he comparing the way the Egyptians and the British travel, or is he dealing with an image of Cairenes that will not be apparent to him, and, consequently, to the reader, when he visits the plague-stricken city? It is true he explains how Cairenes travel in large groups and how they are defenceless and unorganised in facing danger, but otherwise they have no distinguishing features that characterise them or render them human. When they 'professed to be amazed at the ludicrous disproportion between their numerical forces' and his, he uses this as an occasion to theorise about Englishmen and English travellers. Is it not surprising that the accidental encounter with another English traveller happens at this point in the narrative? Perhaps not, since the details that follow are convincing and realistic: the other traveller's profession and route; the mutual coolness with which the two British travellers meet each other; but 'their respective servants [the Arabs] quietly stopped and entered into conversation'.[16] It is through this English traveller that Kinglake announces that the Cairo he is heading to is plague-stricken. The announcement comes in the form of a question that does not surprise the writer: 'I dare say, you wish to know how the

Plague is going on at Cairo?'[17] Nonetheless, his first glimpse of Egypt is conveyed in very romantic terms:

> There appeared a dark line upon the edge of the forward horizon, and soon the line deepened into a delicate fringe, that sparkled here and there as though it were sewn with diamonds. There, then, before me were the gardens, and the minarets of Egypt, and the mighty works of the Nile, I had lived to see, and I saw them.[18]

Kinglake in Cairo

Once Kinglake arrives in Cairo, the romance is shattered. He portrays Cairo as a medieval city, as an image of the past. The salient features of this city are the unpaved streets[19] that are 'narrow and crowded',[20] with no *trottoirs* (pavements), the narrow alleys, the slave market, bazaars with cheap 'pipes and arms', public baths and nothing admirable on the whole. The characters associated with his stay in Cairo and portrayed as human beings are not natives: a Frenchman,[21] a Scotsman,[22] an Osmanlee,[23] a 'Levantine' banker,[24] a 'Bolognese Refugee'[25] and an English doctor.[26] The Cairenes that Kinglake refers to are the dead who do not survive the Plague, 'singers and howlers' in funerals,[27] 'friends and relations' of the dead,[28] 'haggard and woe-begone' men,[29] slaves and slave owners[30] and magicians.[31] Clearly, Kinglake could not see Cairo as a real city and was therefore unable to convey an image that is true to life. The different language, the unfamiliar religion that is the centre of people's lives and the plague did not help. With a sense of guilt, and being conscious that he has not done Cairo justice, he gives a series of indirect excuses. The first is in the Preface, when he says that the travel writer

> tells you of objects, not as he knows them to be, but as they seemed to him. The people, and the things that most concern him personally however mean and insignificant, take large proportions in his picture, because they stand so near to him. He shows you his Dragoman, and the gaunt features of his Arabs – his tent – his kneeling camels – his baggage strewed upon the sand: – but the proper wonders of the land – the cities – the mighty ruins, and the monuments of bygone ages he throws back faintly in the distance.[32]

This is a writer who knows what he is doing: he involves the reader in an animated/animating desert experience, but to him Cairo is not the city with a history or a civilisation, but one under 'the terrible curse of the Plague',[33] one in which 'the Plague was raging so furiously'.[34] Cairo of the nineteenth century becomes a replica of London during the Great Plague of 1665: the spread, ubiquity and violence of the epidemic; the symptoms of the disease and the growing terror; the funerals, burials and lamentable scenes. What takes Kinglake's Cairo further back to the medieval times is the fact that there are no preventive or protective measures taken by the authorities for the sequestration of the sick, no closing of infected houses and no prohibition of assemblies. Furthermore, the estimate made of the total number of deaths is unreliable.[35] (This is a point that Edward Lane discusses with precision in his 'Notes'.)[36]

Another excuse for focusing on 'the power',[37] the 'fear',[38] and 'the progress of the Plague at Cairo'[39] rather than on what he wanted to see or what he saw is his inability to dissociate Cairo from the plague. Before he entered the city, he had not realised how 'ghastly' the experience would be although the man 'of French origin'[40] had warned him from entering the city. Kinglake further points out that he had no difficulty in renting a place 'for there was not one European traveller in Cairo besides myself'.[41] The implication is that the Cairo he is describing might seem 'different', but he is an eye-witness and therefore what he is portraying is real and credible. He is implicitly emphasising a point stressed in his 'Preface' that he is telling 'the truth'.[42] It is true and believable that 'the Plague had now spread horrible havoc'.[43] He adds:

> most of the people with whom I had anything to do, during my stay at Cairo, were seized with Plague, and all of these died . . . my banker, my doctor, my landlord, and my magician, all died of the Plague.[44]

However, what is neither true nor believable is the idea that 'there is not much in the way of public buildings to admire at Cairo'.[45] He mentions 'one handsome mosque, to which an instructive history is attached'.[46] This is not a reference to the Muhammad Ali Mosque, although the story Kinglake narrates coincides with the Muhammad Ali massacre of the Mamelukes at the Citadel. Which mosque is he referring to? Who is the 'Hindostanee merchant' who built it? Why is it singled out as the 'one handsome mosque'? And why did Kinglake overlook the Muhammad Ali, Ibn Tulun and Sultan Hasan mosques? Both Thackeray and Burton, who travelled to Egypt only a few years later, have an altogether different point of view. Thackeray compares the 'new mosque which Mehemet Ali is constructing leisurely' with others:

> The old mosques of the city, of which I entered two, and looked at many, are a thousand times more beautiful. Their variety of ornament is astonishing – the difference in the shape of the domes, the beautiful fancies and caprices in forms of the minarets, which violate the rules of proportion with the most happy, daring grace, must have struck every architect who has seen them. As you go through the streets, these architectural beauties keep the eye continually charmed: now, it is a marble fountain, with its arabesque and carved overhanging roof, which you can look at with as much pleasure as an antique gem, so neat and brilliant is the execution of it.[47]

Burton, who does not admire mosques that were recently built, such as the Sayyida Zaynab and al-Husayn mosques, regards the Ibn Tulun as 'simple and massive, yet elegant',[48] the Sultan al-Hakim mosque as having minarets that are 'remarkable in shape, as well as in size'[49] and the Sultan Hasan mosque as awe-inspiring with 'masculine beauty and a lofty minaret of massive grandeur'.[50]

Kinglake and Islam

Now that mosques have been mentioned, it is appropriate here to deal with Kinglake's distorted image of the Cairene Muslim and of Islam as practised in Cairo and elsewhere. He has quickly become aware that religion is the centre of the lives of Muslims. This is perhaps why Cairo becomes associated in his mind with the Middle Ages, a time in which the Church governed the lives of Europeans. What he fails to understand is that Islam is not only a religion but a social system in which the use of reason and the acquisition of knowledge are duties. Because, as is well known, the Church in the Middle Ages shrouded the West in mental darkness, the Reformation in the sixteenth century was an important movement against the abuses of the Roman Catholic Church. Richard Weekes succinctly puts it:

> While the Dark Ages blanketed Europe, Abbasid [Baghdad 750–950] scientists were exploring the fields of optics (disproving Euclid's theory that the eye emanates rays), chemistry (introducing such words

as alkali, alcohol, and antimony to the world's vocabulary), and medicine (compiling the first medical encyclopedia; Ibn Sina's was the major medical work in Europe until the seventeenth century).[51]

When writing about his stay in Cairo, Kinglake refers to Islam on various occasions: in the course of the history of Osman Effendi,[52] the Kourban Bairam,[53] the burial of those who died of the Plague[54] and the belief in fate.[55] Understandably, Arabic must have been a barrier for him. It must have hindered or prevented him from understanding the fundamentals of Islam. The story he tells of the Muslim convert, Osman Effendi, is inaccurate and misleading:

> He was a Scotchman born, and when very young, being then a drummer-boy, he landed in Egypt, with Fraser's force. He was taken prisoner, and according to Mahometan custom, the alternative of Death, or the Koran, was offered to him; he did not choose Death, and therefore went through the ceremonies which were necessary for turning him into a good Mahometan.[56]

Susan Staffa affirms that in Islam 'differences were not only recognised but respected'[57] and adds:

> Nowhere do we see Islamic tolerance for diversity so vividly expressed as in the explicit recognition of the right of other religious groups 'The People of the Book' (*ahl al-Kitab*), Jews, Christians, and Zoroastrians, to carry on their beliefs and practices.[58]

Butler illustrates this by giving the example of 'Amr ibn al-As, who when conquering Egypt was met with little resistance: the Muslims gave the Egyptians 'security for themselves, their religion, their goods, and their churches and crosses, on land and sea'.[59] The first major mistake Kinglake makes in narrating Osman's history is to assume that there was a Muslim custom that forces non-Muslims to adopt Islam. This did not happen in the early days when Islam was spreading in Mecca and Medina, nor did it happen when the tremendous expansion took political and military form. An often quoted Quranic verse affirms that 'There is no compulsion in Islam.' We may mention here that the Prophet Muhammad established rules and created a system that has been followed by Muslims since the early days of Islam until today. P.J. Stewart in *Unfolding Islam* explains:

there is no doubt in Islam that war against polytheists or disbelievers is justified. It is called *jihad*, which means effort (in God's cause).

The Prophet imposed various restrictions on his warriors. They were not to kill women or children (Bukhari 52:147–8). Prisoners of war were to be treated humanely and provided with what food, drink and clothing they needed, until they were exchanged or ransomed (Bukhari 52:142, 171–2) . . . It is particularly important to note that there was not to be any violence against any person not believed to be at war with Islam. This was a complete break with the Arab tradition of exacting vengeance from any member of the enemy's tribe.[60]

Whoever did not follow Islam at the time simply paid the poll tax or tribute (one dinar per year on an adult male, half a dinar on a female and none on children). Another flaw is the constant use of the term 'Mahometan' when referring to Muslims. Had Kinglake interacted with the local Egyptians, he would have realised that they would object to this designation because it gives the incorrect impression that Muslims worship Muhammad. In proceeding to narrate more details about the young convert Osman, it becomes clear that Kinglake is prejudiced. He says:

> But what amused me most in his history, was this – that very soon after having embraced Islam, he was obliged in practice to become curious and discriminating in his new faith – to make war upon Mahometan dissenters, and follow the orthodox standard of the Prophet in fierce campaigns against the Wahabees, who are the Unitarians of the Mussulman world.[61]

The key words here are 'obliged', 'make war' and 'fierce campaigns'. The question is, who could have obliged him and how? A careful reader will easily and immediately observe that if this convert were forced to convert to Islam for reasons of life and death, it would be beyond anyone to make him 'curious and discriminating', let alone lead him 'to make war' or take part in 'fierce campaigns'. These are all active measures that require an aggressive, ardent believer. But Islam is against ferocity and aggression. Arguing against the misconception that Islam is 'a religion of the sword', Nasr explains that rather than avoid the subject of war, Islam 'limited it by accepting it and providing religious legislation for it'.[62]

Two more issues must be discussed in relation to Osman's history to show how inconsistent Kinglake is. The first relates to Osman's two wives and the second to his library. In attempting to show that Osman is only following Islam in appearances and out of obligation, professionally as well as personally, Kinglake states that Osman 'gave pledge of his sincere alienation from Christianity by keeping a couple of wives'.[63] This is surely an indirect attack on polygamy in Islam, followed by a direct attack on Osman himself:

> The rooms of the hareem reminded me of an English nursery, rather than a Mahometan paradise. One is apt to judge of a woman before one sees her, by the air of elegance, or coarseness, with which she surrounds her home; I judged Osman's wives by this test, and condemned them both.[64]

How and why did the rooms remind him of an English nursery? What is a Mahometan paradise? How are they meant to be the same or different? And since 'the strangest feature in Osman's character was his inextinguishable nationality',[65] as Kinglake claims, why did this not lead him to choose less coarse and less condemnable wives?

On the superficial level Kinglake is writing the 'curious' history of Osman Effendi who was born in Scotland, but has no real name. On the deeper level, Kinglake has created a character that would allow him to praise what is British and attack what is Muslim. Kinglake, the imperialist, says:

> But the strangest feature in Osman's character was his inextinguishable nationality. In vain they had brought him over the seas in early boyhood – in vain had he suffered captivity, conversion, circumcision – in vain they had passed him through fire in their Arabian campaigns – they could not cut away or burn out poor Osman's inborn love of all that was Scotch; in vain men called him Effendi – in vain the rival wives adorned his hareem; the joy of his heart still plainly lay in this, that he had three shelves of books, and that the books were thorough-bred Scotch – the Edinburgh this – the Edinburgh that, and above all, I recollect he prided himself upon the 'Edinburgh Cabinet Library'.[66]

The 'in vain' sequence starts with a false accusation that leads the reader to doubt all that follows, and to ask questions rather than accept the charges Kinglake makes against Muslims. Who are 'they' who brought him from home to Egypt? Why did he come 'in early boyhood'? What could a 'drummer-boy' be doing in Fraser's army? Surely Kinglake cannot be blaming the Muslims for all this, since 'they' can only be a definite reference to the British government and army that sent Fraser and his troops to Rashid (Rosetta) in 1807, in the first British invasion of Egypt. 'Captivity' and 'conversion' have been discussed earlier, but 'circumcision' is a sensitive issue, and if it were really true that Osman had an 'inextinguishable nationality', it is difficult to believe that he could have discussed this with Kinglake, who after all is a total stranger. What also seems unbelievable is the idea that Osman possesses an 'Edinburgh Cabinet Library'. How did he acquire it? Surely, he did not bring it all the way when he came to Egypt as a 'drummer-boy'!

Another aspect of Cairo that is associated with Islam in Kinglake's mind is the recurring funerary scenes that increase in frequency as days go by. He says:

> I believe that about one half of the whole people was carried off by this visitation. The Orientals, however, have more quiet fortitude than Europeans under afflictions of this sort, and they never allow the Plague to interfere with their religious usages . . . Yet at this very time when the Plague was raging so furiously, and on this very ground which resounded so mournfully with the howls of arriving funerals, preparations were going on for the religious festival, called the Kourban Bairam. Tents were pitched, and *swings hung for the amusement of children* – a ghastly holiday! But the Mahometans take a pride, and a just pride in following their ancient customs undisturbed by the shadow of death.[67]

This is a passage that echoes another that is written a week later:

> The deaths came faster than ever they befell in the Plague of London, but the way, the calmness of Orientals under such visitations, and the habit of using biers for interment, instead of burying coffins along with the bodies rendered it practicable to dispose of the Dead in the usual [way] without shocking the people by any unaccustomed spectacle of horror. There was no tumbling of bodies into carts, as in the Plague of Florence, and the Plague of London; every man, according to his station, was properly buried, and that in the usual way, except that he went to his grave in a more hurried pace than might have been adopted under ordinary circumstances.[68]

Here, Kinglake compares Orientals and Europeans in their reactions to death, in their funerary rituals and burials and in the role of religion during such disasters. The word 'visitation' in both passages gives the correct impression that for Cairene Muslims the plague is an affliction regarded as an act of God. This is why, in spite of the howling, which is an ancient Egyptian custom condemned by Islam, it becomes clear to Kinglake that in such circumstances Orientals 'have more quiet fortitude' and 'calmness' than Europeans. He is also explicit in praising the respect shown in burying the dead and the quick pace of the funerals, unaware that these are Islamic obligations.

Despite the commendable qualities Kinglake mentions, he ends the paragraph on a negative note and writes another that is altogether outrageous. Whether out of total incomprehension, or by deliberately misrepresenting what he made of the supplications of the populace, he produces a false image of Islam and of reactions to the plague. Referring to travel writing in general, but relevant and applicable to the passage quoted above from Kinglake's chapter on Cairo, Bernard Lewis puts it bluntly:

> The major disability of the travellers, of which their writings show the clearest evidence and the dimmest awareness, is ignorance. It is of many kinds – diffident and confident, simple and complex, ductile and rigid, elemental and compounded with prejudice, arrogance, and, latterly, guilt. The point was well made by Dr Johnson: 'Books of travel will be good in proportion to what a man has previously in his mind. . . . As the Spanish proverb says: "He, who would bring home the wealth of the Indies, must carry the wealth of the Indies with him." So it is in travelling; a man must carry knowledge with him, if he would bring home knowledge' (conversation of 17 April 1778). For visitors to lands of alien culture, the first essential is that to which Sir William Jones[69] drew attention – knowledge of the language, "the sole means by which they might learn, with any degree of certainty, the sentiments and prejudices" of the people among whom they travel and about whom they write'.[70]

Because of his inability to communicate with the Muslims of Cairo in Arabic, and because of his lack of knowledge that Islam is not simply a religion but a way of life for Muslims, Kinglake cannot observe their life intelligently and is unable to relate to it rationally. He is certainly not sympathetic (although Byron Porter Smith wrongly claims that he is)[71] and does not understand that Muslims mourn, but at the same time proceed with their lives, entertain their children and observe their Muslim feasts. True, the Cairenes are suffering, but should the living give their lives up for the dead? He not only fails to appreciate the real values and the spirit of Islam, but levels an indirect accusation at it of being insensitive and insensible. The criticism is both implicit and explicit of social life and personal mores.

And now the outrageous paragraph:

> I did not hear, whilst I was in Cairo, that any prayer for a remission of the Plague had been offered up in the mosques. I believe that, however frightful the ravages of the disease may be, the Mahometans refrain from approaching Heaven with their complaints until the Plague has endured for a long space, and then at last they pray God not that the Plague may cease, but that it may go to another city![72]

Some might regard the opening statement 'I did not hear' as a redeeming confession, but it certainly is not. In fact it is incriminating, since it is common knowledge that Muslims pray five times a day and Kinglake must have heard the muezzin call to prayers from the many minarets of Cairo. During his three-week stay in 1835, he must have also noticed that the Friday noon prayer is held in public. As Brockelmann puts it:

> [The Friday prayer] is accompanied by the *khutbah*, a pulpit address by the leader of the prayers, later by an official preacher, which, after a silent prayer, runs into the profession of faith and an intercession for Muhammad and his house, for the particularly meritorious among the first adherents of Islam as well as for all believers in general, for the victory of Muslim arms, and later also for the reigning prince, in particular, whom the community recognizes as such by this prayer.[73]

It is, therefore, difficult to believe that during such a calamity, the Muslims would not pray for 'a remission of the Plague'. They must have done so five times a day. An understanding of a different culture is not easy to attain. But the problem here is not one of misunderstanding, misrepresentation, or even ill will, but of the damage Kinglake is doing to Islam.

NOTES

1 Susan Jane Staffa, *Conquest and Fusion: The Social Evolution of Cairo AD 642–1850* (Leiden, E.J. Brill, 1977), p. 13.
2 A.W. Kinglake, *Eōthen, or Traces of Travel Brought Home from the East* (London, John Olivier, 1844).
3 E.W. Lane, *Manners and Customs of the Modern Egyptians* (1836; repr. The Hague and London, East-West Publications, 1981).
4 Richard Burton, *Personal Narrative of a Pilgrimage to El-Madinah and Meccah* (New York, Dover, 1964), p. 88.
5 W.M. Thackeray, *Lovel the Widower and a Journey from Cornhill to Grand Cairo* (London, Collins' Clear-Type Press, 1846), p. 334.
6 Kinglake, *op. cit.*, p. 149.
7 Pritchett, p. xi.
8 Kinglake, *op. cit.*, p. 158.
9 Jonathan Raban, 'Introduction' to A.W. Kinglake, *Eōthen, or Traces of Travel Brought Home from the East* (London, Century, 1982), p. vii.
10 Kinglake, *op. cit.*, p. 131.
11 *Ibid.*, pp. 137–8.
12 *Ibid.*, p. 132.
13 *Ibid.*, p. 129.
14 *Ibid.*, p. 136.
15 *Ibid.*, p. 137.
16 *Ibid.*, p. 143.
17 *Ibid.*
18 *Ibid.*, p. 148.
19 *Ibid.*, p. 158.
20 *Ibid.*, p. 156.
21 *Ibid.*, p. 149.
22 *Ibid.*, p. 150.
23 *Ibid.*, p. 154.
24 *Ibid.*, p. 155.
25 *Ibid.*, p. 165.
26 *Ibid.*, p. 169.
27 *Ibid.*, p. 152.
28 *Ibid.*, p. 153.
29 *Ibid.*, p. 160.
30 *Ibid.*
31 *Ibid.*
32 *Ibid.*, p. xii.
33 *Ibid.*, p. 152.
34 *Ibid.*, p. 153.
35 *Ibid.*, p. 154.
36 Lane, *op. cit.*, p. 561.
37 Kinglake, *op. cit.*, p. 152.
38 *Ibid.*, p. 155.
39 *Ibid.*, p. 154.

40 *Ibid.*, p. 149.
41 *Ibid.*, p. 150.
42 *Ibid.*, p. xi.
43 *Ibid.*, p. 163.
44 *Ibid.*, p. 166.
45 *Ibid.*, p. 159.
46 *Ibid.*
47 Thackeray, *op. cit.*, pp. 347–8.
48 Burton, *op. cit.*, p. 96.
49 *Ibid.*, p. 97.
50 *Ibid.*, p. 98.
51 Richard V. Weekes, *Muslim Peoples: a World Ethnographic Survey* (Westport, Greenwood, 1978), p. 31.
52 Kinglake, *op. cit.*, pp. 151–2.
53 *Ibid.*, pp. 153–4.
54 *Ibid.*, p. 153.
55 *Ibid.*, p. 156.
56 *Ibid.*, p. 151.
57 Staffa, *op. cit.*, p. 9.
58 *Ibid.*, p. 5.
59 A.J. Butler, *The Arab Conquest of Egypt* (Oxford, Clarendon Press, 1902), p. 325.
60 P.J. Stewart, *Unfolding Islam* (Reading, Garnet Publishing, 1994), pp. 75–6.
61 Kinglake, *op. cit.*, p. 151.
62 Seyyed Hossein Nasr, *Ideals and Realities of Islam* (Cairo, American University in Cairo Press, 1989), p. 31.
63 Kinglake, *op. cit.*, p. 151.
64 *Ibid.*
65 *Ibid.*
66 *Ibid.*, pp. 151–2.
67 *Ibid.*, p. 153.
68 *Ibid.*, p. 164.
69 Sir William Jones was an Orientalist who wrote 'A Prefatory Discourse to an Essay on the History of the Turks' in *The Works of Sir William Jones* (London, 1807), vol. 2, pp. 456–7.
70 Bernard Lewis, *Islam in History* (Chicago, Open Court, 1993), p. 27.
71 Byron Porter Smith, *Islam in English Literature* (Beirut, The American Press, 1939), p. 140.
72 Kinglake, *op. cit.*, pp. 153–4.
73 Carl Brockelmann, *History of Islamic Peoples*, trans. Joel Carmichael and Moshe Perlmann (New York, Capricorn, 1960), p. 40.

10

'While I was in Egypt, I finished *Dr. Thorne*'

Nadia Gindy

The title of this paper 'While I was in Egypt, I finished *Dr. Thorne*' comes from Anthony Trollope's *An Autobiography*.[1] The sentence ends with 'and on the following day I began *The Bertrams*'.[2] So obsessed was Trollope with his compulsive writing that he ends the paragraph virtually repeating himself, 'I finished *Dr. Thorne* on one day and began *The Bertrams* on the next.'

Trollope visited Egypt in 1858 at the instigation of his employers, 'the great men at the General Post Office',[3] in order to make a postal treaty with Egypt, with the object of conveying by train instead of on camel-back – within 24 hours – British (not Egyptian) mail through the country from Alexandria to Suez. Curiously, in the ensuing couple of pages devoted to Egypt in *An Autobiography*, Trollope did not register any impression, personal or otherwise, regarding the ambience, the antiquities or the architecture. Briefly, from *An Autobiography*, Egypt seems to have made no impact on him whatsoever – with one exception, and that was his encounter with an 'officer of the Pasha, who was then called Nubar Bey'.[4]

Trollope spent two months negotiating the postal treaty and settling its terms. During that time he was often ensconced with Nubar, discussing, smoking and drinking coffee. The men seemed to have struck up a friendship. Trollope found Nubar 'a most courteous gentleman, an Armenian'.[5] Trollope records this encounter – 25 years later – objectively, with much detail and at some length about how the treaty was finally concluded. More importantly, he produced a succinct but accurate sketch of a skilful negotiator well versed in the art of manipulative statesmanship. Nubar, in Trollope's view, was a man graced with Oriental tranquillity, and when necessary endowed 'with almost more than British energy'.[6] They argued robustly on the 24-hour postal delivery, which was vigorously

[139]

opposed by Nubar, who threatened resignation and prophesied blood and desolation if the 24-hour clause went through. Trollope held his ground, and, in a mirror image, describes himself as taking up a stance of Oriental calm and British doggedness. Later, it transpired that behind the opposition to the express delivery was the powerful British Peninsular and Oriental Steamship Company, which dictated its terms to the Minister of State for Railways, who passed on the message to Nubar Bey. Trollope fair-mindedly writes, 'I often wondered who originated that frightful picture of blood and desolation. That it came from an English heart and an English hand I was always sure.'[7]

Although Trollope was an inveterate and lifelong traveller, who wrote prolifically about his travels, 'I could fill a volume with a tale of my adventures',[8] his two months' stay in Egypt spawned no travel books and no lengthy correspondence of any import. The one letter he wrote from Egypt, in 1858, reads more like a postcard. In a rather superior, peremptory and guidebook-like manner, he advises his correspondent what to do, where to go and what to avoid in Egypt.

Alexandria,
11 March 1858.

My dear Yates,
At Cairo see (above all) the newly-opened catacombs of Sakkara – by taking a horse and mounted guide you may see that and the Pyramids of Ghizeh in one day. Hear the howling dervishes of Cairo at one on Friday, they howl but once a week. Go to the Citadel of Cairo, and mosque of Sultan Hassan. See also the tombs of the Caliphs. Heliopolis is a humbug, so also is the petrified forest. At Alexandria see the new Greek Church they have just excavated. Go to Oriental Hotel at Alexandria and Shepheard's at Cairo.

Yours ever,
Anthony Trollope[9]

However, Trollope used Egypt as the setting for two of his short stories, 'George Walker at Suez'[10] and 'An Unprotected Female at the Pyramids'.[11] It also featured very negatively in one of his least successful novels, *The Bertrams*, which was started in Egypt. Trollope was at the height of his writing fame at this time. Although they were simple and amusing, an in-depth analysis of the two short stories reveals a more sophisticated and complex approach to characters and setting, and perhaps a more balanced attitude towards the Orient. Through placing the English traveller in an Egyptian setting and exposing him or her as being almost completely impervious to the traditional icons of Egypt, Trollope achieves a dual purpose: he deflates the stereotyped notion of the exotic Orient and he ridicules the ordinary British travellers, both en masse and as individuals abroad.

'George Walker at Suez', written in the first person, is set in Suez. The tone of the story is apparent from the outset. Suez is described from George Walker's point of view:

> Of all the spots on the world's surface that I, George Walker, of Friday Street, London, have ever visited, Suez, in Egypt, at the head of the Red Sea, is by far the vilest, the most unpleasant, and least interesting. There are no women there, no water and no vegetation. It is surrounded, and, indeed, often filled, by a world of sand.[12]

George Walker has been in Egypt for four months and is loathing every minute of it. He is there to nurse a prolonged sore throat, as well as a grievance. He is under the impression that his partner, Judkins, wants him out of the way for a while. When in Cairo, he stayed at the Shepheard's Hotel, but no one paid any attention to him, least of all his compatriots:

> I did make attempts to overcome that British exclusiveness . . . with which an Englishman arms himself, and in which he finds it necessary to envelop his wife; but it was in vain; and I found myself sitting down to breakfast and dinner, day after day, as much alone as I should do if I called for a chop at a separate table in the Cathedral Coffee-house.[13]

Out of boredom, George decides to go to Suez with some acquaintances and is stuck there for a week. Everything is horrible: the hotel, the 'sandy, dead-looking open square',[14] the heat, the conveyance they travelled in:

> I remember the Fox Tally-ho coach on the Birmingham road, when Boyce drove it, but, as regards pace the Fox Tally-ho was nothing to these machines in Egypt. On the first going off I was jolted on to Mrs. R and her infant and for a long time that lady had thought that the child had been squeezed out of its proper shape.[15]

Although a Londoner, George Walker of Friday Street, third partner in a small firm is, it is apparent, an unsophisticated provincial at heart. He is in Egypt, miles away from home, unprotected, vulnerable, unable to adapt to the new sounds and the new sights and obviously peeved that he, an Englishman and a Christian, is unable to rise above the incomprehensible situation he finds himself in: 'Was it possible that other human beings were coming into the hotel – Christian human beings at whom I could look, whose voices I could hear, whose words I could understand, and with whom I might possibly associate?'[16]

In short, George Walker is the archetypal British expatriate, complaining of crowds, flies, dust and noise. George Walkers are alive and well in the streets of Egypt today, and are instantly recognisable!

True to type, George has 'a hankering after the homage which is paid to greatness'[17] and, interestingly enough, his finest hour – albeit fleetingly – is thrust upon him in Egypt and by an Egyptian. He is aroused out of his abject misery by a visit from a group of people, at the head of which 'was a stout portly man, dressed from head to foot in Eastern costume of the brightest colours'.[18] George is bowled over by the reception he receives from this vision before him, and patronisingly decides that although 'Arabs, or Copts . . . are immeasurably inferior to us who have Christian teaching',[19] in one aspect they are superior: 'they always know how to maintain their personal dignity'.[20] And though George muses with satisfaction on the shabby figure his ill-natured, vain and arrogant partner, Judkins, would cut when compared to the magnificent bearing and appearance of the Arab gentleman, later on he is discomfited when the aforesaid gentleman, Mahmoud El Ackbar, proceeds to address him in fluent French, of which George of Friday Street understands nothing (neither, it appears, would Judkins, no matter his pretensions). Nothing daunted, Mahmoud tries Italian, Turkish and Armenian but to no avail: George 'could not ask for my dinner in any other language than English, if it were to save me from starvation'.[21]

Finally, through the halting words of a foreign interpreter, George, to his surprise, is invited to go on a luxuriously planned excursion to visit the Well of Moses. All this pomp and ceremony, George vaguely divines, is due to some debt or other that the grand Mahmoud owes him – George Walker! It is interesting that George never questions why he should be singled out for such grandiose treatment. His attitude seems to imply that, simply by virtue of being an Englishman, it is his due to receive such recognition from a native, who is obviously a very distinguished personage. Sadly, it turns out to be a case of mistaken identity. The

morning of the excursion, the distinguished official, George Walker –
the British Governor in Pega for whom our George is mistaken – turns
up and our George is unceremoniously abandoned. Stubbornly, he insists
on making the same trip to the Well of Moses on his own and describes
it as 'a small dirty pool of water . . .'[22] All in all, 'A more wretched day
than that I never spent in my life.'[23] The modern reader cannot but
wonder whether 'the dirty pool of water' would have been transformed
into something more sensational had George Walker seen it under more
auspicious and elaborate conditions – for example, in the cortege of
and accompanied by that colourful figure, Mahmoud El Ackbar. When
it comes to the Orient, is it just a matter of what the foreigner sees, or of·
the circumstances under which he sees it?

In retrospect, despite the horrors of Egypt, George Walker was
consoled by the fact that for a couple of hours he was courted by and
looked upon with favour by the great personage of Mahmoud El Ackbar,
and nobody, not even Judkins, could take that away from him.

There is a strong indication in this short story that Trollope is
intimating that in the encounter between the Arab/Egyptian and the
Englishman there is a reversal of roles. In this instance, George or Trollope
is admitting – albeit grudgingly – that it is the Arab who is in a position
to instruct the rather narrow-minded foreigner, not only on matters
pertaining to dress and bearing ('If only I could have learned that bow, I
might still have been greater than Judkins, with all his French'),[24] but
culturally as well. Our George Walker was certainly not, in the words of
Edward Said, 'a modern Orientalist [who] was in his view rescuing the
Orient from obscurity, alienation and strangeness . . .'[25]

Continuing in the vein of the 'traveller abroad', 'An Unprotected
Female at the Pyramids' is again, seemingly, a very simple and amusing
tale of a group of typical tourists, mostly British but including an
American, Mr Ingram, and a Frenchman, M. de la Bordeau. The British
party is comprised of a family, Mr and Mrs Damer and their daughter
Fanny, their two sons and a Miss Dawkins, a single woman, who has
attached herself to the group. They are bent on an expedition to the
Pyramids, with the intention of climbing one of them. The 'unprotected
female' of the title is at the centre of the story, and Trollope uses her as
a touchstone to express his views on women.

The story starts with a Trollopian preamble on the romantic image
of the Orient in the eyes of the foreigner: 'In the happy days when we

were young, no description conveyed to us so complete an idea of mysterious reality as that of an Oriental . . . I know no place which was to me, in early years, so delightfully mysterious as grand Cairo.'[26] However, all this has changed with the great influx of people passing through Cairo on their way to India and Australia. Cairo is no more the mysterious, sensual, exotic city of the senses and imagination. Its particular atmosphere has disappeared, largely due to the pressure of a foreign population: 'Oriental life is brought home to us, dreadfully diluted by Western customs and the delight of the "Arabian Nights" are shorn of half their value.'[27]

Before he embarks on the story proper, Trollope, the quintessence of the English chronicler whose works, according to W.D. Howells, 'have been written on the strength of beef and through the inspiration of ale',[28] makes an astonishing statement, directly implying that the English may, if they stoop to it, learn a few lessons from the Egyptians:

> It is not much that we deign to learn from these Orientals – we who glory in our civilisation. We do not copy their silence, or their abstemiousness nor that invariable mindfulness of his personal dignity which always adheres to a Turk or an Arab. We chatter as much at Cairo as elsewhere, and eat as much, and drink as much, and dress ourselves in the same old ugly costume.[29]

Has the *mission civilisée* been turned on its head? After writing in this vein for a couple more paragraphs, Trollope proceeds with his story, dealing with the party concerned and its trip to the Pyramids. After much noisy discussion and dissension, each member of the party clambers on donkeys and sets off on the long trek to the Pyramids. As they amble along, they presumably encounter a number of interesting sights: they go through Old Cairo to the Banks of the Nile, pass by the Nilometer . . . but no sight elicits any reaction from the characters, positive or otherwise. Mr Damer is either discussing the prospective Suez Canal project with M. de la Bordeau and denouncing it as a thoroughly ridiculous idea, or he is arguing with the American Mr Ingram on the ills of democracy. The boys are racing ahead on their donkeys, the pretty Miss Damer is flirting with Mr Ingram when he is not arguing with her father, and the helpless, twittering Mrs Damer keeps up a continuous moan about her dreadful donkey and the generally miserable state she is in. As for Sabrina Dawkins, her independent stance, apparent invulnerability, bossiness and imposing nature causes antagonism, and so she is rejected by the party. Miss Dawkins (no one dares call her Sabrina) considers herself a thoroughly modern young woman, very well able to take care of herself: 'peas could grow very well without sticks, and could not only grow thus unsupported but could also make their way about the world without any encumbrance of sticks whatsoever'.[30] Single and unescorted though she may be, she is no plain spinster, but is described as tall, bright-eyed and generally good-looking. She holds her own, comforting Mrs Damer, charming the gentlemen, being kind to the boys and friendly to Fanny, but her brain is working feverishly. Before the day is over she has to wangle for herself an invitation, either to join the Damer group on its trip up the Nile or the de la Bordeau group on its trip to Sinai. Such behaviour warrants a Trollopian quip: 'And this was all very well; but nevertheless she had a strong inclination to use the arms and legs of the people when she could make them serviceable.'[31]

The party proceeds on its way: Mrs Damer is piteously calling for her husband to ride beside her as she pelts along precariously on her spirited little donkey, whereas Miss Dawkins trots along confidently, handling her mount perfectly. When the group of travellers are finally within sight of the Pyramids, their proximity seems to leave them cold. They passed

> . . . through an immense grove of lofty palm trees, looking out from among which our visitors could ever and anon see the heads of the two Great Pyramids; that is such of them could see it as felt any solicitude in the matter.[32]

This provokes Trollope to digress and comment on the timeless and universally blasé attitude of travellers, even when confronted with one of the wonders of the world that they have travelled halfway round the world to see:

> 'Ah! So those are the Pyramids, are they?' says the traveller, when the first glimpse of them is shown to him from the window of a railway carriage. 'Dear me; they don't look so very high do they? For Heaven's sake put the blind down, or we shall be destroyed by the sand.' And then the ecstasy and keen delight of the Pyramids has vanished, and forever.[33]

These travellers are busy with their own thoughts and their private conversations, and it is only when they almost bump into the Pyramids and Sphinx that Miss Dawkins turns her attention to them to finally exclaim, 'Majestic piles are they not?',[34] a remark echoed dully by Mr Ingram, 'Yes they are large.'[35] This scene is strongly reminiscent of Thackeray's own impression at his first glimpse of the Pyramids: 'But, the truth is nobody was seriously moved . . . And why should they, because of an exaggeration of bricks ever so enormous? I confess for my part, that the Pyramids are very big.'[36]

From this point on, it is only Miss Dawkins who evinces any enthusiasm for the Pyramids and their environs. Such slightly pretentious remarks as 'the presence of the stupendous works with which they are connected fill the soul with awe'[37] are rewarded by negative responses and disagreement from the gentlemen. Such reactions seem symbolic of an automatic and implicit rejection of a single woman's independent opinion. As for the women, poor Mrs Damer had fallen off her mount by the time she arrived at the foot of the Pyramids; almost prostrate with fear and exhaustion she is reduced to a frightened whimper. Miss Damer is at her side, ostensibly looking after her, but not unlike Miss Dawkins she, also, has a little scheme afoot! Of course, the Pyramid must be climbed, and after much yelling, gesticulating, bargaining and expostulation a number of guides – two to each gentleman and three to each of the ladies – is assigned and finally the long climb begins. Mr Ingram fights unsuccessfully to get close to Miss Damer, but not one of the 'Christian cavaliers'[38] attempts to go near Miss Dawkins.

When they get to the top all are out of breath except the valiant Miss Dawkins. Feeling that he ought to say something, Mr Damer manages breathlessly to pronounce the word 'wonderful!'[39] However, the dauntless Miss Dawkins rattles on blithely to Mr Damer about the glory of the Ancient Egyptian kings, on the wonderful desert . . . Then, seizing the advantage of his breathlessness and vulnerable position at the apex of the Pyramid – to escape her Mr Damer would have had to step off into oblivion – she corners him and audaciously informs him that she has decided, at the invitation of his wife, to join his party on the boat to Aswan: 'Mr Damer was a man, who in most matters, had his own way. That his wife should have given such an invitation without consulting him, was he knew, quite impossible.'[40] When he recovers both his breath and his senses – making some lame excuse – he rejects her proposal outright. In Mr Damer's patriarchal world, no woman should have so independent a spirit as to make any kind of proposal. Miss Dawkins, rather piqued, flounces off to the extreme corner of the Pyramid 'from which she could look forth alone towards the sands of Libia'.[41]

In another corner on top of the Pyramid a very different proposition is being made – which has also been manipulated, but, ah so cleverly – one that, we assume, will be accepted prettily and gracefully: 'Before she left the top of the Pyramid, Fanny Damer had said that she would try.'[42] Mr Ingram has proposed marriage to the delightful, feminine Fanny, albeit accompanied by the unwelcome addition and noisy presence of a dozen Arabs who will not leave them alone.

Reaching the dizzy heights of the lofty Pyramid may not have instigated in the dulled senses of the tourists any overwhelming sense of the splendour of Ancient Egyptian history. But the exhilaration of standing on the top of a monument symbolic of the greatness of Egypt, surrounded by desert and a limitless horizon, meant that they were in a position of power. This may have, subconsciously, endowed two of them with the necessary courage to make impulsive and outrageous proposals, each of a different nature – to be accepted or refused.

No respectable expedition to the Pyramids would be complete without a visit to the interior of Cheops' Pyramid. Uninviting though the prospect might be, to travel to Egypt from London, New York or Paris omitting such a visit would be an act of dishonour! The ladies, however, with the exception of Miss Dawkins, decline and she joins the men in the dark interior. On their return, the bewildered Mrs Damer, who twitters 'that it is not a place fit for ladies',[43] invites the retort: 'if it be not improper for men to go there, how can it be improper for women?'[44] The men categorically denounce the place ('I never was in such a filthy place in my life said Mr Damer'),[45] upon which Miss Dawkins looks at him with contempt and stalks away.

The obligatory expedition over, the tired and rather joyless party looks forward to returning to Cairo. Again, with the exception of Miss Dawkins, not one member of the party seems to have derived any pleasure or sense of accomplishment from visiting the Pyramids. Mrs Damer, who has weakly succumbed to giving *bakhsheesh* to the Arabs around her, is found, on her companions' return from their climb, 'like a piece of sugar covered with flies'.[46] Although Mrs Damer, the epitome of the hopeless traveller, is seen in a very ironic light, Trollope here is not only referring to colour (white and black) but reducing and comparing the Arabs to an insect of the most disgusting type. Later, Mrs Damer was heard to declare that 'she would not go to the Pyramids again, not if they were to be given to her for herself as ornaments for her garden'.[47]

Throughout the whole trip, Miss Damer had not made any response to the scene around her. Likewise the men, with the exception of one or two banal remarks. Why does Trollope portray Miss Dawkins, whom he treats ironically and clearly does not approve of, as the only one in the group who has the right attitude to travel, is susceptible to the sights and sensations of Egypt, who is observant and not beset by fears of disease and contamination? Despite the fact that she possesses all the qualities that should be admired – an independent spirit, a good education, courage and imagination – why is she not regarded favourably, either by her fellow travellers or by readers? Perhaps the answer lies in the conflict within Trollope himself with regard to his women characters. A careful study of Trollope's attitude to his characterisation of women reveals a dichotomy in his conception of them. His heroines, the faithful helpmates, are ostensibly his ideals. But those that remain within the memory of the reader are the magnificent creatures who rebel against the constraints of traditional womanhood. Similarly, Miss Dawkins, on a more light-hearted level, is one of those females whom Trollope admires but cannot approve. Although he presents her as a person who makes the correct responses, her judgment is not to be considered as sound – for, after all, she is an 'unprotected female' who has appropriated male qualities: decision-making, independent opinions and an apparent disregard for male support. Therefore, her opinions cannot be trusted and her person should be shunned! In addition, she is meted out the greatest of Trollopian punishments – she does not get married! The story ends with, 'when I last heard of Miss Dawkins she was still an unprotected female'.[48]

Since Miss Dawkins is the only one that appreciates Egypt, but her judgment cannot be trusted, it follows logically that Egypt is suspect and should be marginalised – perhaps even considered enemy territory. However, Trollope's conflicting dual attitude to his female characters, including Miss Dawkins, may balance the equation, and, in an ironical twist, the Egypt that Miss Dawkins admires paradoxically mirrors his own reluctant admiration of the country.

In both stories Trollope mercilessly lampoons travellers who resist exposure to a different civilisation and culture. He wittily lays bare their weaknesses and prejudices. At the same time, Egypt and its people are not spared: some of the impressions of George Walker and the experiences of the Damers are obviously his own.

Geoffrey Harvey, in *The Art of Anthony Trollope*, suggests that Trollope is multifaceted, 'the entertainer, the psychological writer, the moralist, the political novelist and the social historian'.[49] Can one add Trollope, the fair-minded traveller? Interestingly, Edward Said excluded him from his scathing castigation of imperialistic nineteenth-century personalities, 'Certainly the Abolitionists, Anthony Trollope . . . were relatively honourable figures among many individual and group move-ments.'[50] However, if one returns to *An Autobiography* it is clear that for Trollope writing assumes connotations of almost religious fervour. As a result, perhaps Egypt was only important to him as a backdrop to a stage on which he could demonstrate his creative skills. Does his use of Egypt parallel the plunder of the archaeological treasures of the nineteenth-century traveller?

1882 was the year of British occupation, and in July 1882, six months before he died, Trollope wrote to his son, 'we have at last walked into those Egyptians and have shown what an ass "'Arabi has been"';[51] again, in August 1882, 'my ideas as to Egypt are that *we are doing the best*'.[52] Sadly Trollope, a Liberal all his life, reverted in old age to the opinions of a diehard old Tory. Although Trollope was a writer who passionately prided himself on accuracy and fairness, he was, in the final analysis, a typical Victorian. Richard Mullen, in his comprehensive biography of Trollope, *A Victorian in His World*, had this to say regarding Trollope's portrayal of Egypt in *The Bertrams*: 'Here we have the Victorian creed: hatred of dirt, a love of progress which was inevitable and the conviction that it would come – through English influence.'

NOTES

1 Anthony Trollope, *An Autobiography* ([hereinafter, Trollope (1928)] 1883; repr. Oxford University Press, 1928), p. 112.
2 Anthony Trollope, *The Bertrams* (1859; repr. London, The Folio Society, 1993). [Hereinafter, Trollope (1859).]
3 Trollope, *op. cit.*, p. 106.
4 *Ibid.*, p. 112.

5 *Ibid.*, p. 113.
6 *Ibid.*
7 *Ibid.*, p. 114.
8 *Ibid.*
9 *The Letters of Anthony Trollope*, ed. Bradford Allen Booth (London, New York, Toronto, Oxford University Press, 1951), p. 41.
10 Anthony Trollope, 'George Walker at Suez' (1861), *Tourists and Colonials* (London, The Folio Society, n.d).
11 Anthony Trollope, 'An Unprotected Female at the Pyramids' (1860) in *ibid.* [Hereinafter, Trollope (1960).]
12 Trollope (1861), *op. cit.*, p. 191.
13 *Ibid.*, p. 192.
14 *Ibid.*, p. 195.
15 *Ibid.*, p. 194.
16 *Ibid.*, p. 196.
17 *Ibid.*, p. 191.
18 *Ibid.*, p. 197.
19 *Ibid.*
20 *Ibid.*
21 *Ibid.*, p. 199.
22 *Ibid.*, p. 208.
23 *Ibid.*
24 *Ibid.*, p. 199.
25 Edward W. Said, *Orientalism* (Harmondsworth, Penguin, 1991), p. 121.
26 Trollope (1860), *op. cit.*, p. 57.
27 *Ibid.*, p. 58.
28 William Dean Howells, *Heroines of Fiction*, ed. John Hall (New Jersey, Barrest and Noble Books, 1981).
29 Trollope (1860), *op. cit.*, p. 58.
30 *Ibid.*, p. 59.
31 *Ibid.*, p. 60.
32 *Ibid.*, p. 67.
33 *Ibid.*
34 *Ibid.*, p. 69.
35 *Ibid.*
36 W.M. Thackeray, *Cornhill to Cairo* (1846; repr. London, Macmillan, 1903), p. 363.
37 Trollope (1860), *op. cit.*, p. 71.
38 *Ibid.*, p. 74.
39 *Ibid.*, p. 75.
40 *Ibid.*, p. 76.
41 *Ibid.*
42 *Ibid.*, p. 79.
43 *Ibid.*, p. 81.
44 *Ibid.*
45 *Ibid.*
46 *Ibid.*, p. 80.
47 *Ibid.*

48 *Ibid.*, p. 85.
49 Geoffrey Harvey, *The Art of Anthony Trollope* (London, Weidenfeld & Nicolson, 1980), p. 1.
50 Edward W. Said, *Culture and Imperialism* (London, Chatto & Windus, 1993), p. 201.
51 *The Letters of Anthony Trollope, op. cit.*, p. 485.
52 *Ibid.*, p. 487.

11

On Translating *The Englishwoman in Egypt* into Arabic

Azza Kararah

When *The Englishwoman in Egypt*, by Sophia Poole, first appeared in London, in 1844,[1] it was very well received, and a version of the book was published in America a year later.[2] The impact it had at the time is best described in the words of Alexander Kinglake, author of *Eōthen*, in *The Quarterly Review* of December 1844, in which he writes, 'The excellent little book which results from her observations gives us, in a few pages, more information on the grand mystery of Oriental homes than we have ever been able to draw from other sources.'[3]

The grand mystery of the Oriental home, the harem,[4] where the women lived in seclusion far from the eyes of male intruders except their husbands and closest relatives, intrigued travellers to the East. The harem was, of course, taboo as far as male travellers were concerned. The only women with whom foreigners could have contact, were the *almeh*s described by Lane as professional singers, and the likes of Flaubert's Kuchuck Hanem, a dancer and prostitute. It is true that Lane, in the chapter on 'Domestic Life' in his *An Account of the Manners and Customs of the Modern Egyptians*, includes a vivid and fascinating account about women in general and all that is pertinent to them, yet it is deficient in many respects. As his sister Sophia comments, she had found his 'account of the hareems and the manners and customs of the women, not only minutely accurate, but of the utmost value still', but she adds, 'his information, however, on these subjects, being derived only from other men, is of course, imperfect'.[5] As regards the middle and lower classes of women, a man could easily glean information, for as Lane remarks, 'Many husbands of the middle classes, and some of the higher orders, freely talk of the affairs of the hareems with one who professes to agree with them in their general moral sentiments, if they have not to converse through the medium of an interpreter.'[6] At the same time he writes, 'there are . . . many women among the lower classes in this country who constantly appear in public with unveiled face'.[7] Lane continues, 'I believe that in Egypt the women are generally under less restraint than in any other country of the Turkish Empire; so that it is not uncommon to see females of the lower orders flirting and jesting with men in public, and men laying their hands upon them very freely.'[8]

But it was the high harem, which belonged to the upper echelon of Egyptian society, where the Turkish element predominated that titillated the imagination of the foreign male traveller. This domain would certainly have to remain a mystery, were it not for the women travellers who could gain access to it and be able to recount what they saw and experienced there. A visit to one of the harems was part of their 'programme' – accompanied by female Christian dragomans, they would pass a few hours in one of them. Such visits usually proved rather disappointing since people of different cultures met briefly, exchanged smiles and exchanged a few polite words through an interpreter.

Harriet Martineau was one of those travellers who, when she visited a harem in Cairo and another in Damascus, could see nothing there but what was apparent on the surface. Unable to converse with the women in their own language, she could, of course, find 'no trace of mind' in the harems. This provoked a commentary on the position of women in Muslim society. She saw that the 'essence of polygamy' was, like slavery, 'the denial to fellow human beings of the right to personal dignity and self-fulfillment'. What most irritated and distressed her was the vacuity and idleness of harem life; the women appeared to her as 'dull, soulless, brutish or peevish'.[9] Likewise, Florence Nightingale was depressed by what she saw as the empty, enclosed life of the harem of Said Pasha at Alexandria. 'Oh', she exclaimed, 'the ennui of that magnificent palace, it will stand in my memory as a circle of hell!'[10] Martineau, Nightingale and other women who visited the harems lacked the essential qualities necessary for a true estimation and understanding of the women they met; they lacked the ability of direct communication as well as more time to bridge the formality of a first visit. Therein lay Sophia Poole's great advantage.

Sophia and her two sons, Stanley and Reginald, lived with her brother, Edward Lane, and his wife, Nefeeseh,[11] in Cairo for seven years from 1842 to 1849. From the beginning of their stay there, Lane's intention was that she should gain access to the 'high Hareem' and supplement his work with her own personal observations 'by learning as much as possible of the state and morals of the women, and of the manner in which they are treated, from their own mouths'.[12] In the meantime, until she could converse in reasonable Arabic, Sophia watched the world go by from the window of the house they rented in a native quarter of the city. She watched weddings, funerals and processions passing by and carefully reported, in letters to a fictitious friend in England, her observations and remarks. It was Arabic she intended to learn and not Turkish, which would have been more appropriate for the 'high hareems', but, as she says, 'After much consideration, . . . I have determined to defer my intended visit to the hareems of the great, until I shall have acquired some little knowledge of Arabic; for, although Turkish is the language usually spoken in those hareems, Arabic is generally understood by the inmates; and as the latter is the common language of Egypt, some knowledge of it is indispensable to me.'[13] In any case, to learn Arabic would be easier for her, living as she did with her brother and Nefeeseh; it would also serve in her daily dealings with servants.[14]

After gaining some fluency in the language, she began to frequent the harems in the company of Mrs Lieder, 'the lady of our most excellent resident missionary, who had gained the confidence of the most distinguished hareems in this country'.[15] Her experience is very different from that of other women travellers; her relationship with the ladies of the harems is more intimate, and she can relate how she 'called on my old friends, the hareem of Habeeb Effendee'. Because of her familiarity with them and because they spoke the same language, 'the ladies in that hareem being particularly well-informed, the conversation during our visit takes always a lively, and often a political turn; and as soon as we were seated yesterday, the passing events were discussed, and the question of liberty of conscience on religious subjects soon introduced'.[16] Clearly we see here a different experience to that of Martineau, when she made her sweeping statement about women in harems who had 'no trace of mind'.

As regards the language used in the high harems, Sophia noticed that the older generation of women were more fluent in Turkish than in Arabic, and she tells how the wife of Habeeb Effendi 'listened with extreme interest to our conversation, which was translated to her into

Turkish by her daughters. In common with all Turkish ladies I have seen in this country, the wife of Habeeb Effendee speaks sufficient Arabic for the usual purposes of conversation; but when any particular topic is discussed, they all like it explained in their own language.'[17]

Sophia had not published anything in her own name before she came to Egypt, nor does she appear to have had any literary ambitions of her own. Except for *The Englishwoman* and *Descriptions* to Francis Frith's *Photographic Views*, she does not appear in print.[18] In her preface to *The Englishwoman*, she expresses her diffidence at 'writing for the press', and were it not for the encouragement of her brother the collection of letters would probably never have seen the light.[19] Sophia was not a Lucie Duff Gordon, whose letters reflect the sophisticated mind of an intellectual and liberal person, who could infuse into her descriptions a force and vehemence completely lacking in 'a Christian wife and mother dressing herself up in turkish "trowsers" and visiting the city's harems'.[20] Sophia was also far from being a Lady Mary Wortley Montagu, writing more than one hundred years earlier about harems and public baths in an Eastern capital. Sophia was the typical Victorian, middle-class Englishwoman of her time; she was not 'an' Englishwoman, but 'The' Englishwoman, addressing ordinary Englishwomen in England. With a typical Victorian sense of prudery, she could not see what Lady Mary had found so fascinating in the public baths: the freedom from distinction of rank imposed by dress; or the 'magestic grace' of the naked, human body with which Milton had described 'our general mother'. Although Sophia enjoyed 'the operation of the bath, which is quite luxurious' yet she condemned the 'perfectly unclothed' state of the bathers, who stood around in groups 'conversing as though full-dressed, with perfect nonchalance . . . it is disgusting'. She remarks that 'the eyes and ears of an Englishwoman must be closed in the public bath in Egypt . . . for besides the very foreign scenes which cannot fail to shock her feeling of propriety, the cries of the children are deafening and incessant'.[21]

A rather pertinent remark by Sophia concerns the costume she wears for her visits to the high harem. She says:

> In visiting those who are the noble of the land, I resume, under my Eastern riding costume, my English dress; thus avoiding the necessity of subjecting myself to any humiliation. In the Turkish in-door costume, the manner of my salutation must have been more submissive than I should have liked; while as an Englishwoman, I

am entertained by the most distinguished, not only as an equal, but generally as a superior[22]

whereas, she continues, 'at home, and when visiting ladies of the middle class, I wear the Turkish dress, which is delightfully comfortable, being admirably adapted to the climate of this country'.[23] Furthermore, it may be significant that Nefeeseh (i.e. Mrs Edward Lane) never accompanied Sophia on her visits to the high harems, whereas she usually went with her on her excursions around Cairo. We know that England and the English occupied a special status in the estimation of Muhammad Ali, Viceroy of Egypt, and this attitude was no doubt reflected in his harems.[24]

In the same way that Sophia had a particular English reading public that she was addressing in the middle of the nineteenth century, an Arabic translation of her book would have to consider the present-day reading public in Egypt and whether what she says is still of interest. Some of the information comprised in her book, derived from Lane's unused notes,[25] is outdated and would not appeal to the modern Egyptian reader:[26] the annual inundation of Lower Egypt by the Nile, the irrigation of fields, the pestilences that visit the country and, in particular, the minute description of the interior of the pyramids. But the information she gives about Cairo, its streets, buildings both private and public, its peoples of all kinds, the way they dress, travel, eat, feast and mourn – in fact, all aspects of their daily life – is fascinating, invaluable and capable of holding the attention of the reader. Her accounts of her visits to the harems of the high and mighty are most entertaining: her minute and detailed descriptions of the interior of the palaces, the furnishings, the colour schemes, the embroideries, the ladies and their costumes with the dazzling jewellery they display; their manner of entertaining guests; their dinner parties; and, most fascinating of all, the eight days' festivities on the occasion of a royal wedding that she was invited to attend in the palace in the Citadel. Sophia's letters vibrate with the life she lived, in a world that still reflected, in many ways, medieval Cairo and the colourful, exuberant world of the *Thousand and One Nights*.[27] In the words of Stanley Lane-Poole:

> Cairo in Lane's time was still emphatically the Arab city . . . Under the Memlook sultans, Cairo, with its Arab art, attained the acme of its splendour; and the kings who left behind them those wonderful monuments of their power and culture in the Mosques of El-Kahirah,

left also an established order of life, stereotyped habits of mind, and a ceremonious etiquette, which three centuries of Turkish rule had not yet effaced when Lane first visited Egypt. The manners, the dwellings and the dress, the traditions and superstitions, the ideas about things in heaven above or in the earth beneath, of the actors in the 'Thousand and One Nights' were those of the people of Cairo under the Memlook Sultans; and Lane was fortunate enough to have seen them before the tide of European innovation had begun to sweep over the picturesque scene.[28]

Sophia's letters complement her brother's book, *Modern Egyptians*, and the two captured a bygone world that would be of great interest to present-day Egyptians. At the same time, modern readers will be amused to hear about some of the superstitions and habits that Sophia mentions, vestiges of which still survive in one way or the other.

Yet a complete and literal translation of *The Englishwoman* would pose some problems; some letters or parts of letters that bear the obvious stamp of 'my brother' and that do not quite fit into the general tenor of the whole, could well be omitted. Likewise, passages such as the following (which illustrate not only the content but also the style of the letters) need some clever juggling to make them palatable to those who are not convinced Christian readers.

> No sound is so imposing as the night-call to prayer from the numerous minarets . . . On some occasions, when the wind is favourable, we can hear perhaps a hundred voices, in solemn, and indeed harmonious, concert.[29] Here the Mueddins, raised between earth and heaven, call on their fellow-creatures to worship Heaven's God; and oh! As their voices are borne on the night-wind, let the silent prayer of every Christian who hears them ascend to a throne of grace for mercy on their behalf. They are more especially objects of pity, because they have the light of the Gospel in their land; but how is that light obscured![30]

> I had no idea that persons of the higher class among the members of the Coptic Church, which was once so famous, and is still venerable for its antiquity, and for the firmness with which it has withstood persecutions too horrible to relate, could be in a state of darkness so deep as to behave in this absurd and shocking manner; and I grieve to tell you of it . . . for the Coptic priesthood is, in general, lamentably degraded by ignorance and superstition.[31]

That Christianity is the only medium through which happiness may be attained by any people is most certain; therefore as the easterns are very far from being Christians, except in the mere dogmas of their faith (inasmuch as they acknowledge the Messiah, though denying his divine nature, and his atonement for sin), so they are very far from being really happy.

The prejudice existing among the Turkish women against the pure doctrines of Christianity is evident from occasional or rather, I should say, from frequent remarks made in my presence, and to my friends. One lady who gave me a general and warm invitation to her hareem, and treated me really affectionately, so far betrayed her opinions, that she exclaimed to me and to my friend, 'What a pity that you are Christians!' Alas! such feelings are too general for our minds to be blinded to the fact of their existence; and so long as martyrdom awaits the convert to our blessed faith, little or no progress will be made by those benevolent men, whose devotion of happiness and of life to our Saviour's cause will secure for them the favour of their God, however unsatisfactory may be the results of their labours.[32]

On one occasion when Sophia expressed her satisfaction at the good health of her son in front of a visitor, the visitor exclaimed in horror, 'Bless the Prophet! Bless the Prophet!' to ward off the evil eye, for, Sophia correctly explains, 'she feared that I had endangered my dear boy's welfare by expressing my opinion of his health and that she earnestly desired I should avert my calamity by doing as she directed'. But Sophia, in all seriousness, assures us that she was not at all 'disposed to bless the Prophet!'[33]

On another occasion, when Sophia looks down from the Citadel at the view below she remarks:

No one with a spark of feelings can look unmoved on such a prospect: the physical sight has enough to charm it; but the deepest interest is felt while, in gazing on this scene, the mind's eye runs rapidly over the historic pages of the Word of God. The oppression and the deliverance of the tribes of Israel, and the miracles which marked that deliverance . . . O! that the power of Almighty God may be present with those who labour for their restoration, and 'may they at length', as Mr Wilberforce beautifully expresses his petition on their behalf, 'may they at length acknowledge their long-neglected Saviour.' Well have they been described as 'tribes of the wandering foot and weary breast'. Often 'houseless, homeless, and proscribed', they endure every indignity and become inured to every hardship; but the eye of God is still upon them, and his ear is open to their prayers. How true it is, that hitherto 'they will not turn to Him that they might receive mercy,' but they are not forsaken; and while we hear with thankfulness of the zeal of many from among their own people in the cause of Christianity, we trust that the day is not far off when rather than

> Weep for those who wept by Babel's stream,
> Whose shrines are desolate, whose land a dream,

we shall rejoice in the prospect of that blessed time when the Lord God shall 'give unto them beauty for the spirit of heaviness,' when all nations of the earth shall 'rejoice with Jerusalem, and be delighted with the abundance of her glory.'[34]

There are several passages such as these that need to be handled with care and understanding when translating them into Arabic. A sense of humour is needed sometimes – as, for example, when Sophia extols the virtues of al-Husayn,[35] grandson of the Prophet, and calls him 'that amiable man, in whom were combined, in an eminent degree so many of the highest Christian[36] virtues'.[37]

Susan Bassnett rightly says that 'the responsibility of the translator is enormous, for it involves a duty to the original writer and to the readers who rely on the translation in order to read that original'.[38] I was very much aware of this dual responsibility when I first undertook the task of translating Sophia's letters into Arabic. This awareness grew as I proceeded with my translation and realised the difficulty of presenting to a post-colonial Arab world, the words of a woman who was so typically conscious of her own Anglo-Christian background. Yet Sophia was not quite the usual English woman either, due to her long stay in Cairo with her brother, Edward Lane, who was so much of an Arab himself. Sophia's letters reflect this duality in her attitude, and therein lies the challenge of choosing the 'right' words with which to express her English snobbishness and at the same time her sympathy and even occasional admiration for things not English or European, while retaining all the time the veracity of the original text.

If 'the translator gives new life to a text, ensuring its survival in another time, another culture',[39] then I hope that my Arabic translation of Sophia Poole's letters may help to throw light on an aspect of the social history of Egypt at a time that still needs exploring and may serve as a suitable complement to Lane's *An Account of the Manners and Customs of the Modern Egyptians*.

Notes

1 Sophia Poole, *The Englishwoman in Egypt: Letters From Cairo, Written during a Residence there in 1842, 3, & 4 with E.W. Lane, Esq., author of 'The Modern Egyptians' by his Sister* [preface signed 'Sophia Poole'] (2 vols., London, Charles Knight, 1844); *The Englishwoman in Egypt: Letters From Cairo, Written during a Residence there in 1845–46, with E.W. Lane . . .* etc., Second Series (1846). [Hereinafter Poole (1846).]

2 *The Englishwoman in Egypt: Letters From Cairo, Written during a Residence there in 1842, 3 & 4, with E.W. Lane Esq., by his sister* [preface signed Sophia Poole] (1 vol. [comprises Eng. edn, 1844, *op. cit.*, minus letters 9 and 16] Philadelphia, G.B. Zieber, 1845). All quotations from Sophia's letters are from this edition, except where stated. [Hereinafter Poole (1845).]

3 'The Rights of Women', *The Quarterly Review* (December 1844), 108.

4 Derived from the Arabic word *haram*, meaning 'sanctuary' or holy place where special rules of behaviour have to be observed as in a mosque or university or law court. The word has degenerated in popular parlance where women are concerned, to imply rigid, unwarranted segregation of the sexes.

5 Poole (1845), *op. cit.*, 'Letter 22' (February 1844), pp. 178–9.

6 E.W. Lane, *Manners and Customs of the Modern Egyptians* (New York, Dover, 1973), p. 175.

7 *Ibid.*, p. 177.

8 *Ibid.*, p. 178.

9 Harriet Martineau, *Eastern Life: Present and Past* (London, 1848), as quoted by Joan Rees, *Writings on the Nile* (London, Rubicon, 1995). Martineau considered harem life as a form of slavery, as did many other European women travellers; this is confirmed by the German Ida Hahn-Hahn, who talks about the 'Joch des Harems' and condemns the 'Reich der Despotie und Sclaverei' in *Orientalische Briefe* (Berlin, 1842), as quoted in 'An den suessen Wassern Asiens' by A. Deeken and M. Boesel (Frankfurt, 1996).

10 Florence Nightingale, *Letters from Egypt* (London, 1854). See also Rees, *op. cit.*

11 At one time a Greek slave in Egypt, bought at an early age by Lane's friend, Hay, who gave her to Lane. Lane took her to England where, with the help of his mother, he undertook her education. Later on he married her. See Leila Ahmed, *Edward W. Lane* (London, Longman, 1978), pp. 33, 38–40.

12 Poole (1845), *op. cit.*, 'Letter 22' (February 1844), pp. 178–9.

13 *Ibid.*, 'Letter 4' (August 1842), p. 45.

14 She had a unique opportunity of learning Turkish from one of the daughters of Habib Effendi, former Governor of Cairo, who suggested that she could teach

her Turkish and learn from her English, and 'we can read and write together.' But Sophia declined the 'honour', feeling that it 'would lead to a considerable waste of time'. And, as 'in all the hareems I have visited, Arabic is understood and spoken; . . . I do not expect any advantage from knowledge of Turkish, unless I could devote to its study considerable attention.' Poole (1845), *op. cit.*, 'Letter 24' (February 1843), p. 128.

15 *Ibid.*, p. 124.

16 *Ibid.*, 'Letter 28' (April 1844), p. 231.

17 *Ibid.*, p. 232.

18 On the title page of Poole (1845), *op. cit.*, she appears as 'the sister of E.W. Lane' and the *Descriptions* to Frith's *Photographic Views* are by 'Mrs. Poole and Reginald Stuart Poole (her son)'. The style of the text sounds more like Reginald than Sophia.

19 He may have had more personal reasons for doing so, besides affection for a beloved sister.

20 Jane Robinson, *Wayward Women: A Guide to English Women Travellers* (Oxford, Oxford University Press, 1990), p. 305.

21 Poole (1845), *op. cit.*, 'Letter 27' (April 1844), pp. 225–8.

22 *Ibid.*, 'Letter 24' (February 1843), p. 125.

23 *Ibid.*, p. 126.

24 From Bowring's *Report on the State of Finances in Egypt* (1840), we learn that Muhammad Ali was sending 15 men to England to 'discover how and why you [i.e. the English] are superior to us.' Cf. James Aldridge, *Cairo* (Boston, Little, Brown, 1969).

25 Cf. MS draft of 'Description of Egypt', Lane Collection, Archives, Griffith Institute, Ashmolean Museum, as mentioned by Jason Thompson in his article, 'Edward William Lane's "Description of Egypt"', *IJMES*, 28 (1996).

26 Their historical value may be important, but no longer relevant nor accurate as in the case of the burning of the ancient library of Alexandria (Poole (1845), *op. cit.*, 'Letter 2', pp. 28–9).

27 Cf. A.J. Arberry, *British Orientalists* (London, W. Collins, 1943), 'From Cairo of the 1830's to Baghdad of the golden days of Haroun Alraschid was not such a very long step', p. 20.

28 Stanley Lane Poole, *Life of Edward Lane* (London, 1877), pp. 92–3. He also mentions that, 'seventeen thousand copies of the *Modern Egyptians* have been sold, a sufficient evidence of its popularity in England', p. 86.

29 Using the human voice alone, as the Prophet had intended, undistorted by modern technological devices!

30 Poole (1845), *op. cit.*, 'Letter 7' (Ramadan, 18 October 1842).

31 Poole (1846), *op. cit.*, 'Letter 3', London, second series (March 1845).

32 Poole (1845), *op. cit.*, 'Letter 20' (December 1843), p. 168.

33 *Ibid.*, p. 169.

34 Poole (1845), *op. cit.*, 'Letter 12' (December 1842), pp. 110–11.

35 As regards the mosque, Sophia, following Lane's example, always refers to it as 'the mosque of the Hasaneyn' and in a footnote explains, as Lane does, that by the Hasaneyn are meant Hasan and Hoseyn [Husayn], the grandsons of the Prophet. I could not trace the mosque called by that name in any Arabic sources; both al-Maqrizi and al-Jabarti refer to it as *Mashhad al-Husayn*.

36 Sophia's intention is, of course, obvious but it stretches the point somewhat to refer to al-Husayn as having '*Christian* virtues'! Another 'hurdle' that faces the translator is the use by Sophia and other travellers of the name 'Arab' to designate a 'Muslim'.

37 Poole (1845), *op. cit.*, 'Letter 10' (November 1842), p. 94.

38 Susan Bassnett, '*Metamorphoses*: New Poems by Ted Hughes', *Literature Matters: Newsletter of the British Council's Literature Department*, 24 (June 1998), 12.

39 *Ibid.*, quoting Walter Benjamin.

12

Amelia Edwards:
From Novelist to Egyptologist

Patricia O'Neill

At the age of twenty, Amelia Blanford Edwards was already an accomplished musician and artist. A cheque from *Chamber's Journal* decided her on a career in writing. She wrote stories and reviews for *Household Words* and *All the Year Round* as well as musical and dramatic reviews for the *Saturday Review* and the *Morning Post*. Edwards' eight novels and several histories and anthologies established her reputation as a popular writer and financed her travel to the Dolomites in 1872. She and her friend, referred to as 'L', travelled the narrow mountain paths on side-saddle, equipped with tea and chocolate, two bottles of cognac and four of Marsala, as well as an Etna stove, which inspired wonder among the local peoples. The story of her adventure, *Untrodden Peaks and Unfrequented Valleys*, published in 1873, included geological observations, advice for future travellers, sketches of the mountains and an account of Edwards' ascent of one peak still unclaimed by the Alpine clubs. It was already a departure from the conventions of novel writing, for although Edwards adopts a self-deprecatory tone when describing the physical hazards and personal discomforts of their journey, she writes authoritatively about what she accomplished as a climber and observer of the landscape. No romantic plot interferes with Edwards' interest in the geological and geographical wonders of the Dolomite region.

Her second travelogue, *A Thousand Miles up the Nile*, published in 1877, marked a transition not only in her life but in the history of women's travel writing. While earlier travelogues had tended to be personal narratives, Edwards uses the genre in order to assert her own authority in the field of scientific exploration. Although Edwards claimed familiarity with Wilkinson's illustrations of Egypt, she arrived in Cairo without any prior knowledge of Arabic and little knowledge of Egyptian history. Nevertheless, Edwards and her companions hired a passenger ship for several months to take them up the Nile to the second cataract and to Abu Simbel. The trip initiated Edwards' programme of intense self-education in ancient Egyptian languages, literature and culture.

Like other Victorian adventuresses, Edwards was middle-class, middle-aged and unmarried. The transition from novelist to travel writer was a crucial step in Edwards' progress from being a conventional literary woman to becoming a founder of British Egyptology. Although she could produce publishable stories, Edwards' intellectual gifts were more analytical and wide-ranging than those demanded of the conventional Victorian lady novelist. Travel writing challenged Edwards to combine instruction with entertainment; it freed her from the necessary conventions regarding plot and character in a novel, while it offered opportunities for a new style of writing. Egypt was at that time at the height of its popularity as a place to visit for amateur archaeologists and antiquarians. As Edwards herself wrote, 'If I were asked to define its [Egypt's] special charm, I would say that it is the remoteness and the mystery of Egyptology which draw me on, even a tyro has the chance of discovering something – etymological or historical or technical.'[1] A self-made woman in several areas of expertise, Edwards eventually applied her talents to journalism, becoming the chief reporter on the expeditions and discoveries of Egyptologists. Travel writing had bridged the gap between literature and science, and initiated her career as an intellectual with an intercontinental audience and considerable influence when it came to organising support for the new field of archaeology.

In this essay, I want to emphasise the importance of travel writing for women writers such as Edwards, as well as the contradictions entailed in her use of ancient Egypt as a means of developing into a Victorian intellectual. To summarise my concerns: on the one hand, many women travelled to escape the patriarchal confines of English drawing rooms; on the other, such independence did not necessarily imply a critique of the patriarchal system in general, either at home or abroad. In an earlier book, called *Victorian Women Travellers*, Dorothy Middleton described her subjects as 'intrepid' ladies whose impetus for travel 'was the growing desire . . . for independence and opportunity, a desire which crystallised in the great movements for women's emancipation and the fight for women's suffrage'.[2] However, although the women who travelled were pushing the limits of proper behaviour for a Victorian woman, their travelogues often reflect the same chauvinism towards foreign peoples and cultures as that of their male counterparts. Women's travel writing, then, must be interpreted in a wider context than the liberal claims of their implied social protest as women. As a traveller and a member of the movement for women's suffrage, Edwards provides an illuminating perspective on recent critical discussions of feminism and Orientalism in women's travel writing.

Feminist analyses of women's travel writing have made the case for recognising the difference gender makes in our understanding of imperialism and discussions about Orientalism. Sara Mills' *Discourses of Difference*, published in 1991, contrasts women's travel writing with that of men in order to emphasise the effects of gender on the writing and reception of travelogues in the nineteenth century. According to Mills, 'because of the way that discourses of femininity circulated within the late nineteenth and early twentieth centuries, women travel writers were unable to adopt the imperialist voice with the ease with which male writers did'.[3] Mills emphasises the importance of the woman's persona as narrator, and the ways in which women defer to male authority while asserting their own superiority to native characters and customs. Susan Morgan's book, *Place Matters*, published in 1996, argues the importance of geography as well as of gender in travel writing. According to Morgan, 'writings about one area of the world cannot simply be transposed to writings about another area, in some sort of global theoretical move. Nor can concepts derived from male-authored travel accounts with male narrators simply be transposed to female-authored accounts with female narrators.'[4] By historicising, Morgan examines the history of colonial relations in South-East Asia in order to understand how women's attitudes and narrative strategies differed from those of women travelling in other regions.

What makes Edwards' *A Thousand Miles Up the Nile* unique is not only its notable contribution to travel literature of the period but also its influence in shaping popular interest in Egyptian history and the new science of archaeology. Published almost three years after her trip, Edwards' travelogue contains eighty illustrations reproduced from her own sketches and watercolours. The second edition, printed in 1888, includes some revisions and numerous footnotes, most of which Edwards added as new discoveries improved her knowledge of the subject. Less a journal of her personal experience than a documentary of regional historical sights, Edwards' representation of Egypt had an underlying agenda: to encourage interest in the excavation and preservation of the tombs and temples.

Unlike most women travellers, Edwards shows little concern for the domestic life of contemporary Egyptians. Aside from making patronising generalisations about Arab and Egyptian character, her scholarly interest is focused on the artefacts and remains of ancient Egypt. Early in her narrative, she describes the squalor of Egyptian villages and compares their poverty and disease to the conditions one might find in an Irish village. Thereafter, Edwards explains, she avoided going to the native towns. According to her, 'the condition of the children is so distressing that one would willingly go any number of miles out of the way rather than witness their suffering, without the power to alleviate it'.[5] Billie Melman has called this attitude 'callous' and concludes that Edwards is 'self-consciously blatant and insensitive on subjects like poverty, disease and child mortality'.[6] Edwards' exclusive concern with ancient Egyptians may be read, then, as a sign of her complicity with an imperialist and Orientalist agenda. Her assumption that the past was more valuable than the present serves British interests in Egypt without regard for the well-being of Egyptians themselves.

We might take a different view of Edwards' attitude, however, if we consider the ways her research and writing about her trip up the Nile challenged the assumptions of her readers and the authority of previous explorers and scholars of Egypt. In his review of *A Thousand Miles Up the Nile*, John Addington Symonds notes Edwards' conjectures about several important areas of Egyptian history and geography: the origins of Philae; the location of the ancient cities of Pithom and Rameses; and the possibility of ancient tributaries below the Second Cataract.[7] These topics excited great interest among Edwards' readers and people who in the future would become supporters of the Egypt Exploration Fund, and they are directly related to religious and social controversies important within Victorian culture. To discover the location of the city of Pithom, the supposed site of Israelite oppression, subsequently became the mission of Édouard Naville, the Egypt Exploration Fund's first archaeological explorer. Later, verification of Edwards' conjecture about an ancient system of canals leading from the Nile to the Red Sea fuelled perhaps her boldest revision of Egyptian history. In a lecture given in England after the 1887 exhibition of Queen Hatshepsut's throne, Edwards claimed that she, not King Seti I, was the scientific ancestress of Ferdinand de Lesseps, the French engineer of the Suez Canal.

By writing about ancient Egypt in the context of a travel narrative, Edwards changed the way a woman might conceive of her role in public or scientific discussions. For it was not as easy for women to make contributions to science as it might be seen to be today. Discussing how women's travel writing was received, Sara Mills points out that Victorian reviewers often accused women of lying about or exaggerating their experiences.[8] Indeed, this had happened to Edwards with regard to her book about the Dolomites. Reviewing it for the *Athenaeum* when it was first published, an anonymous critic accused Edwards of various errors of detail that were based on the critic's own travels to the area. When the book was reprinted in the 1880s, the *Athenaeum* reported it as a new edition of Gilbert's and Churchill's travels to the Dolomites with illustrations by Amelia Edwards. Edwards wrote to the journal to request a retraction and correction. She was answered with a published note in which the error is explained as excusable, since Edwards 'is more indebted to their labours than she is probably herself aware'.[9] Given such scepticism about a woman's accuracy, it is not unreasonable to suspect that Edwards would make sure that she had documented and elicited advice and support for every detail of her Nile travelogue. As Melman admits, Edwards' lack of interest in playing the traditional female role of healer and sympathiser may be part of her strategy to degender her narrative[10] and thereby give authority to her archaeological interests and observations. If this is so, then we must consider Edwards' Orientalism in the context of her outrage at the destruction of Egyptian monuments by official and unofficial treasure-hunters and tomb-robbers.

Although Edwards' narrative is primarily concerned with ancient Egypt, we should also consider whether or not her fascination with Egypt's past leads her to make the present appear more exotic. Unlike most non-academic travellers, male or female, Edwards is a self-conscious narrator. A trained artist as well as novelist, she has an excellent eye for composition. Her work was often praised for its picturesqueness. What has not been remarked upon, however, is her awareness of the way a traveller's account can objectify and distort the reality of the place. Here, for example, is her description of the scene at the First Cataract. She begins, 'An artist might pass a winter there, and not exhaust the pictorial wealth of those five miles which divide Assuan and Philae.' She lists the natural elements of the scene, the water, rocks, sand-slopes, the natural forms of Egyptian pylons or gateways, the wild fowl and the fisherman who spreads his nets and then she continues,

> of camels, and caravans, and camps on shore – of cargo-boats and cangias on the river – of wild figures of half-naked athletes – of dusky women decked with barbaric ornaments, unveiled, swift-guiding, trailing long robes of deepest gentian blue – of ancient crones, and little naked children like live bronzes – of these, and a hundred other subjects, in infinite variety and combination, there is literally no end. It is all so picturesque, indeed, so biblical, so poetical, that one is almost in danger of forgetting that the places are something more than beautiful backgrounds, and that the people are not merely appropriate figures placed there for the delight of sketchers, but are made of living flesh and blood, moved by hopes, and fears, and sorrows, like our own.[11]

In their cadences and attitudes, these sentences reproduce the opening of Elizabeth Barrett Browning's famous epic, *Aurora Leigh*. Like Barrett Browning, Edwards rejects traditional epic poets' authority to catalogue their world or subject. Instead, Edwards imitates a classical style of writing in order to emphasise the subjective nature of such a representation. For Edwards indirectly criticises what the fiction writer or mere fact-finder does – that is, trivialising the landscape or sentimentalising the figures in the scene by reducing them to the exotic background or the conventional perspectives of a dominant culture. Instead, Edwards turns to a scientific study of the past in order to clarify our traditional associations and limit assumptions about both the past and the present. Her impersonal voice and self-consciously poetic style therefore develop the potentially political as well as literary aspects of Egypt for her readers. If the impulse of the novelist in Edwards is to see the mingling together of the past and present in a landscape that she describes as 'biblical', the emerging Egyptologist quickly reminds us that the 'half-wild figures' and 'dusky women' of our imagination are really people with 'hopes, and fears, and sorrows, like our own'. In other words, there is a dual consciousness behind Edwards' description of Egypt: a fascination with the ancient origins of human culture and civilisation and a scepticism toward traditional forms of European culture and authority.

By insisting that travellers must be prepared to read and study Egyptian history in order to appreciate their experience of the tombs and temples, Edwards anticipates her readers' conversion from being passive tourists to becoming active discoverers of knowledge. A scholarly approach to travel allows Edwards to introduce the idea of the antiquity of the Egyptian dynasties – their status as precursors to Greek and Roman civilisations as well as their importance to biblical history. In other words, Edwards relates the experience of travel to the cultural foundations of the classically trained and/or religiously indoctrinated traveller. Whether comparing the art of portraiture in Egypt and Greece, or raising questions about Ramses the Great as the pharaoh who oppressed the Israelites, Edwards provides a highly sophisticated context in which to describe the otherwise awe-inspiring ruins of ancient Egypt. It is no wonder then, that, on the basis of his reading of *A Thousand Miles Up the Nile*, Erasmus Wilson agreed to fund Edwards' proposed Egypt Exploration Fund and, before he died, recruited Edwards to edit and publish his own work on Egyptology.

With the authority that came from having learnt and written about Egypt, Edwards was able to give impetus to the admission of women into the previously masculine realms of scholarship and cultural authority in the late Victorian period. Her lectures on ancient Egyptian women not only created support for the Egypt Exploration Fund, but sparked the interest of women in England and in the United States. In her lecture 'The Social and Political Position of Women in Ancient Egypt', Edwards notes that when it came to Egyptian marriage contracts we seem to have arrived in a world turned upside down. If, in England, it 'has cost us years of agitation and miles of petitions to obtain for the British bride a legal proprietary right in her own property', 'the ancient Egyptian bride stood in no need of agitations and petitions. By the terms of her marriage contract, not only her own property, but her husband's was settled upon her and so settled as to be at her absolute disposal.'[12] Egyptology, then, provided Edwards and other women with a rationale and an historical precedent for both their scholarly and social activism.

For women readers, Edwards' travelogues and essays embodied what the novel could never achieve: the representation of a woman's life outside her marriage. For us, Edwards' own description of her work illuminates the new cultural authority of the novelist turned Egyptologist. In a letter to her American colleague, William Winslow, she wrote:

It is of no use to compare Naville's reports in *The Academy* with mine in *The Times*. You must remember that the Egyptologists do not write a picturesque and popular style like that of A.B.E., who has had thirty years of literary work in the romantic school, and who has especially cultivated style – worked at it as if it was a science – and mastered it. . . . I am the only romanticist in the world who is also an Egyptologist. We must not expect the owl of Athena to warble like the nightingale of Keats.[13]

And yet in her own writing romanticism and Egyptology became formidable allies. In her numerous obituaries, printed in England and America, Edwards is praised for both her erudition and her ability to convey specialist knowledge to non-specialist audiences. Such an ability with regard to Egyptology ensured international and popular support for the excavation and preservation of Egypt's monuments; non-sectarian interest and debate over the interpretation of biblical history; and a more complicated view of Europe's historically diverse cultural heritage. The style that Edwards cultivated as she developed from novelist to travel writer to Egyptologist remained that of a romanticist, making the past live in the imaginations of her readers and listeners. But if style is also related to its historical circumstances, Edwards' style was also indebted, as was British culture generally in the late nineteenth century, to the radical influence of science. With its public insistence on the quest for knowledge without regard to traditional authority, Victorian science provided new opportunities for women's participation in public discussions. By embracing the principles of science, Edwards revolutionised women's travel writing and revealed an Egypt that served eventually to enhance the academic, if not the social and political, position of women in Europe.

NOTES

1 Amelia Blanford Edwards, unpublished letter No. 438, Somerville Archives, Oxford.
2 Dorothy Middleton, *Victorian Lady Travellers* (New York, Dutton, 1965), p. 7.
3 Sara Mills, *Discourses of Difference: An Analysis of Women's Travel Writing and Colonialism* (London, Routledge, 1991), p. 3.
4 Susan Morgan, *Place Matters: Gendered Geography in Victorian Women's Travel Books About Southeast Asia* (London, Rutgers, 1996), p. 3.

5 Amelia Edwards, *A Thousand Miles Up the Nile* (1877; repr. London, Parkway, 1993), p. 86.

6 Billie Melman, *Women's Orients. English Women and the Middle East, 1718–1918: Sexuality, Religion, and Work* (Ann Arbor, University of Michigan, 1992), p. 262.

7 John Addington Symonds, Review of *A Thousand Miles up the Nile*, *The Academy* (7 July 1877), 65–8.

8 Mills, *op. cit.*, pp. 115–18.

9 See *Athenaeum* for 17 and 31 August 1889, 220, 289.

10 Melman, *op. cit.*, p. 263.

11 Edwards (1993), *op. cit.*, p. 201.

12 Amelia Edwards, unpublished manuscript, Egypt Exploration Society, IIIM, London.

13 Quoted in William Copley Winslow's essay 'The Queen of Egyptology', *The American Antiquarian*, 14 (November 1892), 309.

13

Amelia Edwards, Jennie Lane
and Egypt

Brenda E. Moon

It is often claimed, and rightly so, that Amelia Edwards' visit to Egypt in 1873-4 was the turning point in her career – the event that transformed her from popular novelist to champion of Egyptian antiquity. Her book, *A Thousand Miles up the Nile*, first published in 1877, has become a classic of travel literature, combining a careful record of the ancient sites and monuments with a lively description of the events of the journey. Hers is, however, not the only surviving account of this journey: by good fortune the diary of Jennie Lane, the personal maid of Miss Lucy Renshaw, Amelia's friend and travelling companion, survives in private hands.[1] Her diary, with its practical and domestic detail, gives a new insight into certain aspects of the journey and tempers any licence that Amelia exercises in the cause of art.

Amelia claims that 'Never was distant expedition entered upon with less premeditation',[2] and that they had been pursued across France 'by the wettest of wet weather. . . . At Nîmes it poured for a month without stopping',[3] but Jennie does not paint so bleak a picture. She records four wet days at Nîmes, but she also writes of days when 'the weather here is very warm and bright, the people are sitting out like summer'. This alerts us to the possibility that Amelia allowed herself some licence in her presentation.

Jennie's diary is of particular help in matters of chronology and identity. Very few dates are given in *A Thousand Miles up the Nile*, and Amelia admits at one point, 'I do not very distinctly remember the order of our sight-seeing in Cairo',[4] even though she later claims, 'I have been able, in the midst of so much that was new and bewildering, to remember quite circumstantially the dates, and all the events connected with these two days'[5] before embarkation. Any confusion of detail is of no significance in our appreciation of the book, but it is good to have Jennie's diary as a check on any uncertainties.

It is also good to have Jennie fill out the tantalising descriptions and initials of Amelia's companions for us. From her we deduce that 'The Painter' was Mr Andrew McCallum – although we need go no further than Appendix 1 to the book to find his signed letter to *The Times* announcing his discovery of a painted chamber at Abu Simbel. From Jennie we learn that 'The Happy Couple', comprising 'The Idle Man' and 'The Little Lady', were a Mr and Mrs Eyre. The 'M.Bs.' of Amelia's book remain, however, 'the Bagstones ladies' to Jennie. They were, in fact, Miss Brocklehurst, whose nephew, Albert, and groom, George, figure frequently in *A Thousand Miles up the Nile*, and her companion, Miss Booth. Marianne Brocklehurst's diary of the voyage also survives,[6] and provides useful confirmatory, and sometimes complementary, detail. George is the only servant whom Amelia names; there is no mention of Jennie, but this does not necessarily imply indifference. Amelia gave Jennie 'a very nice album for my views' some weeks before they embarked.

Jennie was the only maid travelling with Lucy and Amelia, but she quickly became acquainted with maids in other English parties. 'I met a nice little English maid at supper', she writes on 5 September 1873, while still in France. 'Poor little body, it was her first travelling on the Continent, and she felt very strange.' In Cairo on 8 December she went out with a maid whom she met at the hotel and bought 'a donkey habit and a pair of spectacles'. Once aboard, she looked out for maids travelling in other parties. On 20 December she wrote: 'In the afternoon I went ashore and called on Madame Georgia's maid from the *Cleopatra*.' When, on 24 December, Miss Renshaw and Miss Edwards were joined by others who were to share the *Philae* for the cruise up the Nile, she says of their maids, 'They will be my only companions for the next three months.' She became particularly friendly with one, a Miss Urquhart. On Christmas Day she wrote, 'Miss Urquhart and self have been sitting on deck the whole of the day, at times lost in admiration of the beauties of nature and wondering what it was like in dear old England.' She also enjoyed the company of the dragoman, Mr Tolhamy. While in Cairo preparing for the journey, he bought her some oranges, and when they reached Aswan he bought her feathers.

There were days, however, when 'nothing particular occurred', and she undoubtedly pined for news of home. 'Everyone getting letters but poor me', she writes on 9 January 1874. 'Very unhappy and disappointed in consequence.'

She was thrilled with the *dahabiyeh*, 'I am delighted with our Nile home', she writes on 12 December when they took possession. 'It is a charming boat and beautifully fitted up. . . . My cabin is 4 feet 7 inches wide and 6 feet 6 inches long, a perfect little picture.' When they reached Abu Simbel she records that she could see the faces of the colossi through her window.

Life on board seems to have reproduced life at home as far as possible. On Sundays there were services in the saloon. On Mondays she washed and ironed. Some days the ladies went on excursions with travellers from other boats – especially with the M.Bs.

When the ladies and gentleman were away, she often went for a walk with Miss Urquhart. She was quick to share, however, in many of the excitements of the voyage along with the ladies and gentlemen. The rapids made a tremendous impression on her, 'We were met at the foot of the first rapid by about 250 Arabs waiting to drag us through. Some of them came swimming down to us and coming on board. It was the most exciting day we have had on the Nile.' The downward journey was equally exciting, and her description is as graphic as Amelia's was to be, 'It was really like coming downstairs. One scarcely seems to breathe. . . . As soon as it was over I looked round at our descent. It seemed impossible that we had come through. It looked like a deep hill of snow.'

Jennie Lane was no Egyptologist: she was enchanted by painted temples, but not enthusiastic about less picturesque excavations. 'Nothing much to be seen', she wrote of Memphis, 'but human bones lying about', and again at Dehr el Bahree, 'I hope no one will be shocked, but we have had to walk over the bones of mummies.' But the finding of a new temple at Abu Simbel, by Mr McCallum, the artist, infected the maids as much as the ladies and gentlemen, 'Was able to crawl in on our hands and knees', she wrote on 15 February. 'We are all in a great state of excitement about it.' Two days later the shaykh who had sent a hundred men to help with the excavation 'came to have lunch with us. He did not know how to use a knife and fork so the ladies cut up his food and fed him a little . . . and after lunch they played a few pieces on the piano. He seemed very delighted & pleased with the performance.'

Jennie's diary sheds light on the perplexing incident of the accidental shooting of a boy by the Idle Man. Amelia's wry and ironic tone seems badly misplaced on such a subject. 'Hapless Idle Man', she writes, 'hapless but homicidal. If he had been content to shoot only quail, and had not taken to shooting babies! We heard our sportsman popping away presently in the barley. "Every shot", said we, "means a bird". We little dreamed that one of those shots meant a baby.'[7]

Jennie writes:

> Mr Eyre went out shooting and shot a boy. Did not kill him. We heard the screams and wondered what was the matter. The whole village fell onto Mr Eyre & the sailors who were with him. They took his gun & knocked him about dreadfully & tore nearly all the things off the poor sailors. Mr Tolhamy rushed out to help and brought Mr Eyre on the boat looking more dead than alive. We had the boy brought on the boat. He was about 7 years old and perfectly naked. He was not very badly hurt. A few shots went into his body & one or two into his head & face. The father of the child appeared much the worst. We sponged the boy with warm water and put on some sticking plaster. Mrs Eyre gave the child £1 which the father seemed very pleased to take, & dressed the child up in a shirt of Mr Tolhamy's & the little fellow went trotting off the boat quite pleased in his long white robe.

Five days later, on 9 February, she writes:

> Mr Eyre & Mr Tolhamy went to Assouan today, to see the governor & settle the row with the natives for attacking Mr Eyre when he shot the boy. He got his gun again and about 6 men were bastonarded. Both Mr Eyre and Mr Tolhamy had to stand and see it done. Horrible. Poor wretches. I don't suppose they will want to attack another English gentleman.

It is interesting to compare Amelia's and Jennie's accounts. There are some inconsistencies, but the most striking difference is in the tone. Jennie's two accounts are, as one would expect, straightforward and serious, Amelia's theatrical and almost playful. This may well disguise her embarrassment. Jennie alone shows real sympathy either for the sailors or for the villagers

An incident that appears in Jennie's diary but not in *A Thousand Miles up the Nile* is the shooting of Miss Renshaw's eagle (or hawk, as Marianne Brocklehurst describes it). On 14 January she writes, 'Miss Renshaw bought an eagle' and five days later that 'Miss Renshaw's eagle

escaped and settled on a rock but was caught again by an Arab.' On
30 January she writes again:

> Eagle escaped this afternoon and flew to the desert. Stopped boat
> and Mr McCallum and Mr Tolhamy went with their guns to try
> and get it only by shooting to wound it, and brought it back with a
> broken wing. When we moored we sent to the *Alice* for the doctor
> who was travelling with Sir James [Cathcart] to come and set it,
> and he refused, much to the ladies' disgust.

By 2 February, 'Eagle very bad, and bound up like a mummy. Miss
Renshaw gave it a dose of medicine. Awful fuss.' The next day, 'Miss
Renshaw nursing the eagle. It smells horrible.' By 5 February, 'Eagle still
alive. Dreadful fuss over it. Miss Renshaw has given it beef tea and sherry.
I wish it could die.' It is with relief that we read a later entry that day,
'Mr McCallum shot the eagle – a happy thing – putting it out of its
misery. Mr Tolhamy buried it in the sand. The sailors dug the grave and
were the chief mourners.' It seems extraordinary that this distressing
incident should not be recorded by Amelia, when the shooting of a
boy was given such different treatment. Maybe she found the episode
of the eagle even more unpalatable than that of the boy; moreover Lucy
Renshaw, unlike the Idle Man, was a good friend of hers.

As a bird lover – she regularly wrote to newspapers urging the need
to feed birds in winter – Amelia had little sympathy for those who went
up the Nile for the sport of shooting. The Idle Man and his wife are not
depicted in an entirely sympathetic light. It is established at the outset,
before they join the *dahabiyeh* at Minya, that they are friends of the
Painter and 'we knew nothing of them but their names'.[8] The Idle Man
wins approval, however, when he refrains from pursuing two crocodiles
that they see while they are having breakfast on the journey downstream.
'The crew could not understand how the Idle Man, after lying in wait
for crocodiles at Abou Simbel, should let the rare chance pass without a
shot. But we had heard since then of so much indiscriminate slaughter
that he resolved to have no part in their extermination.'[9]

The Little Lady does not make many independent appearances in
the book. She entertains the Governor of Aswan on the piano, playing
the liveliest thing she could remember, which happened to be a waltz by
Verdi. The Happy Couple never quite come up to Amelia's mark. 'As a
rule', she writes,

people begin to get tired of temples about this time [between Abu Simbel and Philae] and vote them too plentiful . . . the greater number rebel. Our Happy Couple, I grieve to say, went over to the majority. Dead to shame, they declared themselves bored. They even skipped several temples.[10]

But her tone is light-hearted.

L. remains a somewhat shadowy figure in the book, featuring chiefly as a nurse to the crew: she 'soon had a small but steady practice and might have been seen about the lower deck most mornings after breakfast repairing those damaged Alis and Hassans'.[11] She is at one point found 'indulging in that minor vice called afternoon tea' with Mrs Eyre,[12] and while the rest of the party are measuring and sketching the newly discovered temple at Abu Simbel 'L and the Little Lady took their books and their knitting and made a little drawing room of it'.[13]

All this frivolity seems a far cry from the serious motives of Amelia and, it should be said, Andrew McCallum, in taking the Nile journey. For Mr McCallum, 'that indomitable painter, always ready for an afternoon excursion',[14] the one purpose in a journey up the Nile was to paint, and to paint a big picture. His pocket revolver was never loaded and his new fowling-piece never fired. Tents were set up for him day after day for shade when painting. For Amelia, too, painting was one of the pleasures of the cruise, but whereas Andrew McCallum had gallery fame in mind, Amelia was sketching with a view to accurate representation for book illustration. 'When I say that every description which the book contains was written on the spot', she writes in the introduction to the Tauchnitz edition of *A Thousand Miles up the Nile*, 'and every sketch engraved was likewise made and finished on the spot . . . it will be seen that I spared no pains of pen or pencil to ensure such picturesque accuracy as lay in my power'.[15] Following the success of her book on the Dolomites, *Untrodden Peaks and Unfrequented Valleys*, her publisher had suggested that she write another travel book.

Amelia's interest in the preservation of Egyptian antiquities seems, on the other hand, to have developed during the journey. She had visited many a Roman ruin on the continent of Europe without a similar urge to collect or preserve. The difference seems to have been the splendour, remoteness and profusion of Egyptian remains, and the indifference of the majority of the local population to their loss or deterioration. At the start of the tour, however, the need for the preservation of monuments was not uppermost in her mind. 'At Sakkara', she writes,

> the whole plateau was thickly strewn with scraps of broken pottery . . . Presently someone picks up a little noseless head of the common blue ware used for funeral statuettes, and immediately we all fall to work, grubbing for treasure . . . Then with a shock that the present Writer . . . will not soon forget, we suddenly discover that these scattered bones are human . . . Ce n'est pas le premier pas qui coute. We soon become quite hardened to these sights and learned to rummage among dusty sepulchres with no more compunction than would have befitted a gang of professional body snatchers . . . so overmastering is the passion for relic-hunting.[16]

It was only after she had seen painted temples and, above all, experienced the thrill of discovering a new temple at Abu Simbel, that the urgent need for the preservation of such things was brought home. 'I am told', she writes,

> that . . . the wall paintings that we had the happiness of admiring in all their beauty and freshness are already much injured. Such is the fate of every Egyptian monument, great or small. The tourist carves it all over with dates and names and in some instances with caricatures. The student of Egyptology . . . sponges away every vestige of the original colour. The collector buys and carries off everything he can get and the Arab steals for him. The museums of London, of Berlin, of Turin, of Florence tell their own lamentable tale.[17]

This new conviction that the antiquities must be preserved while there was still time gave impetus to her unrelenting activity in this cause on her return. It is interesting to note Jennie Lane's comment on the state of Egypt at that time: 'The poor Egyptians!', she wrote on 24 March 1874, 'How sad to see things at the present day in such a degraded state.'

While preparing her book *A Thousand Miles up the Nile* for publication, in the years 1874–6, Amelia engaged in correspondence with one of the great Egyptologists of the day, Gaston Maspero, checking details of history, hieroglyphics and art. A regular correspondence developed with him, and the idea of launching an appeal to promote excavation in Egypt was formed. She sent a letter to Egyptologists throughout Europe in January 1880, calling on their support, and in

June 1880 she asked Dr Samuel Birch, Keeper of Oriental Antiquities in the British Museum, to call a meeting of interested local people. She never forgave him, nor the British Museum, for his lukewarm response. She did, however, win the sympathetic ear of another of the Keepers, Dr Reginald Stuart Poole. Meetings were held in June 1880 in the British Museum and in University College, London, with Stuart Poole, Édouard Naville and Sir Erasmus Wilson present. The political situation in Egypt was not favourable, however, and it was another two years before the Egypt Exploration Fund was formally created. Amelia Edwards and Stuart Poole were elected joint honorary secretaries and from that time Amelia put virtually all her energies into the promotion of the Fund, acting initially as honorary treasurer as well as joint honorary secretary.

The correspondence that her work for the Fund generated fills many boxes in the archives of the Egypt Exploration Society in London, including evidence of the problems – unpaid subscriptions, non-receipt of papers, and so on – that kept cropping up as Amelia Edwards and Stuart Poole tried to get the infant society off the ground. The joint secretaryship was not without difficulties either, especially since it entailed an exchange of letters, sometimes twice a day, between her home in Westbury on Trym, near Bristol, and his office in the British Museum. On 9 February 1885, Stuart Poole wrote to her:

> Now I have to make a most important suggestion, which I am sure you will carefully consider, recollecting that it is from me, and not suggested in the remotest way by anything anyone else has said. The joint secretaryship is a burden to us both and we should do much better with a single secretary. If you would consent to be promoted to be a Vice-President you would retain an official place and be a more weighty person in our counsels . . . You could do more for us and send the grumbles to me.[18]

But Amelia was having none of it. She enjoyed the daily involvement, and her early letters on Fund matters are eager and lively, and sometimes amusingly illustrated.

In 1883, Flinders Petrie was engaged to work for the Fund as an explorer, and Amelia always took a particular interest in his career. But he was a somewhat prickly man and did not see eye to eye with Édouard Naville, the Fund's first archaeologist, over priorities in excavation. Stuart Poole favoured the more traditional Naville and Amelia the fiery Petrie, and this caused tensions. Yet in spite of many problems – clashes of personality, financial uncertainty and administrative muddles – the Fund prospered, and enthusiasm spread to North America, where nine subscribers were elected as early as 1883. Amelia was excited by this new development and engaged in enthusiastic transatlantic correspondence, especially with the Reverend William Copley Winslow, an Episcopalian minister. Stuart Poole was anxious that the American dimension should not get out of hand, and wrote to Amelia in 1884 that she was enlisting too many American subscribers, but the trend could not be stopped. The administration of the Fund became increasingly complex. Amelia complained that she did not see all the correspondence, while Stuart Poole complained that she acted independently of the Committee.

Fortunately a new opportunity presented itself: in 1886 Amelia attended the Orientalists' Congress in Vienna and presented a paper. She soon found a new vocation in lecturing, and she accepted invitations to speak on behalf of the Fund in the Midlands, the north of England and Scotland. She was now prepared to admit that her work as honorary secretary was more than she could cope with: 'I am fagged out – dead beat', she wrote to Stuart Poole on 23 December 1886, 'The pressure of letters and words is enormous this week'[19] and a week later to Petrie, 'I cannot possibly go on being the literary hack and slave that I am in the Fund. I am willing to remain an Honorary Secretary for America – that much is due to Mr Winslow's loyalty and friendship – but I am heartily sick of the rest of it.'[20]

The following year she had an idea that helped to resolve the problem of overwork: she proposed the creation of a network of local honorary secretaries. This was a stroke of genius. All over the country, enthusiastic members – mostly ladies – were recruited to encourage support in their localities and to publicise the work of the Fund. In this way the workload could be shared, new abilities exploited, and contacts were established that led to lecturing engagements for both Stuart Poole and Amelia Edwards. It left Amelia free to accept an invitation to lecture in America in 1889–90, and she took America by storm. Her lectures were subsequently published as *Pharaohs, Fellahs and Explorers*, in 1891, the year before she died.

Amelia Edwards left the Fund in good shape, as an effective organ for furthering scientific excavation and preserving ancient Egyptian antiquities. Her writings and lectures had brought an awareness of

Egyptian antiquity to a wide public at home and abroad. The thousand miles up the Nile in 1873–4, with Lucy Renshaw and her maid, had been not only a turning point in her career but a starting point for British Egyptology.

NOTES

1 I am indebted to Mr and Mrs J. Martin of Broadstairs, Kent, for access to the manuscript diary of Jennie Lane.
2 Amelia Edwards, *A Thousand Miles up the Nile* (1877; repr. Century Publishing, 1982), p. 2.
3 *Ibid.*
4 *Ibid.*, p. 23.
5 *Ibid.*, p. 33.
6 In the Macclesfield Museum; extracts have been published in *The Macclesfield Collection of Egyptian Antiquities*, by Rosalie David (Warminster, Aris & Phillips, 1980).
7 Edwards (1877), *op. cit.*, p. 382.
8 *Ibid.*, p. 34.
9 *Ibid.*, p. 358.
10 *Ibid.*, p. 354.
11 *Ibid.*, p. 107.
12 *Ibid.*, p. 315.
13 *Ibid.*, p. 333.
14 *Ibid.*, p. 238.
15 Amelia Edwards, *A Thousand Miles up the Nile* (Leipzig, Bernhard Tauchnitz, 1878), p. 6.
16 Edwards (1877), *op. cit.*, p. 51.
17 *Ibid*, p. 353.
18 Egypt Exploration Society, Edwards Papers, III h. 21.
19 *Ibid.*, III a. 54.
20 I am indebted to Miss Peggy Drower for access to a copy of this letter.

14

Oriental Motifs in the Poetry of Nikolay Gumilev

Marianna Taymanova

The interest of European writers and artists, especially the Romantics, in the Orient has been widely discussed. Russian literature, however, as ever followed a path of its own in the nineteenth century. In contrast to Western Europe, Russia did not perceive the East as exotic, for exoticism entails remoteness. By virtue of its geographical situation (Russia has always been an integral part of two continents – Europe and Asia), and of its ethnographic composition (which included, in the words of Pushkin, the 'Tungus and the Kalmyk, the friend of the steppes'), the East has been integral to Russian history. In Russia, the perception of the Orient as exotic was usually applicable to the Indian subcontinent, the Levant and, particularly, Africa, and in this respect it seems to be legitimate to use the term 'Oriental' in relation to African, Madagascan, Indian and Chinese motifs in the works of Russian poets in general, and Nikolay Gumilev in particular.

It is also curious to note that Western Europeans perceived Russia to be part of the Orient. It is significant that in France the Russian language is taught at the École des Langues Orientales, and Théophile Gautier, the French Parnassian, 'poisoned by the Orient', went to Moscow in quest of exoticism. Historically this is related to the Baptism of Russia, when 'Kievan Rus', the first Russian state, in contrast to the Roman Catholic West, adopted the Orthodox Faith from Byzantium, where Oriental cultural traditions had always been strong.

Throughout history Russia has frequently been attacked by nomads from the east and south, and this fact is reflected in both the nation's culture and its language. Serving as a protective shield between East and West, Russia has been culturally infiltrated in the most complex way.

Consequently, the East has never been as distant and alien for Russia as it has been for Western Europe – not to mention the fact that 'the window on Europe' was opened only in the early eighteenth century, by Peter the Great. For this reason, Russian writers and poets have never made a clear-cut distinction between East and West. In the words of Russian poet and philosopher Merezhkovsky: 'The only correct answer to the question "Either East or West?" would be: "Both East and West".'[1]

Practically all Russian poets pay tribute, albeit in various degrees, to Oriental motifs. In Russian poetry, the Orient is primarily a deeply intimate and spiritual topic. It contains allusions to the Old Testament, obviously as a result of the influence of Milton, Blake and Byron, as well as references to a quest for a 'spiritual home' and an attempt to synthesise East and West. The Orient was a part of the internal experience of several poets; in other cases reference to it was a matter of fashion or a convenient form of expression. Yet it had considerable significance, not only because it provided a topographical application of the intellectual quest, but because it fuelled the attempt to establish national identity, which had become particularly necessary at the time of the Russo-Japanese war.

The life of Nikolay Stepanovich Gumilev (1886–1921), who was often referred to as 'the Russian André Chenier', was brief: only a half of the human earthly life specified by Dante. He died, a victim of the Bolsheviks' regime, before reaching the age of 37 – like Pushkin, Rimbaud and Mayakovsky. Russian émigrés considered his works to be classics, but, he became known to readers in Russia itself barely a decade ago.

One can hardly deny that Gumilev appears an outstanding personality amongst Russian poets. Apart from his involvement with Akhmatova, a great Russian poet, Gumilev's first wife, in itself enough to guarantee him a place in the history of literature, he combined three rare qualities: he was a talented poet, a fearless warrior and an observant traveller. As 'The romantic, the wanderer and the poet',[2] he was, according to Russian poet Maximilian Voloshin's definition, an unusual combination.

In 1902, in one of his earlier poems, published in the *Tiflisskii Listok* newspaper, Gumilev expressed his poetic credo, 'I escaped the cities for the woods.' Woods, nature, and Africa attracted the 16-year-old poet, for the romantic world was near to his heart, and the protagonists of his early poems are conquistadors and daredevils. Thus from his adolescence Gumilev was fated to pursue the exotic and his own

Orient. Hence, from his earliest work, Gumilev unerringly established the hero-figure to whom he remained faithful throughout his poetry.

When discussing Gumilev's character, one should note the astonishing courage that earned him the St George Cross, the highest military decoration awarded to private soldiers for gallantry, during the First World War. His personal qualities were strongly reflected in his early poems. On the other hand, there is a clear influence from nineteenth-century Romanticism: not only a deep concern for individual personality, but also an aspiration to create symbolic images (biblical, folkloric and mythological), which then, reworked and reinterpreted, acquired archetypal properties. All these features are perceptible throughout twentieth-century poetry that sought inspiration for its images, religions and themes in the Orient.

The young Gumilev was lured by 'The Muse of Distant Journeys'[3] and by Africa, perhaps because it was less well-trodden by European explorers and still retained its enigmatic and mysterious character. No less important, however, was the fact that it was there, in Abyssinia, that Rimbaud had travelled, and that he, like the Parnassians (Leconte de Lisle, Gautier and Heredia), later greatly influenced Russian poets. Perhaps, indeed, the image of Africa was simply floating in the air at the time. It was not by chance that even the down-to-earth and completely unromantic Chekhovian character, Astrov, was dreaming of Africa.

Gumilev's adolescent romantic dreams were reflected in the second volume of his poetry, published in 1908, entitled *Romantic Flowers*. Out of 32 poems included in the volume, a quarter, either directly or indirectly, contain shades of the Orient. This Orient is an artificial, stagey world, in which realities are replaced by stylised European clichés. One often finds there such worn phrases as 'marmoreality of mountains', 'cheeks, pink pearls of the South', 'corals of pearl lips', 'whiter than oriental lilies', 'a pearly chain . . . of lithe fluttering naiads', 'pearl teeth', 'slender palm-trees' and 'the emerald scales of the crocodile'.[4] By using these phrases, Gumilev paid tribute to the pseudo-Oriental style that had emerged in the nineteenth century, for they are all commonly used poetic clichés devoid of any independent value. One can hardly blame the young poet too severely: even the more famous poets, the Romantics and Parnassians, could not altogether avoid this trap. Probably this is a typical case of stylisation, based on 'secondary' material, namely the fiction on Oriental topics that Gumilev had read in his youth: he had simply assimilated and was now reinterpreting alien images. Gumilev's famous 'elegant giraffe'[5] is a classic example of that phenomenon of stylisation, referred to by Ginzburg as 'the falsification of values'.[6] This image is in no way comparable to the pictures of wild animals that are found in his later poems, or to the naturalistic, crude hunting scenes in his diaries. 'The elegant giraffe from the lake of Chad'[7] sounds like a parody; it is nothing else but an exotic form used for a different content, to create a lyrical poem full of tender sadness. It is reminiscent of Gautier's testimony from his poem 'La vraie esthétique', translated by Gumilev into Russian, 'J'ai dit: "La forme aux yeux donne une fête!/. . . Le parfum envolé, reste la cassolette!"'

In this context, a hypothesis advanced by Davidson in 1992 is particularly significant. Gumilev's biographers date his first trip to Africa to 1907, implying that the poems of this volume were written after this trip and inspired by vivid impressions of Egypt and the Sudan. In this case the naive and mannerist Oriental poems should have been removed by the author. Davidson suggests a solution, and substantiates it convincingly, based on letters and witnesses' records (including those of Akhmatova), that this trip, which was kept secret from his parents, occurred not in 1907, but in 1908, that is, after the publication of the volume. Hence, the first 'African' book by Gumilev was not only raw in style but also based completely on imagination.

Gumilev's next book, which appeared after his African initiation, was *Pearls*, in 1910,[8] a tribute to the Orient of literary convention being perceptible in this title. Out of the 87 poems that make up the volume, only three are related to the Orient. The critics accused Gumilev of slavishly imitating the old masters, yet there are hardly any clichés in his Oriental verses. Here the divergent aspirations of the poet merged: the drive towards realism and precision with the taste for the exotic, the colourful and the unusual. Several of the poems, such as 'The Captains', 'The Way to China' and 'The Old Conquistador', although not formally on the Oriental theme, are redolent of the romantic spirit of long ago and far away, as found in the best poems of Gumilev. These poems are distinguished from the earlier ones by greater perfection of form and decreased stylisation. Why, one may ask, is Gumilev, having accomplished his first journey to the Orient, so much further in this volume (both in quantity and quality) from the exotic palette that he deploys in *The Romantic Flowers*, which was written prior to this voyage?

In my opinion, it is yet another proof that Gumilev visited Africa not in 1907 but in 1908. He returned full of authentic impressions and the details of real life so valued later in the practice and theory of Acmeism, a literary movement established by Gumilev and his friends. He appealed for a return to realism, to concentration on particulars, and an avoidance of mystery and the unsaid. The Acmeists aimed at the creation of an objective picture of the world as it was created. Contemporary writers, such as the Symbolists, prophesied complete and rapid oblivion for this movement. Yet, as often happens, practice proved to be much more fruitful than theory. Although the Acmeist-poets (Gumilev, Akhmatova and Mandelshtam), rapidly outgrew the restriction, adumbrated in their own manifestos, the very fact of their adherence to this movement assumes its place in the history of Russian literature. The poetic forms of the young Gumilev correspond only to the literary surrogate of the Orient; the time of original composition still lay ahead.

The first journey to Abyssinia, which Gumilev undertook at the age of 24, marks the beginning of a new chapter in his life, as Africa remained the subject of his romantic aspirations. It was a short trip, to Jeddah, Djibouti and Harar, and it lasted only a few months from the end of November 1909 until the beginning of February 1910. Gumilev was so impressed by the country of his dreams, however, that less than a year later, in September 1910, he returned to Africa; this time his destination was Lake Rudolf. He set off from Djibouti and decided to travel to Addis Ababa on foot, covering a distance of about 1,000 kilometres experiencing numerous adventures and difficulties.

In a broader context, relations between Russia and Abyssinia were usually for specific purposes. An imagined similarity of religions between Russia and Abyssinia is often mentioned as one of the reasons for this, and the relationship was widely discussed in Russia, both by clergymen and laymen. Later it was proved that such similarity was erroneous: the Ethiopian Orthodox Church had largely followed the Coptic Church doctrine even after it had been condemned by the Council of Chalcedon.[9]

The first Russian mission was sent to Abyssinia in 1847, but only with the opening of the Suez Canal, in 1869, did relations between the two countries became more regular. At the end of the nineteenth century, numerous Russian travellers, including military officers (especially Cossacks), church officials and merchants visited the area that now forms part of Djibouti, Somalia and Ethiopia. Further *rapprochement* occurred in the 1890s, when diplomatic missions were sent first from Russia to Abyssinia and then in the opposite direction. In 1898, a mission from the Russian Red Cross was sent to Abyssinia, and soon afterwards the Russian hospital was opened in Addis Ababa. The same year, a Russian imperial diplomatic mission was set up there – it was the first official mission in East Africa. All these events were largely dictated by political considerations: the two countries were equally interested in preventing British military encroachment into the area.

Gumilev's next volume, *The Foreign Sky*,[10] the first Acmeist book by the poet, appeared in 1912 after his two journeys to Abyssinia, the year when the first attempt to formulate an Acmeist Manifesto was being made. In the 1910s, Symbolism, which had exhausted itself, gradually left the Russian poetic stage, ceding its place to a younger generation of poets – the Acmeists, Imaginists, Futurists and Ego-Futurists. The first issue of the literary almanack *Apollo*, in 1913, carried Acmeist manifestos by Gumilev and Gorodetsky; similar in attitude, they proclaimed the principles of the new literary movement.

Gumilev clearly realised that a brilliant theory is worth nothing if it is not properly expressed. In *The Foreign Sky*, he had to prove the validity of the emerging theory. The very title of the book is a perfect illustration of my theme. Nearly a quarter of the poems are exotic. The book clearly shows the progress of Gumilev as a poet. 'The Pilgrim' is the story of an old pilgrim who believes that Allah himself had summoned him. He dies on his journey, but 'he will see Mecca', as he has done everything it was in his power to do and will be rewarded. Gumilev's use of exotic elements in this poem – in terms of ethnography, religion and place names – is extremely precise and justified, and is combined with a realistic form of expression. Only the finale reveals the philosophy and the personal attitude of Gumilev, precisely what Samson (1979) calls 'meditative lyrics'.[11] Gumilev uses a similar artistic method in his poem 'The Turkestan Generals'. Two other poems, 'At the Fireplace' and 'The Dazzling', anticipate Gumilev's later lyrics. 'The Dazzling' combines all the features of his exotic poetry: a hardly perceptible trend to stylisation and clichés (lonely cypress, naked steppe and so on); impressive scenes of the Orient; and a confessional intonation at the finale, reminiscent of Baudelairean spleen or Petersburg melancholy, 'I will sink my body into the armchair,/I will shade my eyes from the light,/And will weep for the Levant.' The last line could be borrowed as a motto by Romantics,

Symbolists and Acmeists alike: an impractical desire to escape everyday life, a special geography of the soul, proper to poets only.

The four Abyssinian Songs published in this volume are, however, of the greatest interest for the present study. During his missions, Gumilev made a record of the local folklore, later transforming it into the poems which, as he admitted later, were inspired by Abyssinian motifs and the use of local realism. If at an earlier stage of his work his pseudo-oriental poems were purely exercises in style, we now see a different degree of stylisation, inspired by the real sources. These songs sound so authentic that many specialists were convinced that Gumilev had translated them from local dialects into Russian. Yet this was, instead, a fantasy on an Abyssinian theme and an imitation that is common in Russian poetry. Trying to attain maximum authenticity, he often used ethnographic terms not always comprehensible to non-specialists (such as 'durro' [wheat], 'ashker' [soldier], or 'kraal' [cattle-camp]), and numerous place names and tribal names, such as Harar, Tigre, Gabesh and Kaffa.

Apart from this mystification, Gumilev recorded and translated into Russian twelve Abyssinian songs that were never published in his lifetime. Written in free verse, they are able to bring us the true sounds of the original Abyssinian folklore:

> Death is unavoidable; There lived the emperor Aba-Dania
> But the leopard's eyes are sore.
>
> He will not leave his lair.
> If only the horse of Aba-Dania would not grow a coward!
>
> The cowardly horse is afraid of all shadows,
> From that of the elephant to that of the giraffe . . .

In 1913 Gumilev made a third journey to Abyssinia. This time the mission was a scholarly one and was preceded by lengthy preparation. Abyssinia was still poorly studied at the turn of the century; there were few scholars specialising in African studies and very few people were prepared to undertake perilous expeditions in a wild, faraway country. That is why the Academy of Sciences in St Petersburg, after Gumilev had presented his report on the previous expedition to Abyssinia, decided to fund his next mission on behalf of the Museum of Ethnography and Anthropology, with the intention of collecting ethnographic materials and information about the folklore of the Galla. The archives of the museum contain the documents relating to this mission, and include the request to provide Gumilev with five rifles and 1,000 rounds of ammunition, as well as free travel on board a Russian vessel from Odessa to Djibouti for Gumilev and his assistant, his 17-year-old nephew, Nikolay Sverchkov.

The mission started on 7 April 1913 and lasted until September 1913. The original itinerary, including Eritrea and the area now forming part of the Djibouti, was abandoned as being too expensive. Gumilev chose a cheaper route, intending to travel in the south-eastern part of present-day Ethiopia and western Somalia. On arriving at Harar, Gumilev hired four servants and an interpreter and bought mules. In the course of his journey, Gumilev bought local costumes and various artefacts, and recorded Somali songs which he both translated and transliterated. On 26 September 1913 he gave the Museum one of the largest collections of artefacts, with descriptions, ever to be brought back by Russian travellers.

The collection was divided into three parts under three different registration code numbers. The first collection (No. 2154) consists of 46 domestic items from the Harari tribes; the second (No. 2155) of 48 items of weaponry from the Somali tribes, and the third (No. 2156) of 34 household items from the Galla people. The collection also includes 245 photographs, taken mainly by Nikolay Sverchkov, and 250 negatives, which are now in a very poor state. The documentation with each item included its name in the local dialect, its function and a detailed explanation of its use.

It should be noted that these artefacts were rather randomly picked up by the poet, who lacked specialist anthropological training. Nonetheless, they are of considerable interest, especially a stone mortar and a tool-kit for engraving. Several of these items were exhibited in the museum, giving Gumilev the right to say proudly in one of his poems, 'I go there to touch the barbaric objects/That I collected sometime myself.'[12] For more than sixty years following the execution of the poet, in 1921, this collection remained locked up in the museum stores. Now some of the items are again on display at the Museum of Ethnography and Anthropology, while another nine are exhibited at the literary museum dedicated to Gumilev's first wife, Anna Akhmatova.[13]

The *African Diary*, which Gumilev kept in July and August 1913 with the intention of publishing it after his trip, consists of observations and impressions. In style this diary is very similar to those kept by Romantic European travellers to the Orient. The diary mysteriously disappeared after the poet's tragic death and reappeared only recently. It may be reasonably suggested that the impressions put down in this diary served to a certain extent as a basis for his later African poems.

Only two of the 48 poems making up the volume *The Quiver*[14] are Oriental. The years between publication of *The Foreign Sky* and *The Quiver* were very important in the poet's life: they included the journey with Akhmatova to Italy, the birth of their son, the journey to Africa in 1913, the transition to Acmeism and, lastly, the First World War and service as a private soldier. The critics, in most cases, have noticed his progress as a poet. In my opinion, this progress is primarily a reflection of the formation of his personality, both poetic and human.

It is amazing that the greater part of the poems in *The Quiver* are devoted to Italy, despite the recent second journey to Africa. Probably, Italy touched some very sensitive strings in Gumilev's soul, making him turn from barbaric exoticism to the contemplation of a higher civilisation, which always remained close to his European heart.

'The African Night' represents another kind of literary mystification. With its unusually precise rhythm and the energy of a compressed spring it sounds like an authentic battle song of African warriors of yore:

> If tomorrow my dying breath is muffled by the roar of the waves of
>   the Weby
> I shall witness in death, how the god of fire and the god of darkness
>   struggle in the pale sky.

Stringent clear-cut lines, curiously reminiscent of Kipling, convey the message that remains a constant of Gumilev's poetry: the transience and frailty of life, happiness and beauty. In form, 'The African Night' is similar to Gumilev's *Abyssinian Songs*. It is also worth mentioning that his volume *The China Pavilion* (1918), includes translations from the Chinese and a translation of the Babylonian poem, the epic of Gilgamesh. Gumilev was equally in command of formal technique, whether strictly following the original or improvising on a given theme.

By this time, Gumilev's horizons had widened: apart from Italian poems, the volume includes poems of impressions of the war and, probably under its influence, religious motifs (neither of which required an exotic shell). There are also Russian motifs. The Russian theme, which here for the first time becomes perceptible in Gumilev's works, was in itself 'exotic' to his poetry. Yet one can find no trace there of the patriotic feelings that must have led Gumilev to the battlefield; possibly they would not have been in accord with the Acmeist principles of alienation and detachment.

The volume *The Fire*[15] is unique in its almost complete absence of Oriental poems. The exception is the single poem 'Ezbekiah', which concludes the book and amply compensates for the lack of other exotic verses. One finds here an example of the finest psychological lyric of an astonishing sincerity. Gumilev alludes to his first journey to Egypt. As this was mistakenly dated to 1907, it was generally accepted that this undated poem was written in 1917 ('ten years elapsed . . .'). Now, in the light of Davidson's hypothesis, the date of this poem may be moved to 1918. As if summing up, the poem brings together the past and the present. The past is love and dependence on Akhmatova, who repeatedly rejected his love ('I was tormented by a woman then');[16] this brought him to the brink of suicide (an attempt had allegedly been made in Paris). The present is liberation and the change of priorities in the poet's soul. Earlier, visualising the beauty of the Orient, he seemed not to notice its magnificence, grieving for love and meditating on life and death. Now, free from all this, he returns in his thoughts to the Orient: everything is transient and perishable; only the Orient is eternal.

The Tent (1921)[17] includes mainly poems written in 1918. This was the last book Gumilev published in his lifetime, and was dedicated to his nephew, Nikolay Sverchkov, who accompanied him on his Abyssinian journey of 1913. It is the most Oriental of all Gumilev's books, all 15 poems being exotic. Probably after a glance at the list of contents, some critics called it 'a rhymed guidebook'.[18] One can hardly agree with that judgement. All one can assume is that this book represents a new poetic way of looking at Africa and the Orient as a whole. With every right, Gumilev, in his Introduction, calls it '*my* Africa', and indeed he describes here not an imaginary land, but the real Africa, refracted by his poetic vision, explored and experienced by *him* – *his* Africa.

The protagonist of the poem 'At the Fireplace' considers that the greatest honour that could be bestowed on a human in his lifetime would be, 'A river called by my name'.[19] Now the mature poet asks in the poem 'Introduction', 'Let them call by my name a black/as yet undiscovered river.'[20] Africa became a universal measure of values for

Gumilev. The poems are realistic, rich in place names and genuine details. But realistic as the poetry is, it remains expressive, capable of creating such expressive and unexpected images as, 'The Red Sea, a shark soup,/ A Negro's bath, a sandy cauldron'; 'Man's day drunk up by the sun . . .'; 'Floods of red-headed tangled water'; 'The merry children of the Fellaheen'; 'The eye of the sun becomes like the heart of a pomegranate'; 'The grass breathed like the hide of a sweating beast'; or the visible and tragic image: 'Like threatening arms minarets are reared heavenwards.'[21]

It is interesting that the Soviet critics accused Gumilev of all possible evils. They called him 'a colonial poet', or 'a poet of aggressive capitalism, evolving into imperialism'.[22] The poet's verses completely refute this absurd and unscholarly accusation. For the first time, Gumilev addresses social realities (possibly under the influence of events in Russia). In Africa he sees not only beautiful pictures of nature but also the social underpinnings, for example the scene at the slaves' market in the poem 'Sudan'. This 'poet of capitalism' wrote, 'The true tsar of the country is neither Arab, nor White man but the one who with plough and harrow leads black buffaloes to the field.' One finds here yet another previously unknown quality of Gumilev – concern for the destinies of nature and people. In his poem 'Sahara' he records an interesting premonition and an important warning. Based on an archaeological theory, Gumilev predicts the advance of the deserts that is now actually happening in Africa. The poems of the first cycle are in many respects reminiscent of the poet's *African Diaries*. The entire volume and its genre are best characterised by Gumilev himself, who apostrophised his favourite heroine, Africa, 'Listen about your deeds and fantasies, about your animal soul.' The final posthumous volume by Gumilev, *The Pillar Of Fire*, published in August 1921, may only with difficulty be divided into 'purely Oriental' and 'non-Oriental'. It is significant that the Orient is often mentioned in poems of 'neutral' character. This proves that the Orient was no longer a distinct theme for Gumilev, but had become an integral part of his poetry. Reworked through his poetic receptivity, Oriental symbolism had become a form of expression, a part of his system of poetic images. Hence, as before, he uses exotic settings as a background for the resolution of deep philosophical problems. The Oriental poetic form is now a part of his poetic self-expression, both internally and externally. A new 'cosmic' dimension of his philosophy is particularly apparent in the short Oriental narrative poem 'The Star

Horror'. He is summing up his life, expressing an idea that is very important for the understanding of his poetry: the limitlessness of the poetic space, the whole world being 'only a rug beneath the poet's feet'.[23]

Gumilev addressed one of his last poems, 'My Readers', directly to his audience. Biographers of Gumilev have established the identities of the people whom the poet has mentioned: we know the name of the tramp from Addis Ababa, and that of the man who shot the ambassador. It is also interesting that in this literary testament Gumilev clearly shows how important it is to him that his work should be read not only in Russia, but also in Ethiopia, where a part of his soul was left.

His symbolic poem 'The Runaway Tram . . .' is particularly indicative of the role that the Orient played in the formation of the poet's philosophy. Influenced by Oriental culture, he looked at life as a permanent metamorphosis. People may 'change souls' or the soul may remain the same, yet memories of past epochs and spaces may coexist within it. This is one of the most complicated poems by Gumilev, and not all its elements are fully understood. The poet leads the reader into his inner world across 'the abyss of time'. It is amazing that the tram, the prosaic symbol of urbanism, is here a symbol of the 'interrelation of time', rushing like a time machine 'across the years and spaces'. Having gone astray, as implied by the title, it finds its way to the Orient: from Petrograd, passing through a palm forest, it thunders across the Neva, the Nile and the Seine. This combination, or rather trichotomy – the Neva/Nile/Seine – runs through Gumilev's entire work, signifying the three poles of his interest: Russia, the East and the West. In 'Abyssinia', a poem in *The Tent*, the question whether Russia, the East, or the West is more important is no longer asked: 'There is a museum of ethnography in this city, above the Neva as wide as the Nile; at the hour when I tire of being only a poet, I will find nothing more desirable.' The Orient is dissolved into the West, the cold Neva is strangely similar to the Nile and the Museum of Ethnography and Anthropology is a surrogate model of the Orient. In 'The Runaway Tram' one finds the same three rivers and the same tripartite unity (Russia, the East and the West), and these three mainstreams in the life of Gumilev are no longer competing in the consciousness of the poet. The West and the East are reconciled and have merged in the poetic world, in which the Beirut beggar coexists happily with the Petrograd tram conductor. In the poems of this last volume, even in the Oriental poems, Gumilev clearly went beyond the limits of Acmeism. Bringing together the material and spiritual world, and trying to create a panorama of human history in which the East and West, the past and present, merge together, he addresses the universal problems of being, as well as the simple and eternal: Earth, Life and Death.

The Orient proved to be an ideal symbol in the poetry of Gumilev, enabling him to express himself fully. Initially he found in Africa the incarnation of his adolescent romantic dreams; later he found subjects and stories there that were ideally suited by their material reality to the Acmeistic form. The very nature of his talent, which, particularly in his earlier poems, is predominantly epic, required sharp observations and the ability to record what he observed with all its details, nuances and colours. Gumilev was primarily interested in concrete, colourful impressions. Not trying to perceive Africa as the source of all human culture and wisdom, he nevertheless uses his large empirical experience to arrive at an understanding of the vastness and endlessness of the world, both in time and space. This multifaceted world became the essence of his poetry.

NOTES

1 D.S. Merezhkovsky, *It Was and Will Be. Diaries 1910–1925* [in Russian] (Petrograd, 1915), p. 308.
2 M. Voloshin, *Stikhotvorenia* [Poems] (2 vols., Paris, YMCA Press, 1992), vol. 1, p. 103.
3 *Tiflissky Listok* (8 September 1902).
4 N. Gumilev, *Sobranie Sochinenii* (Collected Works) (4 vols., Moscow, Terra, 1991), vol. 1, pp. 68, 72–4, 85.
5 *Ibid.*, vol. 1, p. 76.
6 L. Ginzburg, *On Lyricism* [in Russian] (Moscow & Leningrad, Sovetskii Pisatel, 1964), p. 329.
7 N. Gumilev (1991), vol. 1, p. 76.
8 N. Gumilev, *Zhemtchuga* [Pearls] (St Petersburg, 1910).
9 The Fourth Ecumenical Council of the Christian Church was held in AD 451.
10 N. Gumilev, *Tchuzhoye nebo* [The Foreign Sky] (St Petersburg: Apollon, 1912).
11 E.D. Sampson, *Nikolay Gumilev* (Boston, Twayne, 1979).
12 N. Gumilev (1991), vol. 2, p. 89.
13 Akhmatova Anna (1889–1966), a great Russian poet, the first wife of Gumilev.
14 N. Gumilev, *Koltchan* [The Quiver] (Petrograd, Gyperborei, 1916).
15 N. Gumilev, *Kostior* [The Fire] (Petrograd, Gyperborei, 1918).
16 Gumilev (1991), vol. 2, p. 30.

17 N. Gumilev, *Shatior* [The Tent] (Sevastopol, 1921).
18 E. Gollerbakh, *Zhizn' iskusstva* (30 August 1921).
19 N. Gumilev (1991), vol. 1, p. 180.
20 *Ibid.*, vol. 2, p. 71.
21 *Ibid.*, vol. 2, pp. 72, 78, 83.
22 A. Volkov, *Poeziia Russkogo Imperializma*, Moscow, 1935, p. 175.
23 N. Gumilev (1991), vol. 2, p. 35.

15

'Ah! That the Desert were my Dwelling Place': The Romance of Persia in the Early Writings of Gertrude Bell

Katharine Chubbuck

To those bred under an elaborate social order, few such moments of exhilaration can come as that which stands at the threshold of wild travel. The gates of the enclosed garden are thrown open, the chain at the entrance to the sanctuary is lowered, and with a wary glance to the right and to the left you step forth, and, behold! the immeasurable world. The world of adventure and of enterprise, dark with hurrying storms, glittering in raw sunlight, an unanswered question and an unanswerable doubt hidden in every fold of every hill. Into it you must go alone, separated from the troops of friends that walk the rose alleys, stripped of the purple and of the fine linen that impede the fighting arm, roofless, defenseless, without possessions. The voice of the wind shall be heard instead of the persuasive voices of counsellors, the touch of the rain and the prick of the frost shall be spurs sharper than praise or blame. . . . So you leave the sheltered close, and like the man in the fairy story, you feel the bonds break that were riveted about your heart as you enter the path that stretches around the rounded shoulder of the earth and enter – the desert.[1]

So did Gertrude Bell begin her classic account of eastern travel, *The Desert and the Sown*. Written in 1907, when Bell was 39, her account is full of youthful passion for the 'windless, grey dawns', the wild almond trees bordered by great blooming cyclamen, and 'the glorious cold air [that] intoxicated every sense and set the blood throbbing' as she rode her swaying camel across the moonlit sands.[2] In these early decades of the twentieth century, Bell has become one of Britain's most prominent 'lady explorers'. Having none of the extreme sexual flamboyance of Lady

Jane Digby, nor the sometimes too dry precision of Isabella Bird, Bell captured many readers' imaginations with her lush emotional descriptions of a desolate terrain. While other women rattled on about the importance of sandwich boxes on a journey, or what to do with dirty linen,[3] Bell used her books to portray sympathetically the inhabitants of the East, to appeal to her readers' sense of romance and to their common humanity. She spoke powerfully of the trials of the Kurds, the hospitality of the Druze and the brutality of the Turks. In 1914, when the great decades of desert exploration came temporarily to an end, and this vast and silent pocket of the earth became one of the theatres of war, Bell's help was enlisted by British Intelligence because no one else had such comprehensive knowledge of the desert tribes as she possessed.[4]

It was in these her later years that she won her greatest accolades: as the supporter of Faysal, the first king of Iraq; as the director of the first Iraq Museum in Baghdad, whose antiquities collection of golden headdresses, daggers, lapis lazuli, copper pots and cuneiform tablets amassed under her watchful eye still counts as one of the greatest in the world; and as one of the first western proponents of Arab independence. As Bell noted in a letter to her father at the end of her life, 'Do you know, à propos of nothing at all, that I've been four times mentioned in dispatches for my valuable and distinguished services!' And she said that when she had asked a woman at an 'Arab Ladies Tea Party', 'Who is the smartest lady in Baghdad?', the woman had replied instantly, 'Why you, of course.'[5]

Bell was indeed a great woman, one to be marvelled at. Yet this same woman would never even have entered the East had it not been for her awkward youth, during which she appeared unmarriageable – a time when, as a gangly new graduate from Lady Margaret Hall and the first woman to get a first in Modern History, she had been sent to visit her uncle in Persia to rid her of her 'Oxfordy manner'. She went to Persia, in fact, because her family was having trouble in marrying her off, for Bell was intended to adorn not staterooms but drawing rooms, to produce children not books. Yet the desert did more than simply make Bell an explorer and one of the first female members of the Royal Geographical Society. As Yvonne Ffrench wrote in 1953, 'It was as if by some miracle of transmutation that this English girl, so clever, so decided, apparently so polished with the hard gloss of high society, had, by being drawn into the orbit of desert life, there found her soul.'[6]

It was not as if Gertrude Bell had never travelled before. At 24, she had been to Switzerland, Italy and Germany. She had spent a season in society in Bucharest, where her uncle was ambassador, dancing with princes and emperors at lavish balls. Corseted in whalebone and steel and stuffed into an elaborate *décolleté* gown, Gertrude Bell had put on graceful airs. She had learned to flirt with an ostrich fan and had dined on delicate dishes of caviare and champagne. Yet this hard-nosed Oxford graduate, fluent in Turkish, Persian and Arabic, was of the world, worldly – and not accustomed to keeping her opinions to herself. In the company of a group of diplomats, for example, to her aunt's great horror she told a French statesman that he knew nothing of Germany and that his talk was complete nonsense. When a German prince tried flirting with her by telling her that Shakespeare's plays had never been performed in London, that the Globe Theatre was but a myth propagated abroad, Bell was nothing short of appalled.[7]

Everywhere Bell went she felt her own superiority – and all the young marriageable men learnt to avoid her. One can imagine the frenzied letters – mercifully, perhaps, not preserved – that would have been going back and forth between her mother and her aunt at this time. After a further three seasons in London, when she was barely asked for her hand for a minuet, much less for marriage (she had a tendency to tell young men when they trod on her toes), her uncle was transferred from Bucharest to Tehran. Bell's worried family sent her out with him in the company of her aunt and cousins. Yet while her younger cousin Florence fretted about how to pack her lacy gowns, Gertrude amassed biographies of Browning, Wordsworth and Mary Shelley, accounts of the explorations of Livingstone in Africa, the poetry of Kipling and the novels of Hugo and Balzac. She planned to do a great deal of reading abroad. After all, she reasoned, if Tehran was anything like London, the society was bound to be dull![8]

She could not have been more wrong. Persia worked an amazing transformation in Gertrude Bell. It was a country in which this strong, proud girl felt 'almost ashamed', she wrote, 'before the beggars in the street – they wear their rags with a better grace than I my most becoming habit, and the veils of the commonest women . . . are far better put on than mine'. She felt humble and newly made, intoxicated by the beauty, cloaked with a profound sense of humility, perhaps for the first time. She wrote home to a cousin:

Here there is that which is me, which womanlike is an empty jar . . . is filled with such wine as in England I had never heard of. . . . It is not the person who danced with you at Mansfield St that writes to you to-day from Persia . . . I remember you but as a dear person in a former existence, whom I should like to drag into this one and to guide whose spiritual coming I shall draw paths in ink. . . . How big the world is, how big and how wonderful. It comes to me as richly presumptuous that I should dare to carry my little personality halfway across it and boldly attempt to measure with it things for which no table of measurements could possibly apply. . . . I am not me, that is my only excuse . . . [for] in this country the men wear flaming robes of green and white and brown, and the women lift the veil of a Raphael Madonna to look at you as you pass. Wherever there is water a luxuriant vegetation springs up, and where there is not there is nothing but stone and desert. Oh, the desert round Tehran! Miles and miles of it with nothing, nothing growing, ringed with bleak bare mountains snow crowned and furrowed with the deep courses of torrents. I never knew what desert was till I came here; it is a very wonderful thing![9]

Later in the same letter she wrote: 'We have no hospitality in the West, and no manners. I feel so ashamed.' But this did not stop her from lying 'in a hammock strung between the plane trees of a Persian garden and read[ing] the poems of Hafiz . . . a book curiously bound in stamped leather which you have bought in the bazaars'. It was all, she decided, 'like the Arabian Nights'. 'I am in the Promised Land', she said, and she used a few couplets from Edward Fitzgerald's 1859 translation of *The Rubáiyát of Omar Khayyám* to illustrate her point:

Dreaming when dawn's left hand was in the sky
I heard a voice within the tavern cry
'Awake, my little ones, and fill the cup
Before life's liquor in its cup be dry!'[10]

For if Mark Twain had found the Arab world merely 'lively, picturesque and smells like a police court', and Lord Curzon had declared Persia 'an over-ripe Pear', Gertrude Bell was more likely to sigh after Byron in *Childe Harold's Pilgrimage*, 'Ah! that the desert were my dwelling place!'[11] Persia's talismanic quality became Bell's gateway into a new life far from the Mayfair drawing rooms in which she had so miserably failed. It acted as a revitalising force that was both means and ends in what was to become Bell's lifelong quest for the Eastern romance. 'The East is the birthplace of wonders', she wrote breathlessly in *Safar Nameh: Or, Persian Pictures, A Book of Travel*,[12] and it was among those Eastern wonders that, as Yvonne Ffrench wrote, she was to find her soul.[13]

Published anonymously in 1894 when Bell was 26, the fresh and vibrant *Safar Nameh* is something of an essay version of Bell's Eastern letters, and an attempt to set down as precisely as possible why Persia had taken such hold of her. As with her early letters, the book's outpourings are but witness to the ecstasy of an intelligent young woman set loose for the first time in the country of her imagination. In the constant company of her 16-year-old cousin Florence, not to mention a host of chaperons and guardians, Bell never truly escaped family commitments or Victorian demands for propriety as did other women desert travellers, such as Lady Jane Digby and Freya Stark. Yet in the barren expanses of stones upon stones, Bell too found 'peace and loneliness and beauty', riding astride for the first time and sleeping in goatskin tents, where the desert's 'wild, free spirit', as she called it, reflected the pantheism that pervaded her, seeping like the scent of sandalwood even into the walls of the cobbled towns within its midst.[14] In *Safar Nameh*, Bell wrote lavishly of vibrant desert rides in the gleaming morning air outside Tehran, in the company of the dashing English Legation Secretary, Henry Cadogan:

> Life seized us and inspired us with a mad sense of revelry. The humming wind and the teeming earth shouted 'Life! Life!' as we rode. Life! Life! the beautiful, the magnificent! Age was far from us – death far; we had left him enthroned in his barren mountains, with ghostly cities and outworn faiths to bear him company. For us, the wide plain and the limitless world, for us the beauty and the freshness of the morning! for us youth and the joy of living![15]

Bell also wrote that she was enchanted by the 'strings of camels winding in and out of the streets with all their bells ringing softly – a Persian caravan',[16] and about a garden where she, Cadogan and her cousin Florence, heard a sound of music.

> Presently a door at the side opened and in came a solemn oriental with a little stringed instrument like a zither. The fountain stopped and he sat down opposite us and played weird tunes, sad and a little

discordant . . . We waited silently half expecting a train of slaves to appear bearing a magnificent feast and a one-eyed Kalendar to tell us Arabian Night stories, but no one came, the sunlight faded and the shadows of the trees grew darker and darker; and we went out quietly and rode away.[17]

Safar Nameh is full of such gardens, embroidered cushions and carpets, rose water baths, games of backgammon, feasts of vine leaves stuffed with mincemeat and served with lemon ices, sherbets and heaps of oranges. Bell wrote how delicious it was to lie by the 'wild azaleas . . . and lovely white marsh flowers like clustered snowdrops on a very long stem', which she encountered along the hilltops.[18] Indeed, Bell's love of the wild flowers was such that, fifty years later, on opening her yellowed letters with their cramped, crabbed handwriting forced into every inch of space, her sister Elsa remarked that all the dried blossoms came tumbling out, still faintly fragrant, preserved amid a trickle of sand from the desert.[19] Bell was romanced by these blossoms – Cadogan gathered her long garlands of pomegranate blooms while he taught her Persian poems – as she was romanced by the entire atmosphere. It was appealing, she wrote in *Safar Nameh*, because in Europe she had reached one of those 'moments when the cabined spirit longs for liberty':

> A man stands a-tiptoe on the verge of an unknown world which lures him with its vague promises; the peaceful years behind lose all their value in his dazed eyes. He pines to stand in the great sunlight, the great wide world which is all too narrow for his adventurous energy . . . He remembers the look of the boundless plain stretching before him, the nights when the dome of the sky was his ceiling, when he was awakened by the cold kisses of the wind that flies before the dawn. He cries for the space to fling out his fighting arm; he burns to measure himself unfettered with the forces of God.[20]

Surrounded by these raw materials of romance, by this point Bell was burning for something else, too. Unable to be moved by a single man in Britain – unless it was to be moved in the opposite direction – in Persia Bell fell head over heels in love with the indebted, yet friendly and clever Henry Cadogan, who was addicted to gambling. While a cholera epidemic raged through the countryside, killing thousands, she and Cadogan celebrated life. They sat amid the desert sands, translating poems by Sa'dī of scented maidens, and lounged beside a waterfall, eating wild cherries.[21]

They played tennis, they rode into the mountains, they took walks and on one August afternoon they strolled two miles to a place where Cadogan's servant had spread a picnic for her that was regal enough for a queen. Cadogan helped Bell translate *The Rubáiyát of Omar Khayyám*, and they worked together on *The Divan of Hafiz* – a translation that is still considered among the best English translations from classical Persian poetry.[22] Bell wrote to her parents about her exquisite moments with Cadogan – always chaperoned, of course! – about how 'we left Aunt Mary . . . and lay under some trees in long grasses . . . with a little stream at our feet, looking at the lights changing on the snow mountains and reading Catullus from a tiny volume which Mr Cadogan produced out of his pocket'.[23] It was probably easy to imagine herself as being like her Aunt Mary, the charming, pampered wife of a diplomat, and when Cadogan proposed she happily accepted and sent her parents a letter full of flowers and poetry, rose water and romance. Bell's parents, however, refused Cadogan's offer on the grounds that his gambling debts had made him unworthy and, miserable, she was escorted back to Britain in the care of a younger cousin. She hoped that she could reconcile her father to the match, writing to her mother that, 'some people live all their lives and never have this wonderful thing; at least I have known it and have seen life's possibilities suddenly open in front of me – only one may cry just a little when one has to turn away and take up the old narrow life again. Oh Mother, Mother', she wailed.[24] Cadogan died shortly afterwards from pneumonia; Bell was not to return to the Middle East until six years later, in 1900.

Yet it must be said that although she despaired when her father forbade her marriage with Cadogan, and again later in life when she fell in love with the married Dick Doughty-Wylie, who was killed at Gallipoli, for the most part Bell was happy in the desert life she made for herself. She was calm with the fountain gurgling in the background, the hawks, the roses and the ruined garden of her villa. 'The East has wound itself round my heart', she wrote, 'until I don't know which is me and which is it'.[25] Thus, when Vita Sackville-West, a close friend of Virginia Woolf's, visited her in Baghdad in 1926, she wrote that Gertrude Bell, 'was in her right place . . . in her own house, with her office in the city, and her white pony in a corner of the garden, and her Arab servants, and her English books, and her Babylonian shards on the mantelpiece, and her long thin nose and irrepressible vitality. She had the gift of making you feel that . . . life was full and rich and exciting.'[26] Bell's life had been all that. She was a traveller and a mountaineer, a writer, an historian and an archaeologist who found in the Middle East not merely escape but promise. Even in her earlier years she wrote that 'I found no reason to regret the civilization that I was leaving', making her way into the desert with but 'a hunch of bread, a few olives, a raw onion' as her daily meal.[27]

Constantly catching sandfly fever, and plagued with ill health at the end of her life, Bell could yet write to Lord Hardinge: 'the great pleasure of this country is that I do love the people so much, and they help me through so many things'. She knew she had grown old. She wrote to Lord Hardinge: 'a great deal of water has run under the bridge since I wrote papers on Arab ruins'. Occasionally she was saddened by the transformation of the romantic Persia into the modern state of Iran.[28] But even with the changes that war and heartbreak wrought, Bell maintained to the end that sense of wild exuberance, that feeling that Iraq was the centre of the earth. In fact, one of the principal motives for her suicide, advanced by Janet Wallach in *Desert Queen*, was that Gertrude knew her crumbling health could not last and her family would soon make her leave. The proud unmarried aunt who had nothing to do but crochet sham roses in English drawing rooms was not a role she would willingly play.[29] Instead, curled among the antiquities gathered from girlhood to adulthood in her Baghdad home, the fragments of a life spent among the desert, born of a youthful passion that never died, Bell wrote to Lord Hardinge, 'I almost forget there is a world outside Iraq.'[30] For Gertrude Bell, there was not.

Notes

1 Gertrude Bell, *The Desert and the Sown* (London, William Heinemann, 1907), p. 1.
2 *Ibid.*, pp. 16–18.
3 See, for instance, Lilias Campbell Davidson, *Hints to Lady Travellers at Home and Abroad* (London, Iliffe, 1889).
4 See Bell's unpublished correspondence in the Hardinge collection, Rare Books and Manuscripts Collection, University of Cambridge. [Hereinafter 'Bell, Hardinge'.]

5 'Bell to High Bell, 18 May 1926' in Florence Bell (ed.), *The Letters of Gertrude Bell* (2 vols., London, Ernest Benn, 1927), vol. 2, p. 763.

6 Yvonne Ffrench, *Six Great Englishwomen* (London, Hamish Hamilton, 1953), p. 219.

7 Janet Wallach, *Desert Queen: The Extraordinary Life of Gertrude Bell: Adventurer, Advisor to Kings, Ally of Lawrence of Arabia* (London, Weidenfeld & Nicolson, 1997), p. 27.

8 *Ibid.*, p. 31.

9 'Bell to Horace Marshall, 18 June 1892', Bell (1927), *op. cit.*, vol. 1, p. 31.

10 Bell, cited in Wallach, *op. cit.*, p. 31.

11 Mark Twain, *The Innocents Abroad* (London, J.M. Dent, 1914), p. 69; Lord Byron, *Childe Harold's Pilgrimage* in *The Complete Poetical Works*, ed. J.J. McGann (7 vols., 1814; repr. Oxford, 1980), vol. 2, p. 183.

12 Gertrude Bell, *Safar Nameh: Or, Persian Pictures, A Book of Travel* (London, Richard Bentley, 1894), p. 114

13 Ffrench, *op. cit.*, p. 219.

14 Bell (1907), *op. cit.*, p. 301.

15 Bell (1894), *op. cit.*, pp. 26–7.

16 'Bell to Florence Bell, 18 April 1892' in Elsa Richmond (ed.), *The Earlier Letters of Gertrude Bell* (London, Ernest Benn, 1937), p. 258.

17 'Bell to Florence Bell, 22 May 1892', *ibid.*, p. 278.

18 'Bell to Florence Bell, 18 April 1892', *ibid.*, p. 258.

19 Richmond, 'Introduction', *ibid.*, p. ii.

20 Bell (1894), *op. cit.*, p. 63.

21 'Bell to Hugh Bell, 27 June 1892', Richmond (1937), *op. cit.*, p. 303.

22 See Bell, *Poems from the Divan of Hafiz* (London, William Heinemann, 1897).

23 'Bell to Florence Bell, 18 May 1892', Richmond (1937), *op. cit.*, p. 276.

24 'Bell to Florence Bell, 27 June 1892', *ibid.*, p. 306.

25 'Bell to Hugh Bell, 30 January 1922', Bell (1927), *op. cit.*, p. 510.

26 Vita Sackville-West, cited in Julia Keay, *With Passport and Parasol: The Adventures of Seven Victorian Ladies* (Harmondsworth, Penguin, 1994), p. 80.

27 Bell (1907), *op. cit.*, pp. 8–10.

28 Bell, Hardinge, *op. cit.*

29 Wallach, *op. cit.*, p. 369.

30 Bell, Hardinge, *op. cit.*

16

Orientalism and Gender: The Condition and Status of Women in Morocco

Amy J. Johnson

The Orient – in a paraphrase on Marx – cannot represent itself: so it needs to be represented. It cannot speak for itself, therefore it is 'spoken for'. It is interpreted, by the purveyors of knowledge and agents of power . . . And the inarticulateness of the Orient stands for the silence of marginalised groups in the bourgeois West: women, the poor, racial minorities . . . So Orientalism is characterised as a variant on 'male gender dominance, or patriarchy, in metropolitan societies.' For the West feminised the East and eroticised it. Like the female body in the West, the Orient served as the site of mixed feelings, attraction and repulsion; intimacy and a sense of distance.[1]

Much has been written in recent years about the status of women within Middle Eastern society. As Western society has become more self-conscious and self-critical about the treatment of women within its own sphere, so there has been an increased interest in determining the role of women in other societies and comparing this with the role of Western women. Likewise, the notion of Orientalism, as articulated by Edward Said, has received considerable scholarly attention. Orientalism is defined by Said as encompassing 'a way of coming to terms with the Orient that is based on the Orient's special place in European Western experience'[2] and as 'a style of thought based upon an ontological and epistemological distinction made between "the Orient" and (most of the time) "the Occident"'.[3] Yet, as Billie Melman has observed, the intellectual exchange concerning Orientalism has focused almost exclusively on the ways in which the Oriental Other was viewed by Western men.[4] Melman, in her work *Women's Orients: English Women and the Middle East 1718–1918*, has argued that 'In Edward Said's script of the exchange between the West and the East, the occidental interpretation of the Orient is a symbolic act of appropriation from which Western women are excluded.'[5]

Although Melman's study focuses primarily on the eastern Mediterranean, her argument that the writings of Western women about the Orient have been largely excluded from the debates about Orientalism and from scholarship about the Middle East is equally applicable to the western portion of this geographical region, and especially to the Maghrib. The exclusion of specifically female writing about the Oriental Other from debates on Orientalist discourse is the result of the assumption that Western women experienced and created the Orient[6] in the same way as Western men. In other words, as Melman notes, 'the female experience of the Western expansion and domination outside Europe had been subsumed in a hegemonic and homogenously patriarchal tradition'.[7]

Yet to make such an assumption, to casually accept the notion that all Western writers on and travellers to the Middle East saw essentially the same reality and created essentially the same Orient, is to overlook important differences between Western writers' views about the Middle East, and to ignore the often unique perspective of female authors. In Melman's words,

> the image of the different was never monolithic and, certainly, not androcentric. Women travellers, missionaries, and writers did not perceive the oriental *woman* as the absolutely alien, the 'ultimate other'. Rather oriental *women* became the feminine West's recognisable image in the mirror.[8]

Melman sees the unique contribution of female Western writers as their capacity and tendency to draw parallels between the status of women in the society that they observed and that of women in their own society; in this way, many Western women identified with the Oriental Other in a way that was often absent from male writings on the Orient.

This paper will evaluate Melman's conclusions on the ways in which Western women viewed the women of Morocco. Specifically, it presents and analyses the views of a number of late-nineteenth- and early-twentieth-century female British and American authors' views and notions of the role of women within Moroccan society. Melman's study excludes the western Middle East; it should therefore be instructive to determine whether Melman's conclusions and her contention that Western women often drew parallels between their position within their own society and the status of Oriental women are applicable not only to the eastern Mediterranean, but also to Morocco. Melman writes:

> [My] study of the Western women's Orient has a meaning beyond the discovery of new evidence, the unearthing of the debris of unknown lives, and of an experience 'hidden from history' . . . New evidence may be used to develop a new perspective on the relations between Europe and its 'others' and redefine these relations in terms which are not mostly political.[9]

It is hoped that this study will contribute to the achievement of this goal.

The works that will be analysed and discussed in the remainder of this paper are: *A Winter in Morocco*, by Amelia Perrier; *Seventy-One Days' Camping in Morocco*, by Agnes Grove; *In the Tail of the Peacock*, by Isabel Savory; *In Morocco*, by Edith Wharton; two articles by the Countess of Meath that appeared in the magazine *The Nineteenth Century*; *A Winter in Tangier*, by Mrs Howard-Vyse; *Sketches of Life in Morocco*, by Kathleen Mansel Pleydell; *Holiday in Morocco*, by Eleanor Rigo de Righi; *The Magic of Morocco* by Eleanor Elsner; and *Sixteen Years of an Artist's Life in Morocco, Spain and the Canary Islands*, by Elizabeth Murray. Although this study cannot claim to be an exhaustive analysis of all works written by British and American women about Morocco during the time in question, the works represent a variety of opinions and approaches to viewing Moroccan women, and the topics that these writers discuss can be taken to be representative of those dealt with in the larger body of works by female authors on this topic during the late nineteenth and early twentieth centuries.

The views of the authors will be presented according to the degree of criticism of the treatment of women in Morocco found in their works. Accordingly, there are three basic categories into which the works are divided. The first group consists of those authors who are extremely critical of the role and treatment of women in Morocco; the authors who are included in this group are Perrier, Grove, Savory, Wharton and the Countess of Meath. The second group consists of those authors who are mildly critical of the position of women in Morocco, but who do not treat the topic in much detail; the authors who fall into this category are Howard-Vyse, Pleydell and de Righi. The final group consists of those authors who are essentially uncritical or accepting of the role of women in Moroccan society; these authors are Elsner and Murray. In the next two sections of the paper, the authors and their views will be discussed according to this classification.

About the authors

Before proceeding to discuss the writings of these authors, it may be useful to present a brief overview of their travels, their works and their purposes in writing about Morocco. Unfortunately, very little biographical information about the authors is available, with the exception of those who were well-known authors or from well-known families. Nonetheless, a brief glimpse into the life and travels of each author should help illuminate the circumstances under which they wrote and provide insight into their ways of seeing, understanding and interpreting the lives of the Oriental Other – in this case Moroccan women and their status in Moroccan society.

Amelia Perrier was an Englishwoman who, in addition to *A Winter in Morocco*, was also the author of two earlier books, entitled *Mea Culpa* and *A Good Match*. Perrier's book provides little personal information prior to her experiences in Morocco. That she was British and apparently travelled alone is evident from her narrative; however, little other biographical information is available. Yet this provides some insight in itself: Perrier's book was published in 1873, making it one of the earliest of the works that is examined in this paper, and she is the only author to have travelled to Morocco without any companions. One may infer from her solitary journey that Perrier was probably an independent, unafraid and rather adventurous person who did not find the idea of travelling to a foreign land daunting. As will become evident, she was also keenly aware of gender relations and not at all hesitant to express her views on the condition of women, not only in Moroccan society but also in her own country.

Although she does not give the reader her reasons for travelling to Morocco,[10] Perrier's stated purpose in writing *A Winter in Morocco* is to provide information about a country of which she felt most of her fellow Britons were woefully ignorant. By her own admission, she lacked any substantial knowledge about Morocco prior to her departure. She writes:

> I knew nothing about the country or the people when I went there. Everything I saw was novel and interesting to me. And it is for that

section of the reading public whose minds may be in the same blank condition on the subject that mine was, that I have written down my experiences in Morocco, and described, as well as I could, all that I saw and heard there; in the hope that, even thus at second hand, it may afford some amusement, and perhaps a little instruction, to them also, as it did to me.[11]

Perrier presents a brief sketch of Moroccan history in her introductory chapter; otherwise, the book is entirely devoted to her own voyage, experiences and observations.

Before discussing the other authors, it is worth mentioning that Perrier is also unique in two other areas: her sense of humour and her scepticism about Christianity. Her style of writing is frequently humorous, and many of the anecdotes she relates are extremely amusing, in contrast to most of the other narratives, which are somewhat dry, preoccupied with detailed descriptions, and written wholly in earnest.[12] The author's ability to entertain the reader and to refrain from taking her experiences too seriously is a distinguishing characteristic of her work. Perrier's scepticism about Christianity is also evident. Although she makes broad generalisations about Islam and its effects on society, Perrier apparently does not make such statements out of a sense of religious animosity, and she is herself extremely critical about Christian missionaries and Christian churches.[13]

Lady Agnes Grove is the author of a 1902 work entitled *Seventy-One Days' Camping in Morocco*. Her travels in Morocco took place during the winter of 1899, in the company of her husband, daughter and several other travelling companions. As the title of her book suggests, it is an account of one of her journeys throughout the country, and purports to be nothing more than a record of her own personal experiences during her stay. In contrast to Perrier and some other authors, Grove makes no real attempt to incorporate historical data in her work. Instead, as she writes in the preface to the book, 'I merely relate that which I myself have seen and heard: what has struck me as interesting or humorous. What I have to say, then, is of a rather more than less personal nature, the limited interest of which I fully recognise.'[14]

Like Perrier's work, Grove's narrative demonstrates that the author was sensitive to gender-related issues. Throughout her writing, Grove remarks not only upon the way in which Moroccan women are treated, but also the way in which she was treated by both Europeans and

Moroccans during her travels. Three incidents serve as particularly good examples of this. Commenting on her correspondence with a friend in Britain who drew parallels between women and children, she exclaims 'Alas! even in Morocco I am pursued by the haunting fact that women, children and imbeciles are classed as one, in more matters than the Parliamentary vote.'[15] Similarly, when discussing horseback riding, her attire (consisting of 'Moorish trousers and a Moorish shirt and a sulham') and her use of the 'man's saddle', Grove defends herself by saying that 'on the score of decency, not the most fastidious could object to my costume, because the legs were less outlined than on a side-saddle', yet she remarks offhandedly that 'why legs should convey indecency in a woman is an unsolved mystery'.[16] Finally, Grove relates how her party was discouraged from attempting to cross a river that their local guide thought to be dangerous. Upon being told that the river was unsafe 'for a lady', Grove plunged ahead of the guide and crossed the river alone.[17] These are but a few of the examples of Grove's impatience with what she perceived to be unequal treatment based on gender. The fact that she was keenly aware of gender issues and opposed to gender-based inequality in her own society and elsewhere is important to remember when reading her accounts of Moroccan women.

Like Grove, Isabel Savory journeyed to Morocco and spent much of her time there travelling and camping. Her 1903 book, *In the Tail of the Peacock*, is a record of her adventures. In contrast to Perrier and Grove, however, Savory injects a healthy dose of historical narrative into her personal accounts. Although Savory's elucidation of the purpose of her writing is limited to noting that those who will find interest in her book are those who 'find in other than scenes of peril and excitement their hearts' desire',[18] her decision to include a history of the country and provide an account of her own travels indicates that the work was meant to be more than a mere report of her own activities; it is apparently intended to be a work of history and fact as opposed to one of personal observation. Savory provides little personal information, other than that she travelled and camped primarily with one female friend and their servants.

Edith Wharton's *In Morocco*, published in 1920, was written in the form of a guidebook for visitors to the country. Wharton, the only American author included in this study, was a well-known novelist from a socially prominent family. Known for writing novels concerned with 'values, particularly with reference to the place of woman in society',[19] Wharton's work on Morocco also reflects her awareness of gender roles and the position of women in that society.

An interesting aspect of Wharton's work is her attention to the activities of the French governing authorities in Morocco. Dedicated to General Lyautey, the book in fact contains an entire chapter on the French general's work in Morocco and the 'progress' that had been made in Moroccan society as a result of his policies. Wharton's association with the governing French authorities may have had an influence on the way in which she saw Moroccan society and the views she held on the efficacy and beneficent nature of the French presence in Morocco, but it is difficult to discern what, if any, influence her French connections had on Wharton's views of Moroccan women.

Wharton travelled to Morocco during the First World War. She acknowledges in the preface that the fact that she was able to travel for only one month, in a French military car, and as a result of petrol rationing could only travel on a limited scale, probably made the record of her travels less detailed than otherwise would have been the case. Yet she claims that these limitations are outweighed by the value of her work as the first real guidebook about the country, and the fact that the timing of her journey, carried out at 'the brief moment of transition between [Morocco's] virtually complete subjection to European authority, and the fast approaching hour when it is thrown open to all the banalities and promiscuities of modern travel'[20] was historically unique. Nonetheless, the limited nature of her journeys and the fact that she was often unable to make the 'second visit [to various locations] which alone makes it possible to carry away a definite and detailed impression' of what she saw should be noted.[21]

Also included in this study are two articles written at the turn of the century by the Countess of Meath. The two articles, 'The First Woman's Hospital in Morocco' and 'A Land of Woe', were both published in a magazine called *The Nineteenth Century*. In these articles, the countess clearly expresses her religiosity and makes it known that she is writing from the perspective of a Christian.[22] In addition, she expresses her view that Morocco is rife with barbarism and that Europe is synonymous with civilisation;[23] in fact, she writes: 'truly it is a land of woe, because injustice, cruelty, and oppression prevail . . . when living in Morocco, one is led to feel that death is too often maligned, and that we ought to regard it as a veritable angel of mercy sent to free the sufferer from the cords of anguish'.[24] Through such statements, the countess's prejudices are revealed. As a European and a Christian, she views Morocco as a backward and barbaric land, and her identification of herself in these terms colours her writings.

Another interesting work is Mrs Howard-Vyse's *A Winter in Tangier*, written in 1882 (her first name is not available). Howard-Vyse's narrative is structured as a diary, with entries for each day of her stay in Morocco. The author articulates her purpose in publishing it as follows:

> When I began to keep these Rough Notes, as a journal, I never contemplated producing them in print, and I am only induced to do so at the present time, because I believe that little is known of Tangier, and the surrounding country, and still less of its climate . . . I have therefore thought that the account of our daily life, weather, and expenses, may be useful to some, who seek for a mild winter climate, and, like ourselves, are not over-burdened with this world's goods.[25]

This book is unusual in stating that its purpose is to provide information for travellers and encouraging tourism to Morocco. The author mixed primarily with other Europeans during her stay in Tangier; in fact, one of the principal families with which she and her husband socialised was that of John Drummond Hay, the British consul in Morocco. Because of the lack of biographical information on Mrs Howard-Vyse and the fact that she says little about herself in her book, it is unclear whether her social access to the consul and his family was common to all British travellers in Morocco or was unique to her because of her own social status. Nonetheless, her inclination to confine her social activities largely to interacting with other Europeans and with upper-class Moroccans means that her narrative is limited in scope. Unlike Perrier, Wharton, Savory and Grove, Howard-Vyse either did not have the opportunity to interact with the local population to any great extent or simply chose not to do so, and as a result it should be understood that her observations have a limited application.

Kathleen Mansel Pleydell wrote her book *Sketches of Life in Morocco* in 1907. Unlike the books discussed previously, Pleydell's book has no preface or introduction that provides her reasons for writing and publishing the narrative. Her work is precisely that – a narrative of her personal and family life in Morocco that concerns itself little with anything else. Even more so than Howard-Vyse, Pleydell relates her life in Morocco in a personal manner that is narrow in focus and scope and deals primarily with her relations with other Europeans in Morocco and the activities of the members of her family. She writes little about Moroccans themselves, largely confining her comments to events she witnessed and the people involved in them. Whether this is a result of a lack of interest in Moroccan society or a lack of opportunity to interact with Moroccans socially is not clear. That the author recorded and published an account of her stay in the country indicates a certain interest in Morocco and its people, but the limited scope of her work should be remembered when considering her remarks on Moroccan women and their place within Moroccan society.

Holiday in Morocco was written in 1935 by Eleanor Rigo de Righi and is the most recent of the works included in this study. De Righi's account is both historical and descriptive. While not professing to have produced a comprehensive guidebook to the country, the author claims that the book will provide the average traveller with a brief 'history of the land, its peoples and cities, and . . . the information necessary for travel in the country; the things I myself would have been glad to know on or before arrival'.[26] De Righi does a thorough job of organising and presenting useful information about Moroccan history, hotels, communication systems, climate, restaurants, shopping and points of interest. In sharp contrast to the accounts of Howard-Vyse and Pleydell, de Righi's work is almost devoid of personal experience and instead reads almost like an encyclopaedia entry or basic history text. Nonetheless, she does include several observations about the status of women within Moroccan society, although the lack of a recorded context in which she interacted with Moroccan women makes one wonder whether she arrived at her conclusions through personal experience or whether her remarks are meant to reflect the general opinion of the time.

Eleanor Elsner, a prolific travel author whose other works include *The Romance of the Basque Country and the Pyrenees* and *Romantic France: The Enchanted Land of Provence*, wrote a book in 1928 entitled *The Magic of Morocco*. Elsner, a widow who travelled in the company of several other men and women for the majority of her time in Morocco, journeyed to the country out of a romantic desire to see 'lands where the sun shines and the sky is blue, places where the quietness and dignity of the old life still counts for something'.[27] The first chapter of her book explains her attraction to Morocco, a country which she describes in a highly romanticised way.[28] Elsner's romanticism about faraway places, which she herself admits to feel, may be partially responsible for the way in which she views the women of Morocco. While the authors discussed thus far are generally critical of the treatment of women in Morocco, Elsner tends to dismiss claims of unfair treatment and oppression. This is in keeping with her general romantic views of the country as a whole; since she went to Morocco as a result of its inexplicable attraction as a place in which the old ways were still valued, one is tempted to conclude that Elsner was, from the start, unlikely to see Morocco and Moroccan society through any but the most rose-tinted glasses.

Elizabeth Murray, the last author included in this study, is, like Elsner, disinclined to criticise Morocco on the basis of the position of women in its society. Like the Countess of Meath, Murray draws a sharp distinction between civilisation (in her view, synonymous with Europe) and the rest of the world.[29] Murray, an artist, frequently pokes fun at and even ridicules the aesthetic standards of Moroccans, particularly their ideas of physical beauty. The majority of her remarks about women in Morocco are concerned with their physical appearance, clothing and manners of adorning themselves; she refrains from commenting extensively upon the role of Moroccan women within their society, and the few comments that she does allow herself are not generally of a critical nature.

It should be remembered that the vast majority of these women mixed only with upper- and upper-middle-class Moroccans. Few of the authors discuss any contacts they might have had with lower-middle and lower-class Moroccan families. As a result, their observations, except where noted, should be understood to apply only to the upper- and upper-middle class. Where the authors make distinctions between the treatment of women in different social classes, these distinctions will be noted.

The writings of these authors about women in Morocco, their status in society and their daily activities can be grouped into five loose but overlapping categories. Almost all of the authors discuss marriage and divorce, life in the harem, women's dress and appearance, the economic function of women and women and religion. Each author's views on each of these topics will be presented in order to delineate the similarities and differences between their opinions, their ways of seeing and interpreting the female Oriental Other, and to determine whether Melman's conclusion that Western women often identified with the situation of their counterparts in the eastern Mediterranean is one that can be applied to Morocco with equal validity.

Marriage and divorce

The topic most frequently discussed is that of marriage, wedding customs, relationships between husbands and wives and divorce. More than any other, this topic interested and intrigued these authors, and for most was the area which epitomised for them the unequal treatment of women in Moroccan society. This is particularly true of Amelia Perrier, who devotes one chapter to the discussion of weddings and another to the topic of wives in Morocco. She presents her detailed observations of how weddings and marriages are conducted, then gives the reader her own opinion about the matter. Perrier's is the most descriptive of the various accounts of Moroccan weddings, but other authors in this study who describe the process of marrying in Morocco do not differ from her in any significant aspect.

Perrier's account of a typical Moroccan wedding is as follows. The parents of the groom are responsible for selecting an appropriate bride for their son; neither the groom nor the bride can see each other before the marriage contract is signed and their wedding day is at hand. On the appointed day, the bride's family gathers at the home of the bride's parents, where there is much celebration, including musical entertainment, dancing and ululation. At some point in the evening, the bride is put into an enclosed litter (described by Perrier and several other authors as 'a large square box, about the size of an ordinary tea chest').[30] The bridal box is affixed to the back of a donkey and the procession parades throughout the town, eventually transporting the bride to the home of her future husband.[31]

Perrier also relates what she terms the 'curious custom observed on these occasions that the bride is not permitted to leave her bed for eight days after her marriage; nor . . . may she open her eyes or speak'.[32] After this, the bride is allowed to rise and receives in her new home all her 'married female relations and friends'[33] and another celebration is held. Perrier's chapter, entitled 'Weddings in Tangier', relates the experience of attending one of these celebrations and the observations she made there.

She remarks that she visited one of the new brides in the company of some other Englishwomen who were 'in the frequent habit of visiting Moorish ladies in their prison homes',[34] thus conveying her opinion of the seclusion of women.

Perrier also remarks on the difference in physical appearance between the young and old women whom she observed at the ceremony, and ascribes this difference to the treatment of wives by their husbands after marriage. Noting that the young women were universally plump while the older ones were 'distressingly shrivelled and haggard',[35] she speculates on the reasons for the discrepancy and attributes it to the abusive structure of male–female relations in the society:

> Whether the cause of this is, that the lords and masters of the beings who have the misfortune to be born women in Morocco, when their wives are past the one sole purpose for which according to Mohammedan ideas, they are called into existence, cut them down in their supplies of keskoo [couscous] to a bare sufficiency, I cannot tell. It looks like it. The one little bit of inconsistency however, in Moslem domestic institutions is, that though old wives are regarded as only so much worthless lumber by their husbands, old mothers are held in some respect and affection by their sons. This probably accounts for the fact of old women being kept alive at all.[36]

She also argues that although the marriage customs and treatment of brides 'are intended – so it is said – to preserve and foster female delicacy and modesty, according to Moorish ideas . . . to my mind and the minds of my friends, the result was of a totally opposite nature'.[37] Perrier, noting the bridal box, the seclusion of women, the separation of married from unmarried women in wedding celebrations, forced silence and motionlessness for the first eight days of marriage and what she saw as the excessive painting and adornment of the bride's person, remarks, 'To us, the poor creatures seemed as wanting in womanly delicacy, as they were in human dignity. They appeared quite incapable of conceiving the one, in its true sense, as they were certainly totally devoid of the other.'[38]

After discussing the wedding ceremonies, Perrier treats the topic of relations between husbands and wives in more detail in a later chapter, in which she relates her visit to the *Sharīf* of Wazzan and her visit with his wives. The author was much offended by the *Sharīf*'s failure to introduce his wives to her and the other Englishwomen present, remarking that 'his wives stood behind him; it would, I suppose, have been too great a degradation of Moorish and saintly marital dignity, for him to have introduced them to us'.[39] She also deplores the subordinate status of wives in relation to their husbands. She writes that one of the *Sharif*'s wives was trying to attract his attention: 'The childishly timid demeanour of the girl towards him, and her deferential and humble manner when addressing him, might have been amusing, considering that she was his wife and he was her husband, had it not been so exceedingly painful and humiliating to witness.'[40] Perrier therefore leaves the reader with the distinct impression that the condition of women, in respect of the marriage customs and the treatment of wives by their husbands, is deplorable.

Grove, while criticising the treatment of Moroccan women, does not treat the topic of marriage and divorce specifically in her work. The next author, Isabel Savory, also does not discuss marriage in much detail, yet her limited remarks on the subject are worth noting. Savory speculates that when a Moroccan man leaves his home, 'his house, with his wife, he has locked up: the keys are in his pocket'.[41] Although this remark is not based on her observation that men do, in fact, lock their wives in their homes, it does indicate Savory's impression that men treated their women as property, rather than as people. Based on her observations of one Moroccan family, Savory contends that 'Mohammedans are jealous and suspicious of their wives and daughters.'[42]

In addition to these general remarks, Savory also discusses divorce and polygamy in Morocco. She notes that although Moroccan men, being Muslims, are allowed multiple wives (she contends they may take up to five), the expense involved in maintaining a household with more than one wife makes this a rare practice. Instead, she says that the men 'contented themselves with slaves' and that sexual desires were easily enough gratified by the ease of divorce and remarriage.[43] Yet she does note that divorced women have a certain degree of freedom that other women in Moroccan society lack: 'a Moorish woman does not think for herself until she is divorced. Her father, mother, or brother marries her to whomsoever he or she chooses; but once she is divorced, she is free to marry after her own heart, and no one can interfere with her.'[44] She is also careful to record that divorce is not the exclusive right of the husband; instead, she writes that if husbands 'are away over a year and send no money to the wife, she can claim a divorce'.[45]

Savory, though decidedly critical of the treatment of women in Morocco, thus presents a few positive aspects to it that do not appear in Perrier's work: the right of women to divorce and, once divorced, to freely choose a second husband. Yet Savory, like Perrier, deplores the subjugation of her gender and places the blame squarely on the shoulders of Moroccan husbands. She says that the reason why women in Morocco are often seen as dull, stupid and content lies in their forced and total submission to their husbands:

> If a woman unable to read or write only meets women also unable to read or write, and knows but one man, her husband, who feeds her and values her much like a tame doe-rabbit, it is unreasonable to expect to find in her much intelligence and energy. Wives, when asked if they did not wish to do more, would not like to read or write or work, only laughed derisively. The idea was absurd: they could not understand any one wishing to exert herself in a novel or unnecessary way.[46]

Howard-Vyse also comments upon marriage customs, relating the story of the bridal box in much the same way as Perrier. Like Savory, she also remarks upon Muslim practices regarding divorce and remarriage:

> The Moorish morals as regards marriage and divorce are most peculiar. A man is allowed to have four wives at the same time, though they very rarely avail themselves of this privilege, as they say it is too expensive! But he can divorce them with the greatest ease, and can marry again the same evening if he likes; but the divorced wife must wait for three months before she can marry again, and she cannot be divorced more than four times.[47]

Howard-Vyse thus points out two elements that Savory did not present: the unequal rights of husbands and wives to remarriage after divorce.

Pleydell also treats the topic of marriage, though again, not in much detail. She makes a distinction between the marriage customs of the upper class and those of the lower class, noting that while upper-class couples generally do not meet until the day of their wedding, 'among the villagers, young men and maidens meet and make choice of their mates much as Europeans do'.[48] She does not offer much comment on marriage customs and the treatment of wives by their husbands, except to compare the festive atmosphere that surrounds Moroccan weddings favourably with the sombre, stuffy air of those of the Anglican church.[49]

Elsner, in contrast to the writers examined thus far, presents Moroccan wives as a contented group of women who desire nothing more than a tranquil home life and who treasure their seclusion and lack of involvement in public life to such a great degree that husbands are obliged to promise in the marriage contracts that their wives will never under any circumstances be forced to leave the house.[50] Although Elsner notes that the seclusion of women is not enforced by their husbands in the city of Fez, and that women there had relatively more freedom than their counterparts in other areas of Morocco, Elsner states in no uncertain terms that she sees nothing wrong with the treatment of women in Morocco, as everyone, both men and women, seem content. She remarks that visitors to Morocco should not feel sorry for Moroccan women, because, 'they are, as yet, quite unfitted for any sort of life except one of being taken care of and guarded. They have no desire for liberty, they have not even learned to think.'[51] Elsner was not troubled by this offhand dismissal of the issue of gender equality; it apparently did not concern her, as it did Savory, that when kept in a constant state of isolation, ignorance and seclusion, these women would probably never have the opportunity to 'learn to think' or 'become fitted' for a different lifestyle.

Life in the harem

A related issue often discussed by these authors is the secluded life of the women of the harem. As might be expected from her vehement opposition to Moroccan marriage customs and what she saw as the abusive and degrading nature of relationships between husbands and wives, Perrier also denounces the seclusion of women with equal force. Writing about her attendance at wedding ceremonies, she remarks:

> Some of the women held our gowns while imploring us to remain a little longer, so that we felt that we were really 'tearing ourselves away'. Of course, these poor creatures, do become in a degree, inured, to their life of seclusion; but how little they enjoy it, is plainly seen in the melancholy or fretful expression on the face of every woman . . . and by the evident delight, afforded to all, by the sight of new faces; and even such transitory association with strangers from that outer world from which they are debarred, as visits like ours occasionally supply them with.[52]

This is certainly a different image from the one that Elsner presented. Instead of portraying Moroccan women as content with their lot and their domestic role, Perrier contends that many long for knowledge of and contact with the outside world.

Perrier's work is important in another sense: she compares the actual seclusion of women in Morocco with what she sees as the overwhelming theoretical sentiment in favour of like practices in Britain. Although she is careful to note that seclusion and confinement of British women to the domestic sphere is not a reality, and that the involvement of British women in public life is 'the surest mark of our progress',[53] her comments on the similarity between British rhetoric and Moroccan practice are illuminating:

> If any one took the trouble to consider the matter for a few moments, he[/she] would be astonished to find, on comparing what are still the most general and were until very lately the almost universal *theories*, amongst ourselves, with regard to the social and domestic position of women, with the *practices* in Morocco, what a horribly close resemblance there is between the two . . . It is still by many thought a right and pleasant thing, and agreeable to both sexes, when discussing the subject, to quote texts, 'A woman should be subject unto her husband'; 'Wives, submit yourselves unto your husbands'; adding, as 'moral reflections', 'Women have no need of learning'; 'A woman's weakness is her strength'; 'Home is a woman's *only* sphere'; and others of a like nature.[54]

Such self-criticism and reflection as Perrier engages in on this issue provides a measure of support for Melman's theories. Melman, as noted earlier, argues that Western women were more likely than men to identify with the Oriental Other as a result of the similarities between their own inferior status in Western society and the inferior status of the Orient in the minds of most Westerners; Perrier's remarks can be seen as an example of this tendency.

Grove, like Perrier, also remarks upon the absence of women from the public sphere and contends that the result of such customs can only be to retard the progress and enlightenment of the society. She writes that 'the fact of a woman's existence has to be kept out of ordinary conversation, so much so that there is a recognised formula for inquiring after them, wherein "your house" is substituted for "your womenfolk"'.[55] She argues that the extreme exclusion of women from public life can only result in depravity and barbarism:

> It is no speculative theory but a positive scientific fact that it is impossible for one-half of a human race to progress while the other half remains stagnant . . . All History shows that stagnation must be the inevitable fate of every community, every nation, every people where the women do not fully share the national life and are regarded as incapable of taking an intelligent interest in their country's welfare.[56]

Wharton also attributes the decay of Moroccan society to the seclusion and unequal treatment of women. She refers to the harem of 'one of the chief dignitaries of the Makzen at Fez' as 'a mouldering prison'[57] and laments the lack of topics of conversation that were available between the women of the harem and herself. She writes, 'there are few points of contact between the open-air occidental mind and beings imprisoned in a conception of sexual and domestic life based on slave-service and incessant espionage'.[58]

Dress and appearance

The clothing, makeup and physical appearance of Moroccan women receives a vast amount of attention in the works of virtually every author included in this study. As one might expect, such visual and apparent differences between cultures are the most frequently remarked upon and are often described in great detail. It is likely that such detailed descriptions of women's clothing, their manner of conducting personal hygiene and adornment and methods of applying make-up are topics that are not covered in much, if any, detail in works by male authors, for the simple reason that women alone had access to such personal aspects of the life of Moroccan women.

Several authors remark upon the differing standards of physical beauty of Moroccans and Europeans. The physically ideal Moroccan woman is plump, and would be considered unattractive and even obese by European standards. Perrier observes that once an engagement has been arranged, the prospective bride is methodically fattened for her wedding, 'from the time of her betrothal, she is confined to one room, not permitted to take any exercise, and compelled to swallow large quantities of keskoo [couscous] every day. This system . . . brings her into a condition of what is considered in Morocco becoming obesity.'[59] Murray, in one of her few critical comments about the condition of women in Moroccan society, likens this process to the fattening of poultry for slaughter in Europe.[60]

Perrier also relates the excessive interest in clothing that she asserts the women of Morocco often have. She says that she and her British companions frequently dressed in their finest apparel when visiting Moroccan women, because they were aware of 'the gratification that looking at dress affords these women, who have no other object of interest in life'.[61] The opulence and care with which the majority of Moroccan women with whom the authors interacted dressed inside their own private chambers provides further support for Perrier's conclusions. Without opportunity to participate in public life, and with limited access to the outside world, many Moroccan women apparently had ample time to devote to personal adornment.

The topic of the *haik* is also discussed by the authors. Grove takes the view that the all-enveloping garments in which the women of Morocco dress are demeaning and an indication of their subordinate position within society. She attacks her countrywomen who assent to veiling and virtual seclusion while in Morocco, on the grounds that doing so gives their consent and approval to the subjugation of their gender. She comments forcefully on the issue of appropriate female dress, saying:

> The Mahomedan women veil their faces because to display them is supposed to convey indecent want of modesty. The idea involved in this contention needs no elaboration to prove its bestial tendency; but the English woman by adopting this outward sign of an abominable degradation, degrades and disgraces her countrywomen, and by parading herself as if under the same hideous conditions, bears false witness to the actualities that centuries of enlightenment have established for her . . . from the height of her emancipation for an European woman to perpetuate and encourage in her person the foul wrong that the Mahomedan woman is daily undergoing, seems to me little short of thoughtless and almost criminal folly.[62]

In sharp contrast to this denunciation of the humiliation and degradation inherent in the dress of the women of Morocco, Murray contends that the comfortable anonymity of the *haik* provides Moroccan women with a unique form of freedom. She writes that Christian women, because of their manner of clothing, are easily recognisable and, as a result, their movements are known to anyone who cares to pay attention. Murray argues that 'Mohammedan countries are perhaps the only ones where a woman can be said to possess, in some respects, at least, any advantages of liberty over men'; in her view, this liberty consists of the ability of the Moroccan woman, dressed in her all-encompassing white garments, to 'roam about the town in whatever direction she may choose, without the slightest risk of being recognised'.[63] Despite her assertions about the unrivalled freedom from being recognised in the street and the ability of Moroccan women to move about with anonymity, however, Murray does not discuss how often women are able to leave their homes.

Economic function of women

One of the few areas in which the authors make class-based distinctions about the role of women in Moroccan society is their involvement in economic matters. All authors who comment upon education in Morocco note the complete lack of formal training for Muslim females. Perrier notes that Jewish girls are taught to speak Spanish, and are frequently able to work outside the home, and that Spanish girls attend school in the company of boys and are taught the rudiments of reading and writing in addition to needlework and religious matters. She notes that in each group, the females are educated at a lower level than the males.[64] In addition to the lack of opportunities to involve themselves in public life, the lack of female education in Morocco is considered by Perrier to limit women's role in the economic sector.

Several authors comment upon the apparently widespread custom among lower-class Moroccans of using women to carry goods in much the same way as pack animals are used.[65] Howard-Vyse remarks upon one outing during which she witnessed 'poor women, bent double, with their children and heavy sacks on their backs, the enormous straw hats covering their shoulders; the men generally riding or walking without any kind of burden'.[66]

Various authors also note that lower-class women are seen more frequently in the streets and working as pedlars in the markets,[67] that black women are frequently slaves and so are more visible in public areas and as a commodity perform an economic function;[68] some also remark upon the greater public involvement of Jewish and Berber women, and note the employment of some lower-class women as servants, dancers and musicians.[69]

Women and religion

The last area of consideration for the authors is the relationship between women and religion. Virtually all the authors say that women are prohibited from entering the mosque, although they disagree on whether this prohibition is lifted for major religious festivals.[70] Perrier has the most to say about the effects of Islam on the treatment of women in Moroccan society. She attributes primary responsibility for the subjugation of her gender to religious beliefs, saying that in Islam, 'woman is recognised as existing only for one purpose, the use and benefit – the pleasure and profit – of man. The result of this doctrine being, that she is kept by man in the condition which he believes conduces most to his gain and advantage, viz., absolute slavery and subjection to himself.'[71]

Perrier's remarks on what she terms the slavery of women in Moroccan society, which she says is primarily the fault of Islam, come in the middle of a discussion of racial slavery in Morocco. After discussing the differences and similarities between race-based slavery in North America and the system of slavery in Morocco, Perrier says forcefully:

> But besides this what may be called political slavery, there is another form of slavery existing in Morocco, which I shall lay before my readers, in order that they may consider it, as I did, in comparison with negro slavery; which latter is too generally taken as embodying the whole question of slavery, not only in Morocco, but elsewhere. I mean the enslavement of one sex to the other which is involved in the Moors, in which the female half of the population is kept; and which makes the whole fabric of domestic life in Morocco, nothing more than a system of slavery.[72]

Perrier says that the position of women in Morocco 'is one of the most complete and degrading [systems of] slavery it is possible to imagine';[73] She further contends that women are deprived of every 'mentally and physically healthful employment'[74] and that marriage customs, laws and societal notions of the 'proper' position of women are responsible for this. However, she places the primary responsibility on Islam and on notions of female chastity and women's roles. While admitting that the intentions of the religion to safeguard chastity, decency and morality are not unworthy goals, she says:

> That the means adopted for this end by no means attains it, is affirmed by almost all who have studied or written on this subject. The effect of the system is, on the contrary, totally to destroy all real purity and delicacy of mind, with that natural human pride and self-respect, which are the only real guardians of a woman's virtue. And the very seclusion in which they are kept, affords, as has been frequently shown by previous writers, a thousand facilities for secret immoralities, that it would be next to impossible to carry on undiscovered in a free state of society.[75]

While Perrier, the author most critical of her own religion, is the most vocal of the authors in expressing the view that Islam contributes substantially to the subjugation and ill-treatment of women in Morocco, other authors make the same point. Savory presents Islam's view of women in the following way: 'The Koran speaks of woman as an inferior being, an incomplete creation, needing no education, to be rigorously and jealously guarded all her life, and who after death may or may not be admitted into the Mohammedan heaven.'[76] Likewise, Wharton refers to the passivity of women as 'the soul of Islam',[77] and the Countess of Meath speaks of how 'Mohammedans' believe women must not mix with men.[78]

While it is not the intention of this paper to evaluate whether these authors' claims about the nature of Islam are true or false, a majority of the authors see Islam as the primary social institution responsible for perpetuating the inferior status of women within Moroccan society. Their own religious heritage, and the frequent historical animosity between Christianity and Islam, was probably at least partially responsible for this view.

Conclusions

Melman has argued that the ways in which Western women constructed the Oriental Other differed from the ways in which men constructed the Oriental Other, and that they were coloured by a unique, gender-informed historical experience within Western society. In her study of the eastern

Mediterranean, Melman concludes that European women often interpreted, viewed and constructed the Orient in a unique way. In contrast to the male-dominated historical canon, the writings of Western women about the Orient reflected a concern not only about the position of women within the Oriental society under discussion, but also an identification with the Oriental woman and, on a broader scale, with the subjugated and victimised Orient as well. The purpose of this study has been to elucidate the ways in which Western women viewed Moroccan women, and to determine the validity of Melman's conclusions as they apply to the western Middle East.

The writings of Perrier, Grove, Savory, Wharton, Meath, Howard-Vyse, Pleydell, de Righi, Elsner and Murray about the role of women within Moroccan society in the late nineteenth and early twentieth centuries have been used to determine the ways in which British and American female authors constructed the female Oriental Other and identified their own position with that of the Moroccan women they observed. While a variety of conclusions are drawn, the tendency to see the Orient in terms of their own gender experience is evident in many of their works. Perrier, Grove, Savory and Wharton are the best examples of this tendency; the notion of gender relations informs their work and, particularly in Perrier's case, leads to greater reflection on the role and status of women within their own societies. Melman's view that the creation of the Oriental 'Other' cannot be said to have been exclusively a male enterprise, and that female Western writers often constructed and identified the Oriental 'Other' in unique ways and in light of their own conception of gender relations, seems to have been equally true in the case of Morocco as, she concludes, it has been in the case of the eastern Mediterranean.

NOTES

1 Billie Melman, *Women's Orients: English Women and the Middle East, 1718–1918* (London, Macmillan, 1992).
2 Edward W. Said, *Orientalism* (New York, Vintage Books, 1979), p. 1.
3 *Ibid.*, p. 2.
4 Billie Melman, *op. cit.*, p. 1.
5 *Ibid.*, p. 5.

6 Said, *op. cit.*, p. 4. Said's fundamental argument is that the Orient was produced, or constructed, by the West and that the Orient is not something that can be said to exist objectively. Rather, according to Said, Western ways of seeing, writing, and speaking about the people, history, religion, customs, etc. of the East have resulted in the creation of an entity which has come to be called the Orient.

7 Melman, *op. cit.,* p. 1.

8 *Ibid.*, p. 316.

9 *Ibid.*, p. 6.

10 Amelia Perrier, *A Winter in Morocco* (London, Harvey S. King, 1873), p. v. Perrier does say, however, that her attention was first attracted to Tangier 'by circumstances which afterwards rendered it necessary for me to undertake the journey to, and reside for some length of time in, that town'.

11 *Ibid.*

12 Two examples of Perrier's unique, 'tongue-in-cheek' sense of humour deserve mention. While remarking on the selection of food in Tangier, she writes that 'though beef proper was so exceedingly scarce, ox tongue and brains were, judging by the frequency with which they appeared at the table, remarkably common . . . It is scarcely necessary to say that ordinarily an ox has but one tongue, and, even if he be remarkably intelligent, only brains sufficient to make one dish for a party of six; while he can supply several large joints of sirloin and ribs. How then came this extraordinary disproportion in Tangier? I narrowly scrutinised all the cattle I saw feeding on the Marshen or elsewhere with a view to an elucidation of the mystery. But I saw nothing in the configuration of their heads, to lead me to suppose that any of them had more than one tongue, or such a remarkable superfluity of brains as would enable him to supply an entree to half the dinner-tables in Tangier on the same day.' (p. 149). While remarking on the apothecary shops in Tangier, Perrier also displays her sense of humour, 'A friend of mine once sent for cod-liver oil, and got some rancid brown stuff, that had apparently been intended for burning in lamps, but had got too bad for that, and was now trying its chance as medicine.' (pp. 152–3).

13 Perrier's rather sceptical view of Christianity is evident in her discussion of religion in the context of Christian missionary work in Morocco. She remarks that she 'is not particularly interested in missions' (p. 230) but recognising that a substantial portion of her readership would be interested in the topic, she relates several anecdotes about missionary activity in Tangier. She tells the story of a missionary who, not speaking any Arabic, hired a Jew to translate his remarks to a Muslim audience, in the hopes of converting them to a 'correct' religious viewpoint. Perrier describes the sermon as follows: 'I need not detail it verbatim at third hand, as every one must know what it would be. Any missionary report of any mission will furnish an example. It of course explained to the hearers the complete falsity of the religion they belonged to, and the perfect truth of that of the preacher; and called upon them to immediately renounce their erroneous beliefs, and adopt his true ones instead.' (p. 232). However, in this instance, the Jewish interpreter, possessing a keen sense of humour in addition to an understanding of the delicate nature of his work, instead translated the missionary's comments to say things like 'This is an Englishman who has come to talk to you. Listen to him, and when he has done he will give you coffee. . . . He is a madman. What he is saying is nonsense; but when he is done, he will give you

coffee. . . . Have patience, it will soon be over now. He is getting tired, and then every one can drink as much as he like of coffee.' (pp. 232–3). Perrier remarks that this translation satisfied all parties – the missionary was impressed with the attention he received from his audience, the interpreter was pleased that he had done his job while not offending the audience with an accurate translation, and the audience was content with receiving coffee free of charge; thus, Perrier remarks that 'since all parties were pleased and satisfied, this, I should say, was one of the most successful missions ever undertaken in Tangier'. (p. 234). In addition, while recording her acquaintance with another missionary, she describes him as 'a kindly gentleman who never allowed his Christianity to . . . overcome his humanity'. (p. 242).

14 Agnes Grove, *Seventy-One Days' Camping in Morocco* (London, Longman, Greens, 1902), p. vi.
15 *Ibid.*, p. 7.
16 *Ibid.*, p. 9.
17 *Ibid.*, pp. 13–14.
18 Isabel Savory, *In the Tail of the Peacock* (London, Hutchinson, 1903), p. v.
19 *Chamber's Encyclopaedia* (1973 edn), s. v. 'Wharton, Edith Newbold Jones'.
20 Edith Wharton, *In Morocco* (New York, Charles Scribner's Sons, 1920), p. viii.
21 *Ibid.*
22 Countess of Meath, 'The First Woman's Hospital in Morocco', *The Nineteenth Century*, 43 (June 1898), 1003.
23 Countess of Meath, 'A Land of Woe', *The Nineteenth Century*, 49 (June 1901), 1050.
24 *Ibid.*, 1050–51.
25 Mrs Howard-Vyse, *A Winter in Tangier and Home through Spain* (London, Strangeways, 1882), p. vii.
26 Eleanor Rigo de Righi, *Holiday in Morocco* (London, G.T. Foulis, 1935), p. vi.
27 Eleanor Elsner, *The Magic of Morocco* (London, Herbert Jenkins, 1928), p. 13.
28 *Ibid.*, ch. 1.
29 Elizabeth Murray, *Sixteen Years of an Artist's Life in Morocco, Spain and the Canary Islands* (London, Hurst & Blackett, 1859), p. 34.
30 Perrier, *op. cit.*, p. 173.
31 *Ibid.*, p. 175.
32 *Ibid.*, p. 177.
33 *Ibid.*
34 *Ibid.*, p. 178.
35 *Ibid.*, p. 182.
36 *Ibid.*
37 *Ibid.*, p. 193.
38 *Ibid.*, pp. 193–4.
39 *Ibid.*, p. 292.
40 *Ibid.*, pp. 296–7.
41 Savory, *op. cit.*, p. 19.
42 *Ibid.*, p. 68.
43 *Ibid.*, pp. 77–8.
44 *Ibid.*, pp. 238–9.
45 *Ibid.*, p. 238.

46 *Ibid.*, pp. 239–40.
47 Howard-Vyse, *op. cit.*, p. 84.
48 Kathleen Mansel Pleydell, *Sketches of Life in Morocco* (London, Digby, Long, 1907), p. 150.
49 *Ibid.*, pp. 150–61.
50 Elsner, *op. cit.*, p. 188.
51 *Ibid.*, p. 65.
52 Perrier, *op. cit.*, pp. 305–6.
53 *Ibid.*, p. 350.
54 *Ibid.*, pp. 350–1.
55 Grove, *op. cit.*, p. 82.
56 *Ibid.*, pp. 82, 86.
57 Wharton, *op. cit.*, p. 189.
58 *Ibid.*, p. 193.
59 Perrier, *op. cit.*, p. 177.
60 Murray, *op. cit.*, p. 36.
61 Perrier, *op. cit.*, p. 305.
62 Grove, *op. cit.*, p. 148.
63 Murray, *op. cit.*, p. 36.
64 Perrier, *op. cit.*, pp. 145–7.
65 Savory, *op. cit.*, pp. 110, 127.
66 Howard-Vyse, *op. cit.*, p. 44.
67 Elsner, *op. cit.*, p. 292; Wharton, *op. cit.*, p. 51.
68 Elsner, *op. cit.*, pp. 290–1.
69 Murray, *op. cit.*, pp. 27, 34, 50.
70 For example, Howard-Vyse, *op. cit.*, p. 44; Elsner, *op. cit.*, p. 276.
71 Perrier, *op. cit.*, p. 37.
72 *Ibid.*, p. 336.
73 *Ibid.*, p. 337.
74 *Ibid.*, p. 342.
75 *Ibid.*
76 Savory, *op. cit.*, p. 107.
77 Wharton, *op. cit.*, p. 187.
78 Meath (1898), *op. cit.*, 1002.

Select Bibliography

al-Abbasi, Ali Bey (Domingo Badia-y-Leblich), *Voyages d'Ali Bey al-Abassi en Afrique et en Asie pendant les années 1803–1807* (Paris, Didot, 1814).

—*Travels of Ali Bey: in Morocco, Tripoli, Cyprus, Egypt, Arabia, Syria, and Turkey, between the Years 1803 and 1807* (2 vols., London, Longman, Hurst, Rees, Orme and Brown, 1816; repr. Westmead, Farnborough, Gregg International, 1970).

Abdel-Hakim, Sahar S., 'British Women Writers in Egypt in the Middle Decades of the Nineteenth Century: Sophia Poole, Harriet Martineau and Lucie Duff Gordon', unpublished doctoral thesis, University of Cairo, 1996.

Ahmed, Leila, *Edward W. Lane: A Study of His Life and Work and of British Ideas of the Middle East in the Nineteenth-Century* (London & New York, Longman, 1978).

Akdag, Mustafa, *The Origin of the Great Jelali Disorders* [in Turkish] (Ankara, 1963).

Akinian, Nerses, *Travel Account, Annals and Colophons of Simeon the Scribe of Poland* [in Armenian] (Vienna, 1936).

Aldridge, James, *Cairo* (London, Macmillan, 1969).

Alpini, Prosper, *Historia Ægypti naturalis* (2 vols., Leiden, Lugduni Batavorum apud Gerardum Potvliet, 1735).

Anderson, M.S., *The Eastern Question 1774–1923: A Study in International Relations* (London, Macmillan, 1974).

Anonymous, 'Review of *Incidents of Travel in Egypt, Arabia Petræ, and the Holy Land*', *The North American Review*, 45 (July 1837), 247–50.

—'Review of *Incidents of Travel in Egypt, Arabia Petræ, and the Holy Land*', *The North American Review*, 48 (January 1839), 181–206.

—'The Nile', *Harper's New Monthly Magazine*, 69:410 (July 1884), 165–80.

Antoninus of Piacenza, 'Itinerarium', *Corpus Christianorum*, ed. P. Geyer and O. Cuntz Series Latina 175 (Turhout, Belgium, 1965), 127–74.

Arberry, A.J., *British Orientalists* (London, William Collins, 1943).

Arif Pasha, Mahmud Salih, *Les Anciens Costumes de l'Empire Ottomane depuis l'origine de la monarchie jusqu'à la réforme du Sultan Mahmoud* [*Majmu'at tesavir 'uthmani*] (Paris, Lermercier, 1863–).

Armander, Primrose and Askhain Skipworth, *The Son of a Duck is a Floater* (London, Stacey International, 1985).

al-Armani, Abu Salih, *The Churches and Monasteries of Egypt and Some Neighbouring Countries Attributed to Abu Salih, the Armenian*, trans. from the original Arabic by B.T.A. Evetts, with added notes by Alfred J. Butler (Oxford, Clarendon Press, 1895).

Arnold, Dieter, *Die Tempel Ägyptens – Götterwohnungen, Kultstätten, Baudenkmäler* (Zurich, 1992).

Atiya, Aziz S., *The Copts and Christian Civilization* (Salt Lake City, University of Utah Press, 1979).

Auldjo, John, *Journal of a Visit to Constantinople and Some of the Greek Islands in the Spring and Summer of 1833* (London, Longman, 1835).

Avcioğlu, Nebahat, 'Peripatetics of Style: Travel Literature and the Political Appropriations of Turkish Architecture, 1737–1862', unpublished doctoral thesis, University of Cambridge, 1997.

Baedeker, Karl, *Palestine and Syria* (Leipzig, Baedeker, 1898).

Balzac, Honoré de, *La Lys dans la vallée* (Paris, 1836).

Beaufort, Emily de [afterwards E.A. Smythe, Viscountess Strangford], *Egyptian Sepulchres and Syrian Shrines* (London, Macmillan, 1861).

Beauvan, Henri de, *Relation iovrnaliere dv voyage dv Levant* (Nancy, Iacob Garnic, 1615, 1619).

Behzad, Faramarz, *Adam Olearius' 'Persianischer Rosenthal,' Untersuchungen zur Übersetzung von Saadis 'Golestan' im 17 Jahrhundert* (Göttingen, Vandenhoeck & Ruprecht, 1970).

Bell, Gertrude, *Safar Nameh: Or, Persian Pictures, a Book of Travel* (London, R. Bentley, 1894).

—*Poems from the Divan of Hafiz* (London, W. Heinemann, 1897).

—*Syria: The Desert and the Sown* (London, W. Heinemann, 1907).

—*The Letters of Gertrude Bell*, ed. Lady Florence Bell (London, Ernest Benn, 1927).

—*The Earlier Letters of Gertrude Bell*, ed. Elsa Richmond (London, Ernest Benn, 1937).

Bélon, Pierre, *Les Observations de plusieurs singularitez et choses memorables, trouuées en Grèce, Asie, Iudée, Égypte, Arabie, et autre pays estranges*, redigees en trois Liures, par Pierre Bélon du Mans (Paris, Guillaume Corrozet, 1553).

Belzoni, G., *Narrative of the Operations and Recent Discoveries within the Pyramids, Temples, Tombs, and Excavations in Egypt and Nubia; etc.* (London, John Murray, 1820; 3rd edn, 1822).

Ben Arieh, Yehoshua, *Painting the Holy Land in the Nineteenth Century* (Jerusalem, Tel Aviv & New York, 1996).

Bendiner, Kenneth Paul, 'The Portrayal of the Middle East in British Painting 1835–1860', unpublished doctoral thesis, Columbia University, 1979.

Bevis, Richard (ed.), *Bibliotheca Cisorientalia: An Annotated Checklist of Early English Travel Books on the Near and Middle East* (Boston, J.K. Hall, 1973).

Bierbrier, M.L. (ed.), *Who Was Who in Egyptology*, 3rd revised edn (London, Egypt Exploration Society, 1995).

Binning, Robert B.M., *A Journal of Two Years' Travel in Persia, Ceylon, etc.* (London, W.H. Allen, 1857).

Black, Jeremy, *The British Abroad: The Grand Tour in the Eighteenth Century* (London, Croom Helm, 1985).

Blanch, Lesley, *Pierre Loti: The Legendary Romantic* (New York, Harcourt Brace Jovanich, 1983).

Blashfield, Edwin Holland and E.W., 'Afloat on the Nile', *Scribner's Magazine*, 10 (December 1891), 663–81.

—'Day with the Donkey-boys', *Scribner's Magazine*, 11 (January 1892), 32–50.

Blount, Sir Henry, *A Voyage into the Levant: A Briefe Relation of a Journey, Lately Performed by Master H.B. Gentleman from England by Way of Venice, into Dalmatia, Sclavonia, Bosnah, Hungary, Macedonia, Thessaly, Thrace, Rhodes and Egypt unto Gran [sic] Cairo: With Particular Observations Concerning the Moderne Conditions of the Turkes and Other People under that Empire* (1634; London, printed by I.L. [John Legatt] for Andrew Crooke, 1636). Reprinted in *Collection of Voyages and Travels . . .* (London, printed by assignment from Messierus Churchill, for Thomas Osborne in Gray's Inn, 1752).

Blunt, Anne, *A Pilgrimage to Nejd* (2 vols., London, John Murray, 1881).

Booth, Bradford A. (ed.), *The Letters of Anthony Trollope* (London, Oxford University Press, 1952).

Bourrienne, Louis Antoine Fauvelet de, *Mémoires de Napoléon Bonaparte* (Paris, 1829).

Bowmann, Glenn, 'Contemporary Christian Pilgrim to the Holy Land', *The Christian Heritage in the Holy Land*, ed. Anthony O'Mahony (London, Scorpion Cavendish, 1995).

Bowring, Sir John, *Report on the State of Finances in Egypt* (London, 1840).

Bramsen, John, *Travels in Egypt, Syria, Palestine, Egypt and Greece, in the Years 1814 and 1815* (London, H. Colburn, 1815).

—*Letters of a Prussian Traveller, Descriptive of a Tour through Sweden, Prussia, Austria, Hungary, Istria, the Ionian Islands, Egypt, Syria, Rhodes, the Morea, Greece, Calabria, Italy, the Tyrol, the Banks of the Rhine, Hanover, Holstein, Denmark, Westphalia and Holland* (2 vols., London, H. Colburn. 1818).

Brauer, Erich, *Ethnologie der Jemenitischen Juden* (Heidelberg, 1934).

Brimmer, Martin and Minna (Timmins) Chapman, *Egypt: Three Essays on the History, Religion and Art of Ancient Egypt* (Cambridge, Mass., Houghton, Mifflin, 1892).

Broadhurst, R. (trans.), *The Travels of Ibn Jubayr* (London, Jonathan Cape, 1952).

Brockelmann, Carl, *History of Islamic Peoples*, trans. Joel Carmichael and Moshe Perlmann (New York, Capricorn Books, 1960).

Bronkhurst, Judith, ' "An Interesting Series of Adventures to Look Back Upon": William Holman Hunt's Visit to the Dead Sea in November 1854', *Pre-Raphaelite Papers*, ed. Leslie Parris (London, Tate Gallery/Allen Lane, 1984).

—'Holman Hunt's Picture Frames, Sculpture and Applied Art', *Re-Framing the Pre-Raphaelites: Historical and Theoretical Essays*, ed. Harding and Ellen (Aldershot & Brookfield, Vermont, Scolar Press, 1996).

Browning, Iain, *Palmyra* (Park Ridge, NJ, Noyes Press, 1979).

Buckingham, James Silk, *Travels in Palestine, etc.*, 2nd edn. (2 vols., London, Longman, 1821).

—*Travels among the Arab Tribes* (London, Longman, 1825).

—*Travels in Mesopotamia* (London, H. Colburn, 1827).

—*Travels in Assyria, Media, Persia etc.* (London, H. Colburn & R. Bentley, 1830).

—*Travels in Egypt, Nubia, Syria and the Holy Land* (London, John Murray, 1844).

—*Autobiography of James Silk Buckingham* (2 vols., London, Longman, Brown, Green and Longmans, 1855).

Burckhardt, John Lewis [= Ibraham ibn Abdullah], *Arabic Proverbs; Or, the Manners and Customs of the Modern Egyptians Illustrated from their Proverbial Sayings Current at Cairo, Translated and Explained*, ed. Sir William Ousely (1817; London, H. Colburn, 1830; repr. with an introduction by C.E. Bosworth, London, Curzon Press, 1984).

—*Travels in Nubia: By the Late John Lewis Burckhardt* (London, John Murray, 1819).

—*Travels in Syria and the Holy Land* (London, John Murray, 1822; repr. London, Darf, 1992).

Burton, Sir Richard Francis, *Personal Narrative of a Pilgrimage to Al-Madinah & Mecca*, Memorial Edition (3 vols., London, Longman, Brown, Green and Longmans, 1855–1856; 2 vols., Tylston and Edwards, 1893; repr. New York, Dover Publications, 1964).

Busbecq, Ogier Ghisele de, *The Turkish Letters of Ogier Ghisele de Busbecq* (Oxford University Press, 1927).

Butler, Alfred Joshua, *The Arab Conquest of Egypt* (Oxford, Clarendon Press, 1902).

Butler, Howard Crosby, *Sardis, The Excavations Part I 1910–1914* (Leiden, E.J. Brill, 1922).

Byron, George G.N. [Baron Byron], *Childe Harold's Pilgrimage* (London, John Murray, 1814).

—*Life of Lord Byron, with his Letters and Journals*, ed. Thomas Moore (1844; London, John Murray, 1851).

Cable, Lucy Leffingwell, 'On the Desert with Maude Adams', *The Ladies' Home Journal* (May 1907), 7–8, 72.

Cailliaud, Frédéric, *Voyages à l'oasis de Thèbes et dans les déserts 1815–18* (Paris, Imprimerie Royale, 1821).

Calvert, Frederick [Lord Baltimore], *A Tour to the East in the Years 1763 and 1764, with Remarks on the City of Constantinople and the Turks* (London, W. Richardson & S. Clark, 1767).

Campbell, Mary, *The Witness and the Other World: Exotic European Travel Writing, 400–1600* (Ithaca, Cornell University Press. 1988).

Capper, James, *Observations on the Passage to India, through Egypt, and across the Great Desert with Occasional Remark on the Adjacent*

Countries and also Sketches of the Different Routes (London, printed for W. Faden, Geographer to the King, 1783).

Carne, John, *Letters from the East: Written during a Recent Tour through Turkey, Egypt, Arabia, the Holy Land, Syria and Greece* (2 vols., London, H. Colburn, 1826; repr. 1830).

Casa, Jean Michel, 'Art From a Distance: Van Mour and Guardi', *Cornucopia*, 5 (1993–1994).

Çelebi, E., *Evliya Çelebi in Bitlis*, ed. R. Dankoff (Leiden, New York, Copenhagen, Cologne, 1990).

Chaillé-Long, Charles, *My Life in Four Continents* (London, Hutchinson, 1912).

Chardin, Chevalier, *Voyage en Perse et autres lieux de l'Orient* (London, Moses Pitt, 1686; repr. Amsterdam, 1735).

Chateaubriand, François-René, Vicomte de, *Itinéraire de Paris à Jérusalem* (Paris, Garnier-Flammarion, 1968; 3rd edn, Le Normant, 1812).

Chaudhuri, Nupur and Margaret Strobel (eds.), *Western Women and Imperialism, Complicity and Resistance* (Bloomington and Indianapolis, Indiana University Press, 1992).

Chiego, William J. (ed.), *Sir David Wilkie of Scotland 1785–1841* (Raleigh, NC, North Carolina Museum of Art, 1987).

Chirol, Valentine, *The Occident and the Orient* (Chicago, University of Chicago Press, 1924).

Chwolson, D., *Die Ssabier und der Ssabismus* (St Petersburg, 1856; repr. Amsterdam, 1965).

Clemens, Samuel Langhorne, *The Innocents Abroad* (Hartford, Conn., American Publishing Company, 1869).

Conder, Josiah, *The Modern Traveller* (30 vols., 1827; London, James Duncan, 1825–31), vol. 5.

Conner, Patrick (ed.), 'The Inspiration of Egypt: Its Influence on British Artists, Travellers and Designers', *1700–1900 Exhibition Catalogue* (Brighton, Brighton Borough Council, 1983).

Cook, J.M., *The Troad: An Archaeological and Topographical Study* (Oxford, Clarendon Press, 1973).

Cooley, James Ewing, *The American in Egypt; with Rambles through Arabia Petraea and the Holy Land, during the Years 1839 and 1840* (New York, D. Appleton, 1842).

Coullart, Paul and Jacques Vicari, *Le Sanctuaire de Baalshamin à Palmyre: Topographie et architecture* (Neuchâtel, Institut Suisse de Rome, 1969).

Cox, Percy Z., 'Some Excursions in Oman', *Geographical Journal* (1925).

Craven, Countess of, *A Journey through the Crimea to Constantinople: Letters* (London, H. Colburn, 1814).

Crinson, Mark, *Empire Building: Orientalism and Victorian Architecture* (London, Routledge, 1996).

Cunningham, Allan, *The Life of Sir David Wilkie and His Journals, Tours and Critical Remarks on Works of Art and a Selection from His Correspondence* (2 vols., London, John Murray, 1843).

Curtis, George William, *Nile Notes of a Howadji* (New York, Harper & Brothers, 1851).

Cyril of Jerusalem, 'Catecheses XIII:22', *The Works of Saint Cyril of Jerusalem*, ed. Leo McCauley (Washington, D.C., The Catholic University of America Press, 1968).

Daglish, R. (ed.), *The Cossacks: A Story of the Caucasus* [*Kazaki: Kavkazskasa povesm'*, written 1812–1863], trans. from Russian (Moscow, Foreign Languages Publishing House, n. d.).

Dalrymple, W., *In Xanadu: A Quest* (London, Flamingo/HarperCollins, 1989).

—*City of Djinns: A Year in Delhi* (London, HarperCollins, 1993).

Dalton, Richard, *Antiquities and Views in Greece and Egypt in 1751–2* (London, M. Cooper, 1791–1792).

Damer, Hon. M.G[eorgina] Emma (Seymour) Dawson, *Diary of a Tour in Greece, Turkey, Egypt and the Holy Land* (2 vols., London, H. Colburn, 1841).

Damiani, Anita, *Enlightened Observers: British Travellers to the Near East, 1715–1850* (Beirut, American University of Beirut, 1979).

David, Rosalie, *The Macclesfield Collection of Egyptian Antiquities* (Warminster, Aris & Phillips, 1980).

Davidson, A., *Muse of Wandering of Nikolay Gumilev* [in Russian] (Moscow, Nauka, 1992).

Davidson, Lilias Campbell, *Hints to Lady Travellers at Home and Abroad* (1887; repr. London, Iliffe, 1889).

Davies, W.D., *The Gospel and the Land: Early Christianity and Jewish Territorial Doctrine* (Berkeley, University of California Press, 1974).

Davis, Richard Harding, *The Rulers of the Mediterranean* (New York, Harper & Brothers, 1893).

—'Cairo as a Show-place', *Harper's Weekly*, 37 (8 July 1893), 642–3.

Deeken, A. and M. Boesel, *An den suessen Wassern Asiens* (Frankfurt, 1996).

Degenhard, Ursula, *Exotische Welten, Europäische Phantasien: Entdeckungs- und Forschungsreisen im Spiegel alter Bücher* (Stuttgart, Württembergische Landesbibliothek, 1987).

Demont, [Mrs], *Voyages and Travels of Her Majesty, Caroline Queen of Great Britain* (London, Jones, 1821).

Dye, William McEntyre, *Moslem Egypt and Christian Abyssinia* (New York, Atkin & Prout Printers, 1880).

Ebers, Georg Moritz, *Egypt: Descriptive, Historical and Picturesque*, trans. Samuel Birch with notes by Clare Bell (2 vols., London, Cassell, 1878; repr. 1887).

Edwards, Amelia, *A Thousand Miles up the Nile* (London, Longmans, 1877; repr. Century Publishing, 1982; also Leipzig, Bernhard Tauchnitz, 1878; also repr. London, Parkway, 1993).

—*Pharoahs, Fellahs and Explorers* (New York & London, James R. Osgood & McIlvaine, 1891).

Egeria, *Egeria's Travels*, trans. and ed. John Wilkinson (London, SPCK, 1971).

—'Itinerarium', *Corpus Christianorum*, ed. A. Franceschini and R. Weber, Series Latina 175 (Turnhout, Belgium, 1965).

Egerton, Henrietta Grey, 'Camp Life and Pig-Sticking in Morocco', *The Nineteenth Century*, 182 (April 1892), 623–30.

Elsner, Eleanor, *The Magic of Morocco* (London, Herbert Jenkins, 1928).

Elsner, John, 'Pausanius: A Greek Pilgrim in the Roman World', *Past and Present*, 135 (1992), 3–29.

E.M. [Emile Prisse d'Avennes, fils], *Notice biographique sur Emile Prisse d'Avennes voyageur français, archéologue, égyptologue et publiciste* (Paris, 1896).

Emerson, Ralph Waldo, *The Letters of Ralph Waldo Emerson*, ed. Ralph L. Rusk (6 vols., New York and London, Columbia University Press, 1929).

—*The Journals and Miscellaneous Notebooks of Ralph Waldo Emerson*, ed. William H. Gilman (Cambridge, Mass., Harvard University Press, 1973).

English, George Bethune, *A Narrative of the Expedition to Dongola and Senaar, under the Command of His Excellence Ismael Pasha, Undertaken by Order of His Highness Mehemmed Ali Pasha, Viceroy of Egypt by an American in the Service of the Viceroy* (London, John Murray, 1822).

Eraqi-Kloreman, Bat-Zion, 'Jewish and Muslim Messianism in Yemen', *IJMES*, 22 (1990), 201–28.

Erdbrink, C. Bosscha, *At the Threshold of Felicity: Ottoman-Dutch Relations During the Embassy of Cornelis Calkoen at the Sublime Porte 1726–1744* (Ankara, Türkīrih Kurumu Basimevi, 1975).

Esposito, John L., *Women in Muslim Family Law* (Syracuse University Press, 1982).

Fagan, B. *The Rape of the Nile: Tomb Robbers, Tourists and Archaeologists in Egypt* (New York, Mcdonald & Jane's, 1977).

Farman, Elbert Eli, *Along the Nile with General Grant* (New York, The Grafton Press, 1904).

Favart, Charles Simon, *Les Trois Sultanes* (Paris, 1761; repr. 1826).

Fay, Eliza, *Original Letters from India (1779–1815): Containing a Narrative of a Journey through Egypt, and the Author's Imprisonment at Calicut by Hydar Ally, to which is Added an Abstract of Three Subsequent Voyages to India* (Calcutta, 1817), ed. E.M. Forster (New York, Harcourt, Brace, 1925; repr. London, Hogarth Press, 1986).

Fetridge, William Pembroke, *Harper's Hand-book for Travellers in Europe and the East* (New York, Harper & Brothers, 1871).

Fife, Sir John (ed.), *Manual of the Turkish Bath* (London, Lond, 1865).

Flaubert, G., *Notes de voyages; voyage en Égypte, 1849–1850* (2 vols., Rouen, 1930).

—*Souvenirs, notes et pensées intimes* (Paris, Butchet-Chastel, 1965).

—*Flaubert in Egypt: A Sensibility on Tour*, ed. and trans. Francis Steegmuller (London, Bodley Head and New York, Little, Brown, 1972).

—*Correspondance*, 1re série (2 vols., Paris, 1910), ed. Jean Bruneau (Paris, Gallimard, Bibliothèque de la Pléiade, 1973).

—*Lettres à George Sand. Correspondance* (Paris, G. Charpentier, 1889; new edn, 1981).

Fodor, A., 'The Origins of the Arabic Legends of the Pyramids', *Acta Orientalia Academiae Scientiarum Hungaricae* 23:3 (1970), 335–63.

Forbin, Louis Nicolas Philippe Auguste, comte de, *Travels in Egypt, Being a Continuation of Travels in the Holy Land, in 1817–18* (London, printed for Sir R. Phillips and Co., 1819).

—*Voyage dans le Levant en 1817 et 1818* (Paris, Imprimerie Royale, 1819),

Forster, Charles Thornton and F.H.B. Daniell (trans.), *The Life and Letters of Ogier Ghiselin de Bushecq* (London, C. Kegan Paul, 1881) in *The Orientalists: Delacroix to Matisse. European Painters in North Africa and the Near East* (London, Royal Academy Exhibition Catalogue, 1984).

Forster, Edward Morgan, 'Eliza in Egypt' in *Pharos and Pharillon* (London, Michael Haag, 1983), 59–72.

Frank, Katherine, *Lucie Duff Gordon: A Passage to Egypt* (London, Hamish Hamilton, 1994).

Frankland, Captain Charles Colville, *Travels to and from Constantinople in the Years 1827 and 1828* (2 vols., London, H. Colburn, 1829).

Fresne-Canaye, Philippe du, *Voyage du Levant* (Paris, 1573; repr. 1897).

Frith, F., *Cairo, Sinai, Jerusalem, and the Pyramids of Egypt: A Series of Sixty Photographic Views by Francis Frith with Descriptions by Mrs. Poole and Reginald Stuart Poole*, Issued in 20 pts., 60 albumen prints, approx 8¾" x 6½" 225 x 165mm (London, J.S. Virtue, 1860; repr. 1861).

Gabriel, Alfons, *Die Erforschung Persiens: Die Entwicklung der abendländischen Kenntnis der Geographie Persiens* (Vienna, A. Holzhausen, 1952).

Galt, John, *Letters From the Levant: Containing Views of the State of Society, Manners, Opinions and Commerce in Greece and Several of the Principal Islands of the Archipelago* (London, Galt, 1813).

Geary, G., *Through Asiatic Turkey* (2 vols., London, 1878).

Gendron, Charisse, 'Lucie Duff Gordon's *Letters from Egypt*', *Ariel*, 17 (1986), 4–61.

Ghistele, Joos van, *Le Voyage en Égypte de Joos van Ghistele, 1482–1483*, trans. from the Flemish, introduced and annotated by Renée Bauwens-Préaux (Cairo, IFAO, 1976).

al-Ghoneim, A.Y., *Geography of Egypt from the Book al-Mamalik wa al-masalik* (Kuwait, 1980).

Gibson, Charles Dana, *Sketches in Egypt* (New York, Doubleday & McClure, 1899).

Gibson, Shimon and Joan Taylor, *Beneath the Church of the Holy Sepulchre Jerusalem: The Archaeology and Early History of Traditional Golgotha* (London, Palestine Exploration Fund, 1994).

Gidney, W.T., *The History of the London Society for Promoting Christianity among the Jews from 1809 to 1908* (London, LSPCJ, 1908).

Gilpin, Lillian C., 'To the Pyramids with a Baby Carriage', *Harper's Weekly*, 52 (12 September 1908), 30.

—'City of Noise and Flies', *Harper's Weekly*, 52 (31 October 1908), 17.

Ginzburg, E., *On Lyricism* [in Russian] (Moscow & Leningrad, Sovetskii pisatel, 1964).

Gliddon, George Robins, *Appendix to The American in Egypt* (Philadelphia, Merrihew & Thompson, 1842).

Göhring, L., 'Die Beziehungen des Malers Karl Haag zu seiner Vaterstadt Erlangen', *Erlanger Heimatblätter*, 46 (1930), 185–8.

Gordon, Lucie Duff, *Letters from Egypt 1863–1865* (London, Macmillan, 1865; repr. 1983; repr. Virago, 1986).

—*Last Letters from Egypt to which are Added Letters from the Cape*, ed. Janet Ross (London, Macmillan, 1875).

Greaves, J., *An Account of the Latitude of Constantinople and Rhodes; Written by the Learned Mr. John Greaves, Sometime Professor of Astronomy in the University of Oxford, and Directed to the Most Reverend James Ussher, Archbishop of Ardmagh* in *A Collection of Curious Travels & Voyages*, ed. John Ray (London, 1693).

Grelot, Guillaume-Joseph, *Relation nouvelle d'un voyage de Constantinople* (1680; repr. Paris, 1681).

Grohmann, Adolf, *Studien zur historischen Geographie und Verwaltung des frühmittelalterlichen Ägypten* (Vienna, In Kommission bei R.M. Rohrer, 1959).

Grove, Lady Agnes, *Seventy-One Days Camping in Morocco* (London, Longmans, Green, 1902).

Guiterman, Helen, *David Roberts R.A. 1796–1864* (London, Helen Guiterman, 1978).

Gumilev, N., *Collected works* [in Russian] (4 vols., Moscow, Terra, 1991).

Gurney, J.D., 'Pietro Della Valle: The Limits of Perception', *BSOAS*, 49 (1986), 103–16.

G[ushakian], Th[orgom] E[piskopos], *Ancient and Modern Armenian Churches in Egypt* [in Armenian] (Cairo, 1927).

H., G. S. and R. De P. Tytus, 'On the Nile', *Harper's New Monthly Magazine*, 109 (October 1904), 693–701.

Haarmann, Ulrich (ed.), *Das Pyramidenbuch des Abu Ga'far al-Idrisi* (Beirut-Stuttgart, 1991).

Habachi, Labib, 'The Monument of Biyahmu', *ASAE*, 40 (Cairo, 1940), 721–32.

Habesci, E., *The Present State of the Ottoman Empire* (London, 1984).

Hahn-Hahn, Ida Marie Louise Sophie Friederike Augusta, *Orientalische Briefe* (Berlin, Dunker, 1842).

Halls, John James (ed.), *Life and Correspondence of Henry Salt . . . Consul General in Egypt* (2 vols., London, R. Bentley, 1834).

Halévy, Joseph, 'Voyage au Nedjran', *Bulletin de la Société de Géographie de Paris*, 5 (1873), 5–31.

Halsband, Robert, *The Life of Lady Mary Wortley Montagu* (Oxford, Clarendon Press, 1956)

—(ed.), *The Complete Letters of Lady Mary Wortley Montagu* (3 vols., Oxford, Clarendon Press, 1965–1967).

Hamst, [Olphar Hamst], *Sketches of Turkey in 1831 and 1832* (New York, 1833).

Harman, Henry Martyn, *A Journey to Egypt and the Holy Land, in 1869–1870* (Philadelphia, J.B. Lippincott, 1873).

Hassan, Fekri, 'Town and Village in Ancient Egypt: Ecology, Society and Urbanization', *The Archaeology of Africa*, ed. I. Shaw *et al.* (London, Routledge, 1993), 551–69.

—'The Dynamics of a Riverine Civilization: A Geo-archaeological Perspective on the Nile Valley, Egypt', *World Archaeology*, 29:1 (1997), 51–74.

Hatem, Mervat, 'Through Each Other's Eyes' in N. Chaudhuri and M. Strobel (eds.), *Western Women and Imperialism* (Indiana, Indiana University Press, 1992).

Hentsch, Thierry, *Imagining the Middle East* (Montreal, Black Rose Books, 1992).

Herbert, Th., *Travels in Persia 1627–1629*, abr. and ed. Sir William Foster, with an Introduction and Notes (London, G. Routledge, 1928).

Hobhouse, John Cam, *A Journey through Albania and other Provinces of Turkey in Europe and Asia to Constantinople during the Years 1809 and 1810* (London, J. Cawthorn, 1813).

Hodgson, Marshall, *The Venture of Islam: Conscience and History in a World Civilization* (Chicago, University of Chicago Press, 1974).

Holland, Frederick W., 'Eastern Cities: Cairo the Victorious', *Lippincott's Magazine of Popular Literature and Science*, 7 (February 1871), 197–202.

Holland Sir Henry, *Travels in the Ionian Isles, Albania, Thessaly, Macedonia etc. during the years 1812 and 1813* (2 vols., 1815; repr. London, 1819).

Homayoun, Gholamali, *Iran in europäischen Bildzeugnissen vom Ausgang des Mittelalters bis ins achtzehnte Jahrhundert*, unpublished dissertation (Cologne, 1967).

Hopkins, Hugh E., *Sublime Vagabond: The Life of Joseph Wolff – Missionary Extraordinary* (Worthing, Churchman, 1984).

Howard-Vyse, L., *A Winter in Tangier and Home through Spain* (London, Strangeways, 1882).

Hughes, Rev. T.S., *Travels in Greece and Albania*, 2nd edn (2 vols., London, 1830).

Hunt, William Holman, 'The Pre-Raphaelite Brotherhood: A Fight for Art', *Contemporary Review*, 49 (June 1886), 828.

—*Pre-Raphaelitism and the Pre-Raphaelite Brotherhood* (London, Macmillan, 1905).

Hunter, William, *Travels through France, Turkey and Hungary to Vienna in 1792*, 3rd edn (2 vols., London, 1803).

Hutton, C.A., 'The Travels of "Palmyra" Wood in 1750–51', *Journal of Hellenic Studies*, 47:1 (1927), 102–29.

Ibn al-Akfani, *A Survey of the Muhammedan Sciences*, ed. A. Sprenger (Calcutta, 1849).

Ibn Battuta, *The Travels of Ibn Battuta, A.D. 1325–1354*, trans. H.A.R. Gibb with revisions and notes from the Arabic text, ed. C. Defrémery and B. R. Sanguinetti (Cambridge University Press for the Hakluyt Society, 1958).

Ibn Taymia, *Public Duties in Islam: The Institution of Hisba* (Leicester, Islamic Foundation, 1985).

Inalçik, Halil, 'The Heyday and Decline of the Ottoman Empire' in P.M. Holt, Ann K.S. Lambton and Bernard Lewis (eds.), *The Cambridge History of Islam*, vol. I (Cambridge, Cambridge University Press, 1970), 347–50.

Institut du Monde Arabe, *Jordanie, sur les pas des archéologues,* catalogue of the exhibition, 13 June–5 October 1997 (Paris, Institut du Monde Arabe, 1997).

Irby, Hon. C.L. and J. Mangles, *Travels in Egypt and Nubia, Syria, and Asia Minor, during the Years 1817 and 1818* (London, privately printed, 1823; repr. T. White Printers, 1823).

—*Travels in Egypt, Nubia, Syria, and the Holy Land* (London, John Murray, 1844).

Irwin, Eyles, *A Series of Adventures in the Course of a Voyage up the Red Sea, on the Coasts of Arabia and Egypt and of a Route through the Desarts of Thebais, hitherto Unknown to the European Traveller, in the Year M.DCC.LXXVII in Letters to a Lady* (Dublin, printed for W. Sleater, 1780; London, J. Dodsley, 1787). The two-volume London edition of 1787 contains in addition *A Supplement of a Voyage from Venice to Latichea, and of a Route through the Deserts of Arabia, by Aleppo, Bagdad, and the Tigris to Busrah, in 1780 and 1781* (2 vols., London, J. Dodsley, 1787).

—*Reise auf dem Rothen Meer auf der Arabische und Ægyptische Küste und durch d. Thebaischen Wüste* (Leipzig, Weidmann, 1781).

—*Voyage à la Mer Rouge sur les côtes de l'Arabie, en Égypte et dans les deserts de la Thébaïde; suivi d'un voyage Bassorah, etc. en 1780 et 1781,* trans. from English by J.P. Parraud (2 vols., Paris, 1792).

Isaacs, Albert Augustus, *Biography of the Rev. Henry Aron Stern: For More Than Forty Years a Missionary among the Jews – Containing his Account of his Labours and Travel in Mesopotamia, Persia, Arabia, Turkey, Abyssinia and England* (London, J. Nisbet, 1886).

al-Jabartī, Abd al-Rahmān, *Napoleon in Egypt: al-Jabarti's Chronicle of the French Occupation, 1798* (New York, Markus Wiener, 1993).

J[olliffe], T.R., *Letters from Palestine, Descriptive of a Tour through Galilee and Judaea, with Some Account of the Dead Sea, and of the Present State of Jerusalem,* 2nd edn, to which are added, *Letters from Egypt* (London, James Black, 1820).

Jomier, J., *Le Mahmal et la caravane égyptienne des pèlerins de La Mecque, XIIIᵉ–XXᵉ siècles* (Cairo, 1953).

Jones, George, *Excursions to Cairo, Jerusalem, Damascus, and Balbec from the United States Ship Delaware, during her Recent Cruise* (New York, Van Nostrand & Dwight, 1836).

Jones, Sir William, 'A Prefatory Discourse to an Essay on the History of the Turks', *The Works of Sir William Jones* (13 vols., London, 1807).

Juler, Caroline, *Les Orientalistes de l'école italienne* (Paris, ACR Edition, 1994).

Kabbani, Rana, *Europe's Myths of Orient: Devise and Rule* (London, Macmillan, 1986).

—*Imperial Fictions: Europe's Myths of Orient* (London, Pandora, 1994).

Kamal, Ahmad, *Tarwih al-nafs fī madinat al-Shams* (*Heliopolis*) (Cairo, 1896).

Kapoïan-Kouymjian, Angèle, *L'Égypte vue par des Arméniens, XIᵉ–XVIIᵉ siècles* (Paris, Fondation Singer-Polignac, 1988).

Kardashian, Ardashes H., *Material for the History of the Armenians in Egypt* [in Armenian] (Cairo, 1943).

Keane, John F., *Six Months in the Hejaz: An Account of the Mohammedan Pilgrimage to Meccah and Medinah* (London, Ward and Downey, 1887).

Kendall, James E., 'A Tour in Egypt', *The American Catholic Quarterly Review*, 31 (October 1906), 671–9.

Khalifa, Hajji, *Kashf al-zunun 'an asami al-Kutub wa'l-funun. Lexicon bibliographicum et encyclopaedicum a Mustafa ben Abdallah Katib Jelebi dicto et nomine Haji Khalifa celebrato compositum. Ad codicem Vindobonensium, Parisiensium et Berolinensis fidem primum edidit latine vertit et commentaria indicibusque instruxit Gustavus Fluegel* (7 vols., Leipzig, Leiden, 1835–1858).

al-Kindi, *Fadā'il Misr*, a new edition by Ali Muhammad Umar (repr. Cairo, 1997).

Kinglake, A.W., 'The Rights of Women', *The Quarterly Review* (December 1844).

Kinglake, A.W., *Eōthen, or Traces of Travel Brought Home from the East* (London, John Olivier, 1844; repr. Marlboro, Vt., The Marlboro Press, 1992).

Knecht, Justin, *Belmont und Konstanze* (1787).

Knightley, Phillip and Colin Simpson, *The Secret Lives of Lawrence of Arabia* (London, Nelson, 1969).

Kobak, Annette, *Isabelle: The Life of Isabelle Eberhardt* (New York, Alfred A. Knopf, 1988).

Kosciow, Zbigniew, *Symeon Lehacy (Szymon z Polski). Zapiski Podrozne* (Warsaw, 1991).

Kurz, M. and P. Linant de Bellefonds, 'Linant de Bellefonds: Travels in Egypt, Sudan and Arabia Petraea, 1818–1828' in P. and J. Starkey (eds.), *Travellers in Egypt* (London, I.B. Tauris, 1998).

Laborde, Léon Emmanuel Simon Joseph, Marquis de, *Journey through Arabia Petraea, in Mount Sinai, and the Excavated City of Petra, the Edom of the Prophecies* (London, John Murray, 1836).

—*Pétra retrouvée. Voyage de l'Arabie Pétrée, 1828. Léon de Laborde et Linant de Bellefonds*, preface and notes by Chr. Augé and P. Linant de Bellefonds (Paris, Girard, 1830; repr. Paris, Pygmalion, 1994).

Lamartine, Alphonse de, *Voyage en Orient: souvenirs, impressions, pensées et paysages pendant un voyage en Orient (1832–1833) ou Notes d'un voyageur* (4 vols., Paris, C. Gosselin, 1835; repr. Paris, Firmin Didot, 1849).

Landow, George P., 'William Holman Hunt's "Oriental Mania" and his Uffizi Self-Portrait', *Art Bulletin*, 64 (December 1982), 648.

—'William Holman Hunt's Letters to Thomas Seddon', *Bulletin of The John Rylands University Library of Manchester*, 66 (1983–4), 152.

Lane, Edward William, *An Account of the Manners and Customs of the Modern Egyptians, Written in Egypt during the Years 1833–1835* (2 vols., London, 1836; repr. London, Charles Knight, 1846; repr. The Hague and London, East–West Publications, 1981; also repr. Cairo, Livres de France, 1978; repr. in 2 vols., London, 1849; 5th rev. edn, ed. E. Stanley Poole, London, John Murray, 1860; also repr. New York, Dover 1973).

—trans., *The Thousand and One Nights* (3 vols., London, Charles Knight, 1839–41).

Lansing, Gulian, 'A Visit to the Convent of Sittna (Our Lady), Damiane', *Harper's New Monthly Magazine*, 28:168 (May 1864), 757–74.

Lechevalier, J.-B., *Voyage de la Troade fait dans les années 1785 et 1786* (Paris, 1799).

Le Hay, Jacques, *Recueil de cent estampes representant différentes nations du Levant, tirées sur les tableaux peints d'après nature en 1707 et 1708 par les ordres de M. de Ferriol, ambassadeur du roi à la Porre. Et gravées en 1712 et 1713 par les soins de M. Le Hay*, with new editions in 1714 and 1715 (Paris, St le Hay; Sr Duchange, 1714; Jacques Collomat, 1715).

Leon, Edward De, 'A Bridal Reception in the Hareem of the Queen of Egypt', *Lippincott's Magazine of Popular Literature and Science*, 16 (September 1875), 379–83.

Lermontov, Mikhail Yur'evich, *Geroi Nashego Vremeni* (*A Hero of our Time*), 1841, trans. from the Russian by Vladimir Nabokov in collaboration with Dimitri Nabokov (New York, Doubleday, 1958).

Lewis, Bernard, *The Muslim Discovery of Europe* (New York, Norton, 1982).

—*Islam in History* (Chicago, Open Court, 1993).

Lewis, J.M., *John Frederick Lewis, R.A., 1805–1876* (Leigh-on-Sea, Lewis, 1978).

Lewis, Reina, *Gendering Orientalism: Race, Femininity and Representation* (London, Routledge, 1996).

Light, Capt Henry, *Travels in Egypt, Nubia, Holy Land, Mount Libanan and Cyprus in the Year 1814* (London, printed Weybridge, Rodwell & Martin, 1818).

Linde, Paul and Justin Wintie, *A Dictionary of Arabic and Islamic Proverbs* (London, Routledge & Kegan Paul, 1984).

Lithgow, William, *A Most Delectable and True Discourse of an Admired and Painefull Peregrination from Scotland to the Most Famous Kingdomes in Europe, Asia and Affricke* (London, printed by Nicholas Okes, and are to be sold by Thomas Archer, 1614; 2nd impression 1616; repr. New York and Amsterdam, Da Capo Press and Theatrum Orbis Terrarum, 1971); 2nd edn, *The Total Discourse of the Rare Adventures and Painefull Peregrinations of Long Nineteene Years Travayle From Scotland to the most famous Kingdoms in Europe, Asia and Africa*, 1632; repr. Glasgow, James MacLehose & Sons, Publisher to the University, 1906; new repr. ed. Gilbert Phelps, London, 1974.

Llewellyn, B., 'Petra and the Middle East', *The Connoisseur* (June 1980), 123.

—'The Islamic Inspiration. John Frederick Lewis: Painter of Islamic Egypt', *The Society of Antiquaries of London*, ed. S. Macready and F.H. Thompson, Occasional Paper (New Series), 7 (1985).

—(comp.), *The Orient Observed: Images of the Middle East from the Searight Collection* (London, Victoria & Albert Museum, 1989).

—'Luigi Mayer, Draughtsman to His Majesty's Ambassador at the Ottoman Porte', *Watercolours*, 5:4 (Winter 1990), 9–13.

—'Carl Haag', *The Dictionary of Art* (London, Macmillan, 1996).

—'J.F. Lewis and Frank Dillon: Two Interpretations of Islamic Domestic Interiors in Cairo', *Travellers in Egypt*, ed. P. and J. Starkey (London, I.B. Tauris, 1998).

Lloyd, Christopher, *English Corsairs on the Barbary Coast* (London, Collins, 1981).

Lockhart, Laurence, 'European Contacts with Persia', *The Cambridge History of Iran*, ed. Peter Jackson (Cambridge University Press, 1986).

Longford, Elizabeth, *A Pilgrimage of Passion: The Life of Wilfrid Scawen Blunt* (London, Weidenfeld and Nicolson, 1979).

Lorimer, J.G., *Gazetteer of the Persian Gulf, Omān, and Central Arabia* (2 vols., Calcutta, Government of India, 1908–1915; repr. Farnborough, Gregg International, 1970).

Loring, William Wing, *A Confederate Soldier in Egypt* (New York, Dodd, Mead, 1884).

Lovell, Mary S., *A Scandalous Life: The Biography of Jane Digby el Mezrab* (London, Fourth Estate, 1995).

Lowe, Lisa, *Critical Terrains: French and British Orientalisms* (Ithaca, NY, Cornell University Press, 1992).

Lutyens, Mary (ed.), 'Letters from Sir John Everett Millais, Bart, P.R.A. (1829–1896) and William Holman Hunt, O.M. (1827–1910) in the Henry E. Huntington Library, San Marino, California', *Walpole Society*, 44 (1972–1974).

MacFarlane, Charles, *Constantinople in 1828* (2 vols., London, Saunders & Otley, 1829).

Macgill, Thomas, *Travels in Turkey Italy and Russia during the years 1803, 1804, 1805 and 1806* (2 vols., London, John Murray, 1808).

MacKenzie, John M., *Orientalism: History, Theory and the Arts* (Manchester & New York, Manchester University Press & St Martin's Press, 1995).

Mackintosh-Smith, Tim, *Yemen: Travels in Dictionary Land* (London, John Murray, 1997).

Madden, Richard Robert, *Egypt and Mohammed Ali, Illustrative of the Condition of his Slaves and Subjects* (London, 1841).

—*Travels in Turkey, Egypt, Nubia, and Palestine, in 1824, 1825, 1826 & 1827* (2 vols., London, H. Colburn, 1829).

Madox, John, *Excursions in the Holy Land, Egypt, Nubia, Syria, &c. Including a Visit to the Unfrequented District of the Hauran* (2 vols., London, R. Bentley, 1834).

Manley, Deborah, *The Nile: A Traveller's Anthology* (London, Cassell, 1991).

Manoncourt, C.N. Sonnini de, *Travels in Upper and Lower Egypt*, trans. Henry Hunter (London, J. Debrett, 1800; repr. Westmead Gregg International Publishers, 1972).

—*Voyage en Grèce et en Turquie fait par ordre de Louis XVI* (2 vols., Paris, 1801).

Mans, P. Raphael Du, *Estat de la Perse en 1660, par Le P. Raphael Du Mans, Supérieur de la Mission des Capucins d'Ispahan*, ed. Ch. Schefer (Paris, 1890).

Mansel, Philip, *Constantinople: City of the World's Desire, 1453–1924* (Harmondsworth, Penguin, 1997).

al-Maqrizi, Ahmad ibn 'Ali Taqi al-Din Abu al-'Abbas, *Khitat*, I (Beirut, Dar al-Kutub al-'Ilmiyya, 1998).

Marana, Giovanni Paolo, *The Turkish Spy* (8 vols., 1687–1694; London, printed by J. Leake for Henry Rhodes, 1691).

—*L'Espion des grands seigneurs, dans les cours des princes chrétiens, ou Mémoirs pour servir à l'histoire de ce siècle depuis 1637 jusqu'à 1682* (6 vols., Amsterdam & Paris, 1684).

—*L'Espion du grand Seigneur, et ses relations secrètes envoyées au divan de Constantinople et découvertes à Paris* (2 vols., Amsterdam & Paris, 1684–1686).

—*L'Espion dans les cours des princes chrétiens, ou lettres et mémoires d'un envoyé secret de la Porte dans les cours de l'Europe* (54 vols., Cologne and Paris, 1696).

Markus, Robert, *The End of Ancient Christianity* (Cambridge University Press, 1990).

—'How on Earth Could Places Become Holy? Origins of the Christian Idea of Holy Places', *Journal of Early Christian Studies*, 2:3 (1994), 257–71.

Marsot, Afaf Lutfi al-Sayyid, *Egypt in the Reign of Muhammad Ali* (Cambridge University Press, 1984).

Martin, Abbé, *Voyage à Constantinople fait à l'occasion de l'ambassade de M le Comte de Choiseul-Gouffier à la Porte Ottomane* (1819).

Martineau, Harriet, *Eastern Life: Present and Past* (Philadelphia & London, Lee & Blanchard, 1848).

Masson, Flora, 'Holman Hunt and the Story of a Butterfly', *Cornhill Magazine*, n.s., 39:173 (November 1910), 644.

Masson, Paul R., *Histoire du commerce français dans le Levant au XVIII*
siècle (1896; Paris, 1911; repr. 1967).

Matar, Nabil I., *Islam in Britain, 1558-1685* (Cambridge University
Press, 1998).

Matran, R., *Istanbul dans la seconde moitié du XVII* *siècle. Essai d'histoire*
institutionelle, économique et sociale, Bibliothèque Archéologique et
Historique de l'Institut Français d'Archéologie d'Istanbul, 12 (Paris,
l'Institut Français d'Archéologie d'Istanbul, 1962).

Mayer, Luigi, *Views in Turkey in Europe and Asia Comprising Romelia,*
Bulgaria, Wallachia, Syria and Palestine (London, 1801–1806).

—*Views in Egypt from the Original Drawings in the Possession of Sir Robert*
Ainslie, taken during his Embassy to Constantinople (London, Bowyer,
1801–1804).

—*Views in Palestine* (London, 1801–1804).

—*Views in the Ottoman Empire, Chiefly in Caramania* (London, 1803).

—*Views in the Ottoman Dominions* (London, 1810).

—*A Series of Twenty-Four Views Illustrative of the Holy Scriptures Selected*
from Sir Robert Ainslie's Celebrated Collection of Drawings (London,
1833).

Mazuel, J., *L'Oeuvre géographique de Linant de Bellefonds: étude de géographie*
historique (Cairo, Société Royale Géographie d'Égypte, 1937).

McClellan, George B., 'The War in Egypt', *Century Illustrated Monthly*
Magazine, 24 (1882), 784–88.

Meath, Countess of, 'The First Woman's Hospital in Morocco', *The*
Nineteenth Century, 43 (June 1898), 1002–7.

—'A Land of Woe', *The Nineteenth Century*, 49 (June 1901), 1050–5.

Melman, Billie, *Women's Orients: English Women and the Middle East,*
1718–1918. Sexuality, Religion, and Work (Ann Arbor, University
of Michigan, 1992; London, Macmillan, 1992).

Melville, Lewis, pseud. [i.e. Lewis Saul Benjamin], *Lady Mary Wortley*
Montagu, Her Life and Letters 1689–1762 (Boston and New York,
Houghton Mifflin and London, Hutchinson, 1925).

Merezhkovsky, D.S., *It Was and Will Be. Diaries 1910–1925* [in
Russian], (Petrograd, 1915).

Meynell, Alice, 'William Holman Hunt, Part III, The Artist's Home and
Studio', *Art Annual* (1893), 28.

Middleton, Dorothy, *Victorian Lady Travellers* (New York, Dutton,
1965).

Miles, S.L., 'On the Route between Sohar and el-Bereymi in Oman', *Journal of the Asiatic Society of Bengal,* 46 (1877).

—'Journal of an Excursion in Oman', *Geographical Journal,* 7 (1896).

—'Across the Green Mountains of Oman', *Geographical Journal,* 18 (1901).

—*The Countries and Tribes of the Persian Gulf* (London, Harrison, 1919; 2nd edn (London, Frank Cass, 1966).

Mills, Sara, *Discourses of Difference: An Analysis of Women's Travel Writing and Colonialism* (London, Routledge, 1991).

Mitchell, Timothy, *Colonising Egypt* (Cambridge University Press, 1988).

Monro, Rev. Vere, *A Summer Ramble in Syria, with a Tartar Trip from Aleppo to Stamboul* (2 vols., London, R. Bentley, 1835).

Montagu, John, *A Voyage Performed by the Late Earl of Sandwich Round the Mediterranean in the Years 1713 and 1739* (London, 1799).

Montagu, Lady Mary Wortley, *Complete Letters,* ed. Robert Halsband (Oxford, Clarendon Press, 1965).

—*The Turkish Embassy Letters,* ed. Malcolm Jack (London, Virago, 1994).

Montulé, Edouard de, *Travels in Egypt during 1818 and 1819* (London, printed for R. Phillips, 1821).

Morgan, David, *Medieval Persia 1040–1797* (London, Longman, 1988).

Morritt, J.B.S., *A Grand Tour: Letters and Journeys 1794–1796* (London, Century, 1985).

Murray, Elizabeth, *Sixteen Years of an Artist's Life in Morocco, Spain, and the Canary Islands* (London, Hurst and Blackett, 1859).

Musckau, Hermann Ludwig Heinrich Puckler, Prince, *Egypt and Mehemet Ali* (3 vols., London, T.C. Newby, 1845).

Nasr, Seyyed Hossein, *Ideals and Realities of Islam* (Cairo, American University in Cairo Press, 1989).

Nemoy, Leon, ed. and trans., 'The Treatise on the Egyptian Pyramids (*Tuhfat al-kiram fi khabar al-ahram*) by Jalal al-Din al-Suyuti', *ISIS,* 30 (1939), 17–37.

Netton, I.R., *Golden Roads: Migration, Pilgrimage and Travel in Medieval and Modern Islam* (Richmond, Curzon Press, 1993).

—(ed.), *Seek Knowledge: Thought and Travel in the House of Islam* (Richmond, Curzon Press, 1996).

Niebuhr, Carsten, *Travels through Arabia and Other Countries in the East,* trans. and ed. Robert Heron (Edinburgh, R. Morison, 1792).

Nightingale, Florence, *Letters from Egypt*, ed. Antony Sattin (London, A. & G.A. Spottiswoode, 1854; repr. London, Barrie & Jenkins, 1987).

Nochlin, Linda, 'The Imaginary Orient', *The Politics of Vision* (New York, Harper and Row, 1989), 35–59.

Norden, Frederic Louïs, *Voyage d'Égypte et de Nubie* (2 vols., Copenhagen, Imprimerie de la Maison Royale, 1755).

Oddie, E.M., *Portrait of Ianthe: Being a Study of Jane Digby, Lady Ellenborough* (London, Jonathan Cape, 1935).

Oelwein, Cornelia, 'Carl Haag (1820–1915). Ein Erlanger Künstler – "Well-Known" in England', *Bayernspiegel*, 4 (Munich, 1995).

—*Lady Jane Ellenborough. Eine Frau beeindruckt ihr Jahrhundert* (Munich, 1996).

Olearius, Adam, *The Travels of Olearius in Seventeenth-century Russia*, trans. and ed. Samuel Baron (Stanford, Stanford University Press, 1967).

—*Vermehrte Newe Beschreibung der Muscowitischen und Persischen Reyse* (1656), ed. Dieter Lohmeier, Deutsche Neudrucke 21 (Tübingen, Max Niemeyer, 1971).

—[*Vermehrte Newe Beschreibung der Muscowitischen und Persischen Reyse*] *Moskowitische und persische Reise: die holsteinische Gesandtschaft beim Schah, 1633–1639*, ed. Detlef Haberland (Stuttgart, Thienemann, 1986).

Olivier, G.A., *Voyage dans l'empire Othoman, l'Égypte et la Perse* (Paris, H. Agosse, (1801–7).

Ollier, Edmund, *Cassell's Illustrated History of the Russo-Turkish War* (2 vols., London, Paris, New York, 1885–1886).

Osterhammel, Jürgen, 'Reisen an die Grenzen der Alten Welt: Asien im Reisebericht des 17. und 18. Jahrhunderts', *Der Reisebericht*, ed. Peter Brenner (Frankfurt am Main, Suhrkamp, 1989), 224–60.

Packard, J.F., *Grant's Tour Around the World* (Cincinnati, Forshee & McMakin, 1880).

Palmer, Loomis T., *General U.S. Grant's Tour around the World* (Chicago, W.M. Farrar, 1880).

Pardoe, Julia S.H., *The City of the Sultan and Domestic Manners of the Turks in 1836* (2 vols., London, H. Colburn, 1837).

Paton, A.A., *A History of the Egyptian Revolution from the Period of the Mamelukes to the Death of Mohammed Ali*, 2nd edn, enlarged (2 vols., 1863; repr. London, Truebner, 1870).

Perrier, Amelia, *A Winter in Morocco* (London, Harvey S. King, 1873).

Peters, F.E., *Jerusalem: The Holy City in the Eyes of Chroniclers, Visitors, Pilgrims and Prophets from the Days of Abraham to the Beginnings of Modern Times* (Princeton, Princeton University Press, 1985).

Petherick, John, *Egypt the Soudan and Central Africa* (London & Edinburgh, William Blackwood, 1861).

Philippe, Beatrice (ed.), *Voir Jérusalem: pèlerins, conquérants, voyageurs* (Paris, 1997).

Phipps-Jackson, M., 'Cairo in London: Carl Haag's Studio', *Art Journal* (1883).

Pick, Christopher (ed.), *Embassy to Constantinople: The Travels of Lady Mary Wortley Montagu* (London, Century, 1988).

Pigafetta, Marc Antonio, *Itinerario da Vienna a Constantinopoli di Marc'Antonio Pigafetta gentil'huomo Vicentino* (London, Giovanni Wolfio, 1585).

Piloti, Emmanuel, *L'Égypte au commencement du XVe siècle d'après le Traité d'Emmanuel Piloti de Crète (Incipit, 1420)*, ed. P.- H. Dopp (Cairo, 1950).

Pilz, Gerg, ed., *Paul Gavarni* (Berlin, Eulenspiegel Verlag, 1971).

Pleydell, Kathleen Mansel, *Sketches of Life in Morocco* (London, Digby, Long, 1907).

Pococke, Richard, Bishop of Meath, *A Description of the East and Some Other Countries* (2 vols., London, J. & R. Knapton, 1743–1745).

Poole, Sophia, *The Englishwoman in Egypt: Letters from Cairo, Written during a Residence there in 1842, 3, & 4, with E.W. Lane, Esq., Author of 'The Modern Egyptians'* (2 vols., London, Charles Knight, 1844).

—*The Englishwoman in Egypt: Letters from Cairo Written during a Residence there in 1842, 3, & 4, with E.W. Lane, Esq.* (3 vols., 1844; repr. London, C. Cox, 1851).

—*The Englishwoman in Egypt: Letters from Cairo, Written during a Residence there in 1845–46, with E.W. Lane . . . etc.*, 2nd Series (London, Charles Knight, 1846).

Poole, Stanley Lane (ed.), *The Thousand and One Nights, Commonly Called in England, The Arabian Nights' Entertainments, a New Translation from the Arabic, with Copious Notes by Edward William Lane* (London, Charles Knight, 1859).

—*Life of Edward William Lane* (London, Williams & Norgate, 1877).

—*Cairo: Sketches of its History, Monuments and Social Life* (1898; repr. New York, Arno Press, 1973).

Postel, Guillaume, *Des Histoires orientales et principalement des Turkes ou Turchiques* (Paris, H. de Marnef & G. Cauellat, 1575).

Potocki, Jan, Le Comte de, *Voyage en Turquie et en Egypte, fait en l'année 1784* (Varsovie, 1788).

Potter, W. (proprietor of the Turkish Bath, Manchester), *The Roman or Turkish Bath: Its Hygienic and Curative Properties* (Manchester and London, 1859).

Pratt, Mary Louise, 'Fieldwork in Common Places', *Writing Culture: The Poetics and Politics of Ethnography*, ed. James Clifford and George Marcus (Berkeley, University of Berkeley Press, 1986).

—*Imperial Eyes: Travel Writing and Transculturation* (London, Routledge, 1992).

Prime, William Cowper, 'Passages of Eastern Travel', *Harper's New Monthly Magazine*, 12:68 (1856), 224–34, 371–80, 482–90.

—'Passages of Eastern Travel', *Harper's New Monthly Magazine*, 13 (1856), 191–201, 323–35, 473–84, 609–18, 773–82; also 14 (1856), 32–44.

—'From Thebes to the Pyramids', *Harper's New Monthly Magazine*, 14:82 (March 1857), 463–77.

—*Boat Life in Egypt and Nubia* (New York, Harper, 1857).

Prisse d'Avennes, Emile, *Atlas de l'histoire de l'art Égyptien d'après les monuments depuis le temps les plus reculés, jusqu'à la domination romaine* (Paris, A. Bertrand, 1868–1878).

Quataert, Donald, 'Clothing Laws, State and Society in the Ottoman Empire, 1720–1829', *IJMES*, 29 (August 1997).

al-Qudsi, *Al-Fada'il al-bahira fi mahasin Misr wa-al-Qahira* (formerly attributed to Ibn Zahira), ed. M. al-Saqqa and K. al-Muhandis (Cairo, National Library Press, 1969).

Raguse, Marechal, Duc de, *Voyage en Hongrie, en Turquie . . . et en Egypte* (4 vols., Brussels, Société Typographique Belge, 1837).

Rapelje, George, *A Narrative of Excursions, Voyages, and Travels, Performed at Different Periods in America, Europe, Asia, and Africa* (New York, printed for the author, 1834).

Ray, John (ed.), *A Collection of Curious Travels and Voyages* (2 vols., London, S. Smith & B. Walford, 1693).

Rees, Joan, *Writings on the Nile* (London, Rubicon, 1995).

Repplier, Agnes, 'Christmas Shopping in Assuân', *Atlantic Monthly*, 75 (May 1895), 681–95.

Ribeiro, Aileen, 'Turquerie: Turkish Dress and English Fashion in the Eighteenth Century', *Connoisseur* (May 1979), 17–23.

Rice, Edward, *Captain Sir Richard Francis Burton: The Secret Agent Who Made the Pilgrimage to Mecca, Discovered the* Kama Sutra *and Brought* The Arabian Nights *to the West* (New York, Harper, 1990).

Richard, F., 'Raphaël du Mans missionaire en Perse au XVIIᵉ siècle', *Moyen Orient & Océan Indien XVIᵉ–XIXᵉ siècle*, 9 (2 vols., 1995).

Richardson, Robert R., *Travel along the Mediterranean, and Parts Adjacent: In Company with the Earl of Belmore, during the Years 1816, 1817, and 1818, Extending as Far as the Second Cataract of the Nile, Jerusalem, Damascus, Balbec, etc.* (2 vols., London, printed for T. Cadell, 1822).

Richmond, J.C.B., *Egypt 1798–1952: Her Advance towards a Modern Identity* (London, Methuen, 1977).

Riedesel, Johann Hermann von, Baron, *Voyage en Sicile, dans la Grande Grèce et au Levant* [in German, 1771] (Paris, 1802).

Righi, Eleanor Rigo de, *Holiday in Morocco* (London, G.T. Foulis, 1935).

Roberts, Chalmers, 'Where East and West Meet', *Harper's New Monthly Magazine*, 100:596 (January 1900), 245–56.

Roberts, David, *The Holy Land, Syria, Idumea, Arabia, Egypt & Nubia* (2 vols., London, F.G. Moon, 1842–1849).

Robinson, Edward H.T., *Lawrence: The Story of His Life* (London, Oxford University Press, 1933).

—*Lawrence the Rebel* (London, Lincolns-Praeger, 1946).

Robinson, Gertrude, *David Urquhart* (Oxford, Basil Blackwell, 1920).

Robinson, Jane, *Wayward Women: A Guide to Women Travellers* (Oxford & New York, Oxford University Press, 1990).

Roche, Max, *Éducation, assistance et culture françaises dans l'empire Ottoman* (Istanbul, 1989).

Rodenbeck, Max, *Cairo: The City Victorious* (London, Picador, 1998).

Rodkey, Frederick Stanley, 'The Turko-Egyptian Question in the Relations of England, France and Russia, 1823–41', *University of Illinois Studies in the Social Sciences*, 11:3–4 (September–December 1923).

Rottiers, Colonel E.A., *Itinéraire de Tiflis à Constantinople* (Brussels, 1829).

Rozière and Rouyer, 'Mémoire sur l'art de faire éclore les poulets en Égypte par le moyen des fours', *Description de l'Égypte* (2nd edn, Paris, Panckoucke, 1822).

Rushdy, Rashad, *The Lure of Egypt for English Writers and Travellers during the Nineteenth Century* (Cairo, Anglo-Egyptian Bookshop, 1954).

Russell, Alexander, *The Natural History of Aleppo and Parts Adjacent* (1756; repr. London, G. & J. Robinson, 1794).

Said, Edward W., *Orientalism: Western Concepts of the Orient* (London, Routledge & Kegan Paul, 1978; New York, Pantheon, 1978, repr. New York, Vintage Books, 1979; and London, Penguin Books, 1991 & 1995).

—*Culture and Imperialism* (London, Chatto and Windus, 1993; New York, Alfred A. Knopf, 1993; repr. London, Vintage, 1994).

Sampson, E.D., *Nikolay Gumilev* (Boston, Twayne, 1979).

Sanderson, John, *Travels of John Sanderson in the Levant, 1584–1602*, ed. Sir William Forster (London, printed for the Hakluyt Society, 1931).

Sattin, Anthony, *Lifting the Veil: British Society in Egypt 1768–1956* (London, J.M. Dent & Sons, 1988).

Sauneron, Serge, 'Le Temple d'Akhmim décrit par Ibn Jobeir', *BIFAO*, 51 (Cairo, 1952), 123–35.

Sauveboeuf, L. Ferrières, Comte de, *Mémoires historiques, politiques et géographiques des voyages du comte de Ferrières-Sauveboeuf faits en Turquie, en Perse et en Arabie, depuis 1782 jusqu'en 1789* (2 vols., Paris, 1790).

Savory, Isabel, *In the Tail of the Peacock* (London, Hutchinson, 1903).

Savory, Roger, *Iran under the Safavids* (Cambridge University Press, 1980).

Sayyid, Ayman Fuad, *Le Manuscrit autographe d'al-Mawa'iz wa-al-i'tibar fi dhikr al-khitat wa-al-athar de Taqi al-Din Ahmed b. Ali b. Abd al-Qadir al-Maqrizi* (London, al-Furqan Islamic Heritage Foundation, 1995).

Schmidt, Margaret Fox, *Passion's Child: The Extraordinary Life of Jane Digby* (London, Hamilton, 1977).

Schuster-Walser, Sibylla, *Das Safawidische Persien im Spiegel Europäischer Reiseberichte (1502–1722): Untersuchungen zur Wirtschafts- und Handelspolitik* (Baden-Baden, Bruno Grimm, 1970).

Searight, Sarah, *The British in the Middle East* (London, Weidenfeld and Nicolson, 1969; New York, Atheneum, 1970; repr. 1979).

—*Steaming East: The Forging of Steamship and Rail Links between Europe and Asia* (London, The Bodley Head, 1991).

Seddon, [John Pollard], *Memoir and Letters of the Late Thomas Seddon, Artist by his Brother* (London, James Nisbet, 1858).

Sezgin, Ursula, *Light on the Voluminous Bodies to Reveal the Secrets of the Pyramids by Abu Ja'far al-Idrisi* (Frankfurt am Main, Institute For the History of Arabic-Islamic Science, 1988).

Shaw, Stanford, *History of the Ottoman Empire and Modern Turkey: Empire of the Gazis: The Rise and Decline of the Ottoman Empire, 1280–1808* (Cambridge University Press, 1978).

al-Shenawy, Abdel-Aziz M., *Qanat al-Suways* (Cairo, Maahad al-Buhuth wa al-Dirasat al-Arabiyya, 1971).

Shepheard's Hotel, *Cairo and Egypt: A Practical Handbook for Visitors to the Land of the Pharaohs* (Cairo, Shepheard's Hotel, *c.* 1897–1917).

Shirazi, Mosleh al-Din Sa' di-ye, *The Gulistan or Rose Garden of Sa'di*, trans. Edward Rehatsek (London, George Allen & Unwin, 1964).

Simeon of Poland, *Travel Account, Annals and Colophons of Simeon the Scribe of Poland* [in Armenian] (Vienna, 1936), with a German résumé, 485–93.

Skeet, Ian, *Muscat and Oman* (London, Faber and Faber, 1974).

Skilliter, S.A., *William Harborne and the Trade with Turkey, 1578–1582* (Oxford University Press, for British Academy, 1977).

Slade, Adolphus, *Turkey, Greece and Malta* (2 vols., London, 1837).

Slatter, Enid M., 'The Princess, the Sultan and the Pasha', *Art and Artists* (November 1987), 1417.

Smith, Byron Porter, *Islam in English Literature* (Beirut, The American Press, 1939).

Smith, Thomas, *Remarks upon the Manners, Religion and Government of the Turks* (London, Moses Pitt, 1678).

—*Historical Observations Relating to Constantinople by the Reverend and Learned Tho. Smith, D.D. Fellow of Magd. Coll. Oxon, and of the Royal Society* in *A Collection of Curious Travels & Voyages*, ed. John Ray (London, 1693).

Spitzer, Leo, 'The Epic Style of the Pilgrim Aetheria', *Comparative Literature*, 1:3 (1949), 225–58.

Spivak, G.C., *In Other Worlds: Essays in Cultural Politics* (London, Routledge, 1988).

—*The Post-Colonial Critic* (London, Routledge, 1990).

—'Can the Subaltern Speak?', *Colonial Discourse and Post-Colonial Theory*, ed. P. Williams and L. Chrisman (New York & London, Wheatsheaf & Harvester, 1993).

St John, James Augustus, *Egypt and Mohammed Ali: Or, Travels in the Valley of the Nile* (2 vols., London, Rees, Orme, Brown, Green & Longman, 1834).

Staffa, Susan Jane, *Conquest and Fusion: The Social Evolution of Cairo AD 642–1850* (Leiden, E.J. Brill, 1977).

Stanford, W.B. and E.J. Finopoulo, *The Travels of Lord Charlemont in Greece and Turkey in 1749* (London, Trigraph for A.G. Leventis Foundation, 1985).

Stephens, John Lloyd, *Incidents of Travel in Egypt, Arabia Petræ and the Holy Land* (New York, Harper, 1837).

Stern, Henry A., *Dawnings of Light in the East* (London, C.H. Purday, 1854).

—*Journal of a Missionary Journey into Arabia Felix: Undertaken in 1856* (London, 1858).

Stevens, Mary-Anne (ed.), *The Orientalists: Delacroix to Matisse, European Painters in North Africa and the Near East*, Exhibition Catalogue (London, Royal Academy of Arts, and Washington, National Gallery of Art, 1984).

Stevenson, Catherine B., *Victorian Women Travel Writers in Africa* (Boston, Twayne, 1982).

Stewart, Aubrey (ed.), *Itinerary from Bordeaux to Jerusalem: 'The Bordeaux Pilgrim' [AD 333]* (London, Palestine Exploration Fund, 1896.)

Stewart, Desmond, *T.E. Lawrence* (London, Paladin, 1979).

Stewart, Frederick William Robert [Lord Castlereagh, 4th Marquess of Londonderry], *A Journey to Damascus, through Egypt, Nubia, Arabia Petraea, Palestine and Syria* (2 vols., London, Henry Colburn, 1847).

Stoneman, Richard (ed.), *Across the Hellespont: A Literary Guide to Turkey* (London, Hutchinson, 1987).

Strack, Thomas, *Exotische Erfahrung und Intersubjektivität. Reiseberichte im 17. und 18. Jahrhundert. Genregeschichtliche Untersuchung zu Adam Olearius – Hans Egede – Georg Forster* (Paderborn, Igel Verlag, 1994).

Stucky, R.A. and N.N. Lewis, 'Johan Ludwig Burckhardt und Williams John Bankes', *Petra*, ed. Th. Weber and R. Wenning (Mainz, 1997), 5–12.

Sweetman, John, *The Oriental Obsession* (Cambridge University Press, 1988).

Symonds, John Addington, Review of *A Thousand Miles up the Nile*, *The Academy* (7 July 1877), 65–8.

Tabachnick, Stephen E. and Christopher Matherson, *Images of Lawrence* (London, Jonathan Cape, 1988).

Taylor, Bayard, *A Journey to Central Africa: Or, Life and Landscapes From Egypt to the Negro Kingdoms of the White Nile* (New York, G.P. Putnam, 1854).

Teixeira, Pedro [Muhammad ibn Khavand Shah, called Mir Khavand], *Relaciones de Pedro Teixeira d'el Origen Descendencia y Succession de los Reyes de Persia y de Harmuz y de un Viage hecho por el mismo Autor dende la India Oriental hasta Italia por tierra*, En Amberes En can de Hieronymo Verdussen (2 vols., Amberes, Hieronugmo, 1610).

—*The Travels of Pedro Teixeira*, ed. W.F. Sinclair and D. Ferguson (London, Hakluyt Society, 1902).

Temple Bt., Major Sir Grenville, *Travels in Greece and Turkey* (2 vols., London, 1836).

Thackeray, W.M., *Lovel the Widower and Notes of a Journey from Cornhill to Grand Cairo* (London, Collins' Clear-Type Press, 1846).

—*Notes of a Journey from Cornhill to Grand Cairo* (London, Chapman & Hall, 1846; repr. London, Macmillan, 1903; illus. repr. Heathfield, Cockbird Press, 1991).

Thesiger, W., *Arabian Sands* (London, Longmans, 1959).

Thévenot, Jean de, *Relation d'un voyage fait au Levant* (3 vols., Paris & Rouen, chez Thomas Jolly, 1665–1684).

Thomas, Bertram, 'The Musandam Peninsula and its Inhabitants: The Shihuh', *Journal of the Royal Central Asian Society*, 15 (1928).

—'Among Some Unknown Tribes of South Arabia', *JRAS* (1929).

—'Musandam and its People', *Journal of the Royal Central Asian Society* (1929).

Thompson, Jason, *Sir Gardner Wilkinson and His Circle* (Austin, University of Texas Press, 1992).

—'"OF THE OSMANLEES, OR TURKS": An Unpublished Chapter From Edward William Lane's Manners and Customs of the Modern Egyptians', *Turkish Studies Association Bulletin*, 19 (Autumn 1995), 19–39.

—'Edward William Lane's "Description of Egypt"', *IJMES*, 28 (November 1996).

—'Edward William Lane in Egypt', *JARCE*, 34 (1997), 243–61.

Thornton, Lynne, *Women as Portrayed in Orientalist Painting* (Paris, 1988).

—*La Femme dans la peinture orientaliste* (Paris, ACR Éditions Internationales, 1993).

Tidrick, Kathryn, *Heart-beguiling Araby: The English Romance with Arabia*, revised edn (London, I,B. Tauris, 1989).

Tillett, Selwyn, *Egypt Itself: The Career of Robert Hay, Esquire of Linplum and Nunraw, 1799–1863* (London, SD Books, 1984).

Tregaskis, Hugh, *Beyond the Grand Tour: The Levant Lunatics* (London, Ascent Books, 1979).

Trollope, Anthony, *Doctor Thorne. A Novel* (1858; New York, Harper and brothers).

—*The Bertrams* (1859; repr. London, The Folio Society, 1993).

—'An Unprotected Female at the Pyramids' (1860), *Tourists and Colonials* (London, The Folio Society, n.d.).

—'George Walker at Suez' (1861), *Tourists and Colonials* (London, The Folio Society, n.d.).

—*An Autobiography* (1883; repr. Oxford, Oxford University Press, 1928).

Tucker, Judith, 'Muftis and Matrimony: Islamic Law and Gender in Ottoman Syria and Palestine,' *Islamic Law and Society*, 1:3 (1994).

Turner, William, *Journal of a Tour in the Levant* (3 vols., London, John Murray, 1820).

Tuson, Penelope, *Records of the British Residency and Agencies in the Persian Gulf* (London, India Office Library and Records, 1979).

Twain, Mark pseud. (i.e. S.L. Clemens) *The Innocents Abroad* (Leipzig, Bernhard Tauchnitz, 1879; repr. London, 1914).

Urquhart, D., *The Spirit of the East: Illustrated in a Journal of Travels through Roumelia during an Eventful Period* (2 vols., London, 1838).

—*The Pillars of Hercules: Or, A Narrative of Travels in Spain and Morocco in 1848* (2 vols., London, 1850).

Valle, Petri della, *Petri della Valle: Eines vornehmen Roemischen Patritii Reiß-Beschreibung in unterschiedliche Theile der Welt* (3 pts., Genff, J.H. Widerhold, 1674).

Vann, R.L., *The Unexcavated Buildings of Sardis*, BAR International Series 538 (Hildesheim and New York, George Olms Verlag, 1976; Oxford, BAR, 1989).

Varthema, Ludovico de, *Itinerario . . . nello Egitto, nella Sorria, nella Arabia deserta e felice, nella Persia, nella India e nella Ethiopia* (Venice, 1525).

Vittone, Bernardo Antonio, *Corso d'architettura civile sopra li cinque ordini di Giacomo Barozzio da Vignola, disegnato da Giambatista Borra . . .* (Turin, 1737).

Volney, Constantin François Chassboeuf, Comte de, *Voyage en Syrie et en Égypte pendant les années 1783, 1784 et 1785*, 2nd edn, revue et corrigée (2 vols., Paris, Volland et Desenne, 1787).

Walker Art Gallery, *Collective Exhibition of the Art of W. Holman Hunt, O.M., D.C.L.* (Liverpool, Walker Art Gallery, 1907).

Walker, Peter, *Holy City, Holy Places? Christian Attitudes to Jerusalem and the Holy Land in the Fourth Century*, Oxford Early Christian Studies (Oxford, Clarendon Press, 1990).

Wallach, Janet, *Desert Queen: The Extraordinary Life of Gertrude Bell: Adventurer, Adviser to Kings, Ally of Lawrence of Arabia* (London, Weidenfeld & Nicolson, 1996).

Walsh, Rev. Robert A., *Residence at Constantinople, during . . . the Commencement, Progress, and Termination of the Greek and Turkish Revolutions* (2 vols., London, F. Westley & A.H. Davis, 1836).

Warburton, Eliot, *The Crescent and the Cross: Or, Romance and Realities of Eastern Travel* (2 vols., London, Henry Colburn, 1845; repr. London, Maclaren, 1908).

Ward, Philip, *Travels in Oman: On the Track of Early Explorers* (Cambridge, Oleander, *c.*1987).

Warner, Charles Dudley, 'At the Gates of the East', *Atlantic Monthly*, 36.

—'Cataracts of the Nile', *Atlantic Monthly*, 31.

—*My Winter on the Nile: Among the Mummies and Moslems in Egypt 1874–75* (Hartford, Conn., American Publishing Co., 1876).

Warner, Nicholas (ed.), *An Egyptian Panorama: Reports from the Nineteenth-Century British Press* (Cairo, Zeitouna, 1994).

Waterfield, Robin E., *Christians in Persia: Assyrians, Armenians, Roman Catholics and Protestants* (London, Allen & Unwin, 1973).

Wattins, Thomas, *Tour through Swisserland . . . to Constantinople* (2 vols., London, 1792).

Webster, James, *Travels through the Crimea, Turkey, and Egypt; Performed during the Years 1825–28, Including Particulars of the Last Illness and Death of the Emperor Alexander, and of the Russian Conspiracy in 1825* (London, H. Colburn, 1830).

Wedmore, F., 'Carl Haag R.W.S.', *The Magazine of Art* (December 1889), 52–61.

Weekes, Richard V., *Muslim Peoples: A World Ethnographic Survey* (Westport, Greenwood Press, 1978).

Weiss, Gerhard, 'In Search of Silk: Adam Olearius' Mission to Russia and Persia', *James Ford Bell Lectures*, 20 (Minneapolis, University of Minnesota, 1983).

Wellsted, Lt James Raymond, *Travels in Arabia* (2 vols., London, John Murray, 1838).

Wesseling, P., *Vetera Romanorum Itinera* (Amsterdam, 1735).

Whaley, Buck, *Buck Whaley's Memoirs, Including his Journey to Jerusalem* (London, Alexander Moring, 1906).

Wharncliffe, Lord (ed.), *Embassy to Constantinople: The Letters and Works of Lady Mary Wortley Montagu* (2 vols., London, Swan Sonnenschein & Co., New York, Macmillan & Co., 1893).

Wharton, Annabel, *Refiguring the Post-Classical City: Dura Europos, Jerash, Jerusalem and Ravenna* (Cambridge University Press, 1995).

Wharton, Edith, *In Morocco* (New York, Charles Scribner's Sons, 1920).

Wilbour, Charles Edwin, *Travels in Egypt (December 1880 to May 1891)*, ed. Jean Capart (Brooklyn, NY, Brooklyn Museum, 1936).

Wilken, Robert, *The Land Called Holy: Palestine in Christian History and Thought* (New Haven, Yale University Press, 1992).

Wilkie, Sir David, *Sir David Wilkie's Sketches in Turkey, Syria and Egypt 1840–41. Drawn on Stone by Joseph Nash* (London, Graves & Warmsley, 1843).

Wilkinson, John, *Jerusalem Pilgrims before the Crusades* (Warminster, Aris and Phillips, 1977).

Williamson, Capt. T., *The East India Vade-Mecum: Or, Complete Guide to Gentlemen Intended for the Civil, Military or Naval Service of the East India Company* (2 vols., London, 1810).

Wilson, C.W., 'Introduction', *Itinerary from Bordeaux to Jerusalem* (London, Palestine Exploration Fund, 1896).

Wilson, E., *The Eastern or Turkish Bath: Its History, Revival in Britain, and Application to the Purposes of Health* (London, 1861).

Wilson, Edward L., 'Sinai and the Wilderness', *Century Illustrated Monthly Magazine*, 36 (July 1888), 324–40.

—'From Sinai to Shechem', *Century Illustrated Monthly Magazine*, 37, 193–208.

Wilson, Jeremy, *T.E. Lawrence: The Authorised Biography* (London, Minerva, 1990).

Wilson, William Rae, *Travels in Egypt and the Holy Land* (London, printed for Longman, Hurst, Reese, Orme and Browne, 1823).

Winslow, William Copley, 'The Queen of Egyptology', *The American Antiquarian*, 14 (November 1892).

Wolff, Joseph, *Missionary Journal of the Rev. Joseph Wolff* (London, 1827–1829).

—*Researches and Missionary Labours among the Jews, Mohammedans and other Sects* (London, J. Nisbet, 1835; Philadelphia, 1837).

—*Journal of the Rev. Joseph Wolff in a Series of Letters to Sir Thomas Baring Bart.: Account of his Missionary Labours from the Years 1827 to 1831; and from the Years 1835 to 1838* (London, printed Leeds, 1839).

Wood, Alfred C., 'The British Embassy in Constantinople', *English Historical Review*, 40 (1925).

—*A History of the Levant Company* (Oxford University Press, 1935; repr. London, Frank Cass, 1964).

Wood, Robert, *The Ruins of Palmyra, Otherwise Tedmor, in the Desart* (London, 1753; repr. Westmead, Farnborough, Gregg, 1971).

—*The Ruins of Balbec, Otherwise Heliopolis in Coelosyria* (London, 1757; repr. Westmead, Farnborough, Gregg, 1971).

Woolson, Constance Fenimore, 'Cairo in 1890', *Harper's New Monthly Magazine*, 83 (October 1891), 651–74 (part II in November 1891 issue, 828–55).

Wright, William, *An Account of Palmyra and Zenobia* (London, Thomas Nelson, 1895).

Wustenfeld, F., *Die Geographie und Verwaltung von Ägypten nach dem Arabischen des Abul Abbas Ahmed ben Ali el-Calcaschandi* (Göttingen, 1879).

Ya'ari, Avraham, *Jacob Saphir: Sefer Masa Teiman* [in Hebrew] (Tel Aviv, 1941), abr. from Saphir's account, *Even Saphir* (2 vols., Lyck, 1866; Mainz, 1874).

Yegül, Fikret K., *The Bath-Gymnasium Complex at Sardis*, Archaeological Exploration of Sardis Report 3 (Cambridge, Mass. and London, Harvard University Press, 1986).

Yohannan, John, *The Poet Sa'di: A Persian Humanist* (Lanham, MD, University Press of America, 1987).

Zand, K.H. *et al.*, *The Eastern Key*, Arabic text published with translation and some notes (London, Allen & Unwin, 1965). Arabic text ed. Paul Ghalioungui (Cairo, General Book Organisation, 1985).

Zoller, Olga, *Der Architekt und der Ingenieur Giovanni Battista Borra (1713–1770)* (Bamberg, Wissenschaftlicher Verlag Bamberg, 1996).

Zulalyan, M.K., *The Jelali Movement and the Condition of the Armenians in the Ottoman Empire* [in Armenian] (Erevan, 1966).

Index

Also available

Ithaca Press

Unfolding the Orient: Travellers in Egypt and the Near East
2001 • 328pp • 235 x 155 mm • Cased £35.00 • ISBN 0 86372 257 1

In a Sea of Knowledge: The British Arabists in the 20th Century
2001 • 252pp • 235 x 155 mm • Cased £35.00 • ISBN 0 86372 288 1

Sexual Encounters in the Middle East
1999 • 332pp • 235 x 155 mm • Cased £35.00 • ISBN 0 86372 253 9

Garnet Publishing

Egypt: Caught in Time
1997 • 160pp • 260 x 210 mm • 17 colour & 155 duotone pictures • Cased £19.95 • ISBN 1 873938 95 0

Narrative of the Residence of Fatalla Sayeghir among the Wandering Arabs of the Great Desert
1996 • 216pp • 210 x 120 mm • Cased £19.95 • ISBN 1 85964 0885

Travels of Ali Bey in Morocco, Tripoli, Cyprus, Egypt, Arabia, Syria and Turkey
Vol. I • 1993 • 383pp • 235 x 168 mm • 44 engravings, 2 maps • Cased £30.00 • ISBN 1 873938 39 X
Vol. II • 1993 • 388pp • 235 x 168 mm • Cased £30.00 • ISBN 1 873938 40 3

Available from your local bookshop; alternatively, contact our Sales Department on +44 (0)118 959 7847 or e-mail on **orders@garnet-ithaca.demon.co.uk** to order copies of these books.